Science Fiction Writers of The Golden Age

Writers of English: Lives and Works

SCIENCE FICTION WRITERS OF THE GOLDEN AGE

Edited and with an Introduction by

Harold Bloom

CHELSEA HOUSE PUBLISHERS
New York   Philadelphia

Jacket illustration: David A. Hardy, *Floating City* (Science Photo Library/Photo Researchers Inc.).

CHELSEA HOUSE PUBLISHERS

Editorial Director Richard Rennert
Executive Managing Editor Karyn Gullen Browne
Picture Editor Adrian G. Allen
Copy Chief Robin James
Creative Director Robert Mitchell
Art Director Joan Ferrigno
Manufacturing Director Gerald Levine

Writers of English: Lives and Works

Senior Editor S. T. Joshi
Series Design Rae Grant

Staff for SCIENCE FICTION WRITERS OF THE GOLDEN AGE

Assistant Editor Mary Sisson
Research Peter Cannon, Stefan Dziemianowicz
Picture Researcher Sandy Jones

Printed and bound in the United States of America.

First Printing

1 3 5 7 9 8 6 4 2

Library of Congress Cataloging-in-Publication Data

Science fiction writers of the golden age / edited and with an introduction by Harold Bloom.
    p. cm.—(Writers of English)
    Includes bibliographical references.
    ISBN 0-7910-2199-8.—ISBN 0-7910-2198-X (pbk.)
  1. Science fiction, American—History and criticism. 2. Science fiction, American—Bio-bibliography. 3. Science fiction, English—History and criticism. 4. Science fiction, English—Bio-bibliography. I. Bloom, Harold. II. Series.
PS374.S35S38 1994
813'.0876209—dc20   94-4322
[B]   CIP

 Contents

▣ User's Guide

THIS VOLUME PROVIDES biographical, critical, and bibliographical information on the thirteen most significant science fiction writers of the Golden Age. Each chapter consists of three parts: a biography of the author; a selection of brief critical extracts about the author; and a bibliography of the author's published books.

The biography supplies a detailed outline of the important events in the author's life, including his or her major writings. The critical extracts are taken from a wide array of books and periodicals, from the author's lifetime to the present, and range in content from biographical to critical to historical. The extracts are arranged in chronological order by date of writing or publication, and a full bibliographical citation is provided at the end of each extract. Editorial additions or deletions are indicated within carets.

The author bibliographies list every separate publication—including books, pamphlets, broadsides, collaborations, and works edited or translated by the author—for works published in the author's lifetime; selected important posthumous publications are also listed. Titles are those of the first edition; variant titles are supplied within carets. In selected instances dates of revised editions are given where these are significant. Pseudonymous works are listed, but not the pseudonyms under which these works were published. Periodicals edited by the author are listed only when the author has written most or all of the contents. Titles enclosed in square brackets are of doubtful authenticity. All works by the author, whether in English or in other languages, have been listed; English translations of foreign-language works are not listed unless the author has done the translation.

The Life of the Author
Harold Bloom

NIETZSCHE, WITH EXULTANT ANGUISH, famously proclaimed that God was dead. Whatever the consequences of this for the ethical life, its ultimate literary effect certainly would have surprised the author Nietzsche. His French disciples, Foucault most prominent among them, developed the Nietzschean proclamation into the dogma that all authors, God included, were dead. The death of the author, which is no more than a Parisian trope, another metaphor for fashion's setting of skirt-lengths, is now accepted as literal truth by most of our current apostles of what should be called French Nietzsche, to distinguish it from the merely original Nietzsche. We also have French Freud or Lacan, which has little to do with the actual thought of Sigmund Freud, and even French Joyce, which interprets *Finnegans Wake* as the major work of Jacques Derrida. But all this is as nothing compared to the final triumph of the doctrine of the death of the author: French Shakespeare. That delicious absurdity is given us by the New Historicism, which blends Foucault and California fruit juice to give us the Word that Renaissance "social energies," and not William Shakespeare, composed *Hamlet* and *King Lear*. It seems a proper moment to murmur "enough" and to return to a study of the life of the author.

Sometimes it troubles me that there are so few masterpieces in the vast ocean of literary biography that stretches between James Boswell's great *Life* of Dr. Samuel Johnson and the late Richard Ellmann's wonderful *Oscar Wilde*. Literary biography is a crucial genre, and clearly a difficult one in which to excel. The actual nature of the lives of the poets seems to have little effect upon the quality of their biographies. Everything happened to Lord Byron and nothing at all to Wallace Stevens, and yet their biographers seem equally daunted by them. But even inadequate biographies of strong writers, or of weak ones, are of immense use. I have never read a literary biography from which I have not profited, a statement I cannot make about any other genre whatsoever. And when it comes to figures who are central to us—Dante, Shakespeare, Cervantes, Montaigne, Goethe, Whitman, Tolstoi, Freud, Joyce, Kafka among them—we reach out eagerly for every scrap that the biographers have gleaned. Concerning Dante and Shakespeare we know much too little, yet when we come to Goethe and Freud, where we seem to know more than everything, we still want to know more. The death of the author, despite our

current resentniks, clearly was only a momentary fad. Something vital in every
authentic lover of literature responds to Emerson's battle-cry sentence: "There is
no history, only biography." Beyond that there is a deeper truth, difficult to come
at and requiring a lifetime to understand, which is that there is no literature,
only autobiography, however mediated, however veiled, however transformed. The
events of Shakespeare's life included the composition of *Hamlet,* and that act of
writing was itself a crucial act of living, though we do not yet know altogether
how to read so doubled an act. When an author takes up a more overtly autobiographical stance, as so many do in their youth, again we still do not know precisely how
to accommodate the vexed relation between life and work. T. S. Eliot, meditating
upon James Joyce, made a classic statement as to such accommodation:

> We want to know who are the originals of his characters, and what were
> the origins of his episodes, so that we may unravel the web of memory
> and invention and discover how far and in what ways the crude material
> has been transformed.

When a writer is not even covertly autobiographical, the web of memory and
invention is still there, but so subtly woven that we may never unravel it. And yet
we want deeply never to stop trying, and not merely because we are curious, but
because each of us is caught in her own network of memory and invention. We
do not always recall our inventions, and long before we age we cease to be certain
of the extent to which we have invented our memories. Perhaps one motive for
reading is our need to unravel our own webs. If our masters could make, from their
lives, what we read, then we can be moved by them to ask: What have we made
or lived in relation to what we have read? The answers may be sad, or confused,
but the question is likely, implicitly, to go on being asked as long as we read. In
Freudian terms, we are asking: What is it that we have repressed? What have we
forgotten, unconsciously but purposively: What is it that we flee? Art, literature
necessarily included, is regression in the service of the ego, according to a famous
Freudian formula. I doubt the Freudian wisdom here, but indubitably it is profoundly
suggestive. When we read, something in us keeps asking the equivalent of the
Freudian questions: From what or whom is the author in flight, and to what earlier
stages in her life is she returning, and why?

Reading, whether as an art or a pastime, has been damaged by the visual media,
television in particular, and might be in some danger of extinction in the age of
the computer, except that the psychic need for it continues to endure, presumably
because it alone can assuage a central loneliness in elitist society. Despite all
sophisticated or resentful denials, the reading of imaginative literature remains a
quest to overcome the isolation of the individual consciousness. We can read for
information, or entertainment, or for love of the language, but in the end we seek,
in the author, the person whom we have not found, whether in ourselves or in

others. In that quest, there always are elements at once aggressive and defensive, so that reading, even in childhood, is rarely free of hidden anxieties. And yet it remains one of the few activities not contaminated by an entropy of spirit. We read in hope, because we lack companionship, and the author can become the object of the most idealistic elements in our search for the wit and inventiveness we so desperately require. We read biography, not as a supplement to reading the author, but as a second, fresh attempt to understand what always seems to evade us in the work, our drive towards a kind of identity with the author.

This will-to-identity, though recently much deprecated, is a prime basis for the experience of sublimity in reading. *Hamlet* retains its unique position in the Western canon not because most readers and playgoers identify themselves with the prince, who clearly is beyond them, but rather because they find themselves again in the power of the language that represents him with such immediacy and force. Yet we know that neither language nor social energy created Hamlet. Our curiosity about Shakespeare is endless, and never will be appeased. That curiosity itself is a value, and cannot be separated from the value of *Hamlet* the tragedy, or Hamlet the literary character. It provokes us that Shakespeare the man seems so unknowable, at once everyone and no one as Borges shrewdly observes. Critics keep telling us otherwise, yet something valid in us keeps believing that we would know Hamlet better if Shakespeare's life were as fully known as the lives of Goethe and Freud, Byron and Oscar Wilde, or best of all, Dr. Samuel Johnson. Shakespeare never will have his Boswell, and Dante never will have his Richard Ellmann. How much one would give for a detailed and candid *Life of Dante* by Petrarch, or an outspoken memoir of Shakespeare by Ben Jonson! Or, in the age just past, how superb would be rival studies of one another by Hemingway and Scott Fitzgerald! But the list is endless: think of *Oscar Wilde* by Lord Alfred Douglas, or a joint biography of Shelley by Mary Godwin, Emilia Viviani, and Jane Williams. More than our insatiable desire for scandal would be satisfied. The literary rivals and the lovers of the great writers possessed perspectives we will never enjoy, and without those perspectives we dwell in some poverty in regard to the writers with whom we ourselves never can be done.

There is a sense in which imaginative literature *is* perspectivism, so that the reader is likely to be overwhelmed by the work's difficulty unless its multiple perspectives are mastered. Literary biography matters most because it is a storehouse of perspectives, frequently far surpassing any that are grasped by the particular biographer. There are relations between authors' lives and their works of kinds we have yet to discover, because our analytical instruments are not yet advanced enough to perform the necessary labor. Perhaps a novel, poem, or play is not so much a regression in the service of the ego, as it is an amalgam of *all* the Freudian mechanisms of defense, all working together for the apotheosis of the ego. Freud valued art highly, but thought that the aesthetic enterprise was no rival for psychoanalysis, unlike religion and philosophy. Clearly Freud was mistaken; his own anxieties about his indebtedness to Shakespeare helped produce the weirdness of his joining in the lunacy that argued for the Earl of Oxford as the author of Shakespeare's plays. It was Shakespeare, and not "the poets," who was there before Freud arrived at his depth psychology, and it is Shakespeare who is there still, well out ahead of psychoanalysis. We see what Freud would not see, that psychoanalysis is Shakespeare prosified and systematized. Freud is part of literature, not of "science," and the biography of Freud has the same relations to psychoanalysis as the biography of Shakespeare has to *Hamlet* and *King Lear*, if only we knew more of the life of Shakespeare.

Western literature, particularly since Shakespeare, is marked by the representation of internalized change in its characters. A literature of the ever-growing inner self is in itself a large form of biography, even though this is the biography of imaginary beings, from Hamlet to the sometimes nameless protagonists of Kafka and Beckett. Skeptics might want to argue that all literary biography concerns imaginary beings, since authors make themselves up, and every biographer gives us a creation curiously different from the same author as seen by the writer of a rival *Life*. Boswell's Johnson is not quite anyone else's Johnson, though it is now very difficult for us to disentangle the great Doctor from his gifted Scottish friend and follower. The life of the author is not merely a metaphor or a fiction, as is "the Death of the Author," but it always does contain metaphorical or fictive elements. Those elements are a part of the value of literary biography, but not the largest or the crucial part, which is the separation of the mask from the man or woman who hid behind it. James Joyce and Samuel Beckett, master and sometime disciple, were both of them enigmatic personalities, and their biographers have not, as yet, fully expounded the mystery of these contrasting natures. Beckett seems very nearly to have been a secular saint: personally disinterested, heroic in the French Resistance, as humane a person ever to have composed major fictions and dramas. Joyce, self-obsessed even as Beckett was preternaturally selfless, was the Milton of the twentieth century. Beckett was perhaps the least egoistic post-Joycean, post-Proustian, post-Kafkan of writers. Does that illuminate the problematical nature of his work, or does it simply constitute another problem? Whatever the cause, the question matters. The only death of the author that is other than literal, and that matters, is the fate only of weak writers. The strong, who become canonical, never die, which is what the canon truly is about. To be read forever is the Life of the Author.

⬡ *Introduction*

THE "GOLDEN AGE" OF SCIENCE FICTION is generally taken to be 1939–1950, with Arthur C. Clarke, Ray Bradbury, and Fritz Leiber being perhaps its most representative figures. Clarke, my subject here, is a very mixed writer, aesthetically considered, but his importance transcends his literary achievement. He may be best remembered for his association with the communications satellite, his work on Stanley Kubrick's film, *2001*, and for his strenuous campaign to keep an American space program going, despite all its disappointments. His best novels do not come at his origins, but the early works interest me the most, so I will center here upon *Against the Fall of Night* (1948, 1953), *Childhood's End* (1953), and the revision and expansion of *Against the Fall of Night* in *The City and the Stars* (1956). All three fictions show the acknowledged influence of Olaf Stapledon's *Last and First Men* (1930), at once Clarke's overwhelming precursor and perhaps also finally as much an inhibitor as an inspirer, if only because Stapledon sets an unsurpassable standard for future cosmological history. Stapledon has an imaginatively persuasive force that rises from obsessive conviction; his dying worlds and visions of the end of mankind can be said to have formed Clarke's imagination, once and for all.

Yet Clarke's early fictions survive as more than period pieces; they prefigure a popular mythology concerning space travel that does not seem to leave us even now, when no signals have reached us from across the seas of space and when it seems dubious that we can afford a continued quest for we-know-not-what. The Kubrick-Clarke *2001* increasingly seems a sadly optimistic title, seven years from the Millennium. Most of Clarke's secular prophecies have not been realized, but as Millennium beckons, one appreciates Clarke's firmly secular disposition. *Against the Fall of Night* locates Alvin, Clarke's characteristic quester, in the ageless city of Diaspar, an island in the wilderness of sand that constitutes the remainder of Earth. Glorious Diaspar is a prison-paradise of "gracious decadence" excluding the wonder of the unknown, of the star-world from which mankind has been driven back. As a city of the Immortals, with perpetually renewable life-cycles, Diaspar is not fully developed until its revision in *The City and the Stars*, where it does possess a certain grim, almost grotesque splendor. But here Clarke's literary flaws rather sadly enter in; his ironies are too obvious and uncontrolled, and he is seriously deficient in humor. To think of the city in Borges's story, "The Immortal," is to destroy Clarke's Diaspar as an imaginative conception. Borges's city of the Immortals is a complex and powerful irony, unforgettable as a critique of all Utopias, including the aesthetic ones. Clarke's own aesthetic Utopia, Comarre, in the early *The Lion of Comarre* (1948), like Diaspar cannot sustain comparison with Borges's Swiftian depiction of what it would mean never to die.

I find that, of early Clarke, *Childhood's End* best sustains rereading, perhaps because it catches so precisely Olaf Stapledon's speculative intensity as he broods on the saga of millions of years of ruined worlds. *Childhood's End* completes itself with a veritable apocalypse of Earth, as the human race pulses out to join the Overmind, which devours us, substance and spirit, and our world, in order to accomplish purposes beyond our ken. There is a singular dearth of affect at the novel's close, reminding us that Clarke lacks command of significant pathos even as he is rather deficient in irony. Though he helped establish the science fiction genre that is our modern mode of visionary romance, Clarke simply lacks the literary power of such great modern fantasies, with science fiction overtones, as David Lindsay's *A Voyage to Arcturus*, Ursula K. Le Guin's *The Left Hand of Darkness*, and John Crowley's *Little, Big*. Yet it would be difficult to overestimate the pragmatic influence of Clarke's work, not only upon other writers but upon our lives, particularly upon our ventures into space, the few that have been, and perhaps (if he has his way) the many yet to come.

—H. B.

Poul Anderson
b. 1926

POUL WILLIAM ANDERSON was born on November 25, 1926, in Bristol, Pennsylvania, to a Scandinavian family. Interest in his family's heritage, stimulated in part by a brief stay in Denmark before the outbreak of World War II, resulted in a lifelong appreciation of Scandinavian culture and literature evident in much of his writing. His interest in science led him to enroll in the physics program at the University of Minnesota and to read and try writing science fiction.

Encouraged by his roommate and fellow science fiction writer Gordon R. Dickson, Anderson sold his first science fiction story, a collaboration with F. N. Waldrop entitled "Tomorrow's Children," to *Astounding Science-Fiction* in 1947, a little more than a year before he took his undergraduate degree. Anderson joined the Minnesota Fantasy Society and dabbled in science fiction for several years until 1950, when poor job prospects in the physics field spurred him to try writing full time.

Anderson married his occasional collaborator, Karen, in 1952. That same year, his first novel, *Vault of the Ages*, a science fiction juvenile set in a post-apocalyptic future, was published. His second novel, *Brain Wave* (1954), describes what happens when the earth emerges from an intergalactic cloud that has inhibited human thought since the dawn of time and human beings are suddenly forced to cope with newly acquired genius in a world not built to accommodate it. The novel was praised for the meticulous detail with which Anderson showed how such an event would permeate all levels of civilization.

In the prolific burst of novels and stories that followed and has continued ever since, Anderson has distinguished himself as a student of the old-fashioned science fiction schools of space opera and extrapolated hard science, one who can condense historical, anthropological, and scientific concepts into vivid narratives filled with fully realized characters. His ambitious Technics Civilization saga, which comprises nearly a dozen novels and numerous short stories, chronicles five thousand years of humanity's

1

colonization of the universe and recapitulates the European Age of Exploration through the exploits of two major characters: twenty-third-century
merchant Nicholas van Rijn, hero of *War of the Wing-Men* (1958), and
twenty-ninth-century naval intelligence agent Nicholas Flandry, whose
adventures extend from *Ensign Flandry* (1966) to *The Game of Empire* (1985).
Both characters are recognized as mouthpieces for Anderson's conservative
politics and his guarded optimism regarding human progress.

Anderson's many other series include the comic Hoka stories, written in
collaboration with Gordon R. Dickson and set on a planet whose inhabitants
interpret all language literally, and the alternate world tales that comprise
his Time Patrol sequence. Among his highly regarded nonseries novels are
The High Crusade (1960), a blend of fantasy and science fiction that tells
of an extraterrestrial visit to Earth during the Dark Ages; *Tau Zero* (1970),
in which a space ship forced to travel at near–light speed witnesses the
birth of a new universe following a second "big bang"; and *The Boat of a
Million Years* (1989), which tracks the experiences of a group of immortals
over several millennia of Earth history. Anderson has also written detective
fiction and straight fantasy novels, many derived from Scandinavian lore.

Anderson has won the Hugo Award seven times and the Nebula twice
for his short fiction. He has one daughter and lives with his wife in San
Francisco.

❖ *Critical Extracts*

LESLIE FLOOD   The one brightly gleaming experience this month
is Poul Anderson's supremely effective *Brain Wave*. Here the author, one
of America's newest young talents, takes an intriguing concept—the sudden
releasing of the brake on neural responses in all Earthly animal life (including
man) caused by our planet moving out of a blanketing force field which
has affected it for millions of years. I.Q.s jump to a norm of 500, and while
former morons become intelligent by previous standards, the lower forms
of animal life start climbing the bottom rungs of human intelligence. On
this premise, Poul Anderson weaves a powerful and entertaining story. To
do the theme full justice the scope of the novel should have been enlarged
four-fold and built into a more emotional climax in perhaps surer hands

than Anderson's. Then I think it would have been one of the finest science fiction books of our time. As it is, in two hundred pages, the author carefully and ingeniously works out the probable effects of the "brain wave"—the disruption of metropolitan life and its rescue by the new brilliant minds, the calamity in rural areas with the revolt of farm animals, the rising of the coloured peoples against the white oppressors—and scattered incidents all over the world. Then the rebuilding of a new civilization with its incredible science and new ways of speech communications, the building of the first star ship and its fantastic voyage, the subversive plot to synthesize the old order of dimmed thinking in a misguided (or was it?) attempt to avoid the unknown but possibly glorious future of unleashed mankind. A tender emotional ending, and a serene feeling of magic entertainment is the reward for the reader. *Brain Wave* is a convincing, humanly realistic example of the wonders of the science fiction novel at its literary and thought-provoking best.

Leslie Flood, [Review of *Brain Wave*], *New Worlds* No. 44 (February 1956): 127–28

MICHAEL KING   If the term "space opera" didn't have almost universal connotations of "juvenile" and "comic strip" I'd have listed this novel ⟨*Star Ways*⟩ as such. Then I could have made the point that *good* space opera very definitely has its place among the many mansions of science fiction. However, I'd better not use the dread term, lest some readers assume that this novel of a far-flung future—where a Nomad society is caught between the outspread of integrated civilization and the encroachment of a totally different culture whose existence has been heretofore unsuspected by either—is Captain Future stuff. *Star Ways* isn't juvenile at all; it would have been a credit to any of the top science fiction magazines as a serial. In the intricate philosophy of the alien culture, Anderson approaches the excellence of S. Fowler Wright ⟨. . .⟩

Michael King, [Review of *Star Ways*], *Future Science Fiction* No. 31 (Winter 1957–57): 101–2

DAMON KNIGHT   *The Enemy Stars*, by Poul Anderson, is another recent book that gives me to hope, even if only marginally. The story, serialized in *Astounding* as "We Have Fed Our Sea," follows a familiar pattern: spacemen go out, wreck their ship, undergo prodigious hardships to repair it and get back to Earth.

Anderson's version is chiefly notable for its painstaking scientific background. Almost alone among active s. f. writers today, Anderson is a man with graduate training in science, and this novel, like some of the stories of James Blish and Hal Clement, fairly bristles with accurate and abstruse technical reasoning. ⟨. . .⟩

The story does not always break free of its pulp origins. Anderson's prose is sometimes graceless, occasionally drops into pulp jargon. But at his best he is poetically penetrating: in one swift image he can show you the heart of a character, or spread a landscape before your eyes.

Damon Knight, [Review of *The Enemy Stars*], *Magazine of Fantasy and Science Fiction* 16, No. 5 (May 1959): 75–76

ANTHONY BOUCHER   Poul Anderson is a prolific young man who has long been recognized as one of the most literate and inventive of science fiction writers and who has recently become almost equally successful with mysteries and historicals. Now he passes the bounds of such specialized fields with a splendid story of imaginative adventure calculated to appeal to any but the most crusty and inhibited reader of fiction.

Three Hearts and Three Lions tells of a young Dane, an underground worker in World War Two, who finds himself pulled from this world's conflict into that of another and even stranger world, where the eternal battle between Law and Chaos is fought with forces including, on the side of Chaos, werewolves and trolls and firedrakes and Morgan le Fay herself and, on the side of law, a swanmay, a valiant dwarf and a baptized Saracen.

It is, in short, the world of Carolingian romance, operating under its own magical rules as strict as the physical rules of our own universe. Holger Carlson must learn those rules and more: he must learn to know himself and the vital role that he is to play (in both universes) in the eternal war.

This novel of the world of the romances is itself a perfect modern romance: an exciting adventure story which is also rich in humor and poetry, in allusive wit and fantastic invention. (It is, incidentally, twice as long and twice as good as a magazine version which appeared 8 years ago.) The publishers label it "science fiction" and perhaps, by the broadest possible stretching of definitions, it might be so classified; but primarily this book is for those readers who rejoiced in T. H. White's *The Once and Future King* and J. R. R. Tolkien's *The Lord of the Rings* and have ever since then thirsted for comparable delights.

> Anthony Boucher (as "H. H. Holmes"), "Into Another World," *New York Herald Tribune Books*, 17 September 1961, p. 14

ALGIS BUDRYS   "Escape from Orbit" ⟨in *Time and Stars*⟩ is a technique-problem story; the consulting expert is called in to resolve the emergency in space, where three men are trapped and doomed to die unless he can, by exercising technical ingenuity in an office on Earth's surface, so arrange the available materials and data as to bring them safely down.

As we all know, this story when well done affirms many ideals for us. It is done very well here. But it isn't the real story. What Anderson has really been doing with this structure is brought forward and recapitulated at the end, when the exhausted hero, his dealings with the inflexible Universe satisfactorily concluded, now has to go home and get his kid off to school. The wife who has been phoning him for help with her routine household problems while he was figuring orbits has been so drained by her difficulties that she has slept through the ringing of the alarm clock.

Anderson's technical execution of this story is superb. The most important of the many subtle objectives he set out to reach—and he reached every one I could detect at all—was to make this a profoundly optimistic and ennobling story. He has at least added a new dimension to what seemed to be a completely rounded science-fiction form. I actually believe he has wiped it out and substituted something much more genuinely satisfying and truer to life, but that remains to be seen.

One thing that impresses me most distinctly is that Anderson shows the hero manipulating the supposedly difficult problem by wireless, but having to fend off the wife's problems with stopgaps and finally having to go home in person, not to solve but merely to alleviate one specific among them. I doubt very much whether this story was intended to be merely about one man and one wife, or cabbages and kings; I believe it was intended to be about whatever energy-sink each of us has; we all have them—so do our wives, kids and kings. I think one thing you could say about this story, if you had only one thing to say, would be that it is about where entropy really lives. And I think it is a piece of literature that could only have been written by a man thoroughly steeped in the traditions of science fiction, and which consequently could not possibly be fully understood by the editors or readers of "mainstream" anthologies of noteworthy contemporary writing, which is one of the places where this piece of work otherwise belongs.

> Algis Budrys, [Review of *Trader to the Stars* and *Time and Stars*], *Galaxy* 23, No. 3 (February 1965): 155–56

JOANNA RUSS   I think Poul Anderson sees the world as an unhappy place of much vulnerability and little splendor and that he ought to say so. One of the striking things about ⟨Satan's⟩ *World* (and this is usual lately with this author) is that the book's evocations of joy, strength, and freedom fall very flat indeed. ⟨. . .⟩

In short, when asked to invoke the joy of life, the author carries on like the Scand of Minneapolis (to use William Atheling, Jr.'s phrase), while the book's descriptions of misery, failure, weakness, and pain, especially emotional pain, are considerably more convincing. One wrests from life, with great effort, a kind of bleak, minimal happiness—this is the unspoken message of the novel. There are no equals in this story and no love, although space adventure does not automatically preclude either ⟨. . .⟩ There is a conventional, stylized camaraderie between shipmates Falkayn, Adzel, and Chee: otherwise everything in this world is seen as a question of hierarchy, or perhaps it would be better to say a question of dominance—one of the horrors in the story is "Brainscrub," the taking over of one's very personality, and I think it no accident that such complete control of one person over another is spoken of as a rape. Nor is it a matter of chance that the heroine-victim, Thea (the only fully developed new character in the book, aside from the aliens), is seen as tragically vulnerable, vulnerable through her feelings, responsive, affectionate (not only to her master but to van Rijn *and* Falkayn *and* someone who is actually an employee), and far more interesting than the successful characters. If only the weak can feel, only the weak are real. Success anesthetizes and isolates.

> Joanna Russ, [Review of *Satan's World*], *Magazine of Fantasy and Science Fiction* 39, No. 1 (July 1970): 43–44

JAMES BLISH   The sense of tragedy is ⟨. . .⟩ extremely rare in science fiction. To Poul Anderson it is a living entity. For him, it does not inhere in such commonplaces as the losses of old age, the deaths of lovers, the slaughters of war or Nature; as a physicist, he knows that the entropy gradient goes inexorably in only one direction, and he wastes no time sniveling about it. For Anderson, the tragic hero is a man ⟨. . .⟩ who is driven partly by circumstance, but mostly by his own conscience, to do the wrong thing for the right reason—and then has to live with the consequences. A fully fleshed-out example is "Sister Planet," in which the hero, foreseeing that a friendly alien race whom he loves are going to be ruthlessly exploited by man, bombs their Holy Place to teach them eternal suspicion. His exit line is: *Oh God, please exist. Please make a hell for me.* And in a way, the prayer is answered, for when the man's body is found much later, he is carrying a Bible in which Ezekiel 7:3, 4 are marked. Look it up.

I have never reread that story; it tore me to pieces the first time, and that was enough. But I am richer for it. And I can only stand in awe of a man who could not only entertain the insight, but write it out. It is utterly pitiless, as genuine tragedy must be; very few writers, and almost no sf writers, know the difference.

James Blish, "Poul Anderson: The Enduring Explosion" (1971), *The Tale That Wags the God*, ed. Cy Chauvin (Chicago: Advent, 1987), pp. 90–91

SANDRA MEISEL   *The Enemy Stars* is far richer in conscious symbolism than most of Anderson's work. Throughout this novel, the material represents the immaterial. Specific technical problems stand for universal human concerns—solving the former illuminates the latter. The awfulness of their beauty makes the cosmos womanly and a woman cosmic. Crossing the trackless gulfs between suns bridges the lonely gaps between men. Emptiness within and without has seldom been so starkly rendered as in this book, yet Anderson makes the eternal silence of the infinite spaces ring with shouts of human victory.

Alpha Crucis is the lodestar of the expedition, object of a generation-spanning quest that has outlasted the rise and fall of empires. The target constellation Crux Australis gives its name to the explorers' starship *Southern Cross*, a gibbet upon which three men are crucified for the sake of their race. For centuries the craft has fallen toward its goal by the force of its own inertia. But its diversion to inspect the dark star, an act which requires positive intervention, is a decision which changes the course of history. By turning aside from a predetermined path, men find a greater good than the one they sought. The error that wrecks the *Southern Cross* is in the long run a *felix culpa*. It occasions heroic deeds which would not have otherwise occurred, and so forges triumph out of tragedy.

The voyage of the *Cross* as a metaphor for human progress is complemented by parallels drawn between space and sea. These resonances affect Anderson personally since he is a space advocate, a sailing enthusiast, and a sea-captain's grandson. Both space and sea are fascinating (" 'Any ocean is, is too—big, bold, blind for us—too beautiful' ") but pitiless environments (" 'The sea never forgives you' ") which men must master in order to achieve the fullness of their being. As Kipling says, "By the bones about the wayside ye shall come into your own!" Space incubates substance as the sea does life, both are mothers who devour what they have brought forth. Each demands feeding, and "she calls us still unfed," no matter how many worlds or sailors are consumed. But there will always be some "dreamers dreaming greatly" to take risks. There is no substitute for sacrifice. Starfaring spacemen buy admiralty with their blood as their seagoing ancestors did in ages past. But Anderson believes that "our enterprise beyond the sky will keep alive that sense of bravery, wonder, and achievement without which man would hardly be himself."

Sandra Meisel, *Against Time's Arrow: The High Crusade of Poul Anderson* (San Bernadino, CA: Borgo Press, 1978), pp. 45–46

ANDREW KAVENEY   There is a set of ideas quite common among more commercially oriented sf authors which has produced hackwork from hacks, entertainments perfect of their kind from authors of minor gifts, and, from authors of real talent, as often as not slack potboilers full of lazy writing and pasteboard characters. These ideas might be summarised as a belief in intellectual and technical slickness and viscerally exciting, well-paced storytelling as replacements for, rather than adjuncts to, sensitivity to language and three-dimensional characterisation. This belief is dressed up with ⟨Kingsley⟩ Amis's idea that in sf the idea is hero and dignified with the claim that since all art is basically in competition with the breweries for the public's loose change, elevated ideas about the artist's role and responsibility are a presumptuous intellectual fad.

In the recent novels of Poul Anderson these views lead to a number of bad habits and technical shortcuts. To send your characters careering around the Universe for a hundred pages may provide entertainment but it is several hundred years since it passed for satisfactory plotting. Anderson has also become content with a sort of stock-company characterisation—cheer the hero, hiss the bureaucrat—in which complex differences of nationality or species are indicated by different varieties of broken English. A further deterioration has been caused by the singleminded preaching of a bizarre and inconsistent set of political views—a "libertarian" horror of governments and an idealisation of feudalism that owes a lot to the rancher-hands relationship in old Westerns; Anderson's singleminded preparedness to be boring almost indicates that he is aware of the essential shoddiness of his thought.

For there is more to him than this. There is a poetic fascination with words and sensations that can at times turn into a routine appeal to each sense in turn or into the cutesy-pie whimsy of A *Midsummer Tempest* but informs a routine tale like "We Have Fed Our Sea" with tragic grandeur. His silly political solutions, and the narcissistically unscrupulous way that his heroes defend them, go along with a capacity to convey movingly the importance of social obligation and of freedom, though the latter tends to be seen exclusively in terms of the wild emptiness of forests, mountains and deep space. It is not enough to dismiss Anderson unread; he is terribly flawed by overproduction but his real gifts often shine through.

Andrew Kaveney, [Review of *The Avatar*], *Foundation* No. 16 (May 1979): 71–72

ROALD D. TWEET   Dominic Flandry is the subject of seven novels and seven shorter pieces set about 600 years after van Rijn's time. A Naval Intelligence agent sworn to support the Terran Empire, he is Anderson's best example of the hero who is forced to discover the meaning and responsibility of the individualist placed in situations where he must choose between what is good for himself, for a small group of friends or lovers, and for the civilization he serves. How does one serve oneself and others?

In *The Rebel Worlds*, for example, Flandry falls in love with Kathryn McCormac, wife of an admiral who is in revolt against the Empire. In the end it is she who makes the choice when she permits her husband's rebellion to fail, then follows him into exile, at the expense of personal happiness. Flandry's personal life seldom works out, but his efforts prolong the Empire by one hundred years more than it would otherwise have lasted.

Flandry and van Rijn represent, as do many other of Anderson's characters, a belief in enlightened self-interest operating within a free—that is, laissez-faire—capitalist system. He has been criticized for his conservative political views, but his response is that such a system has gotten most of the world's work done most effectively. Anderson does not put forth these views thoughtlessly. As Flandry's personality has developed, he has gained both depth of character and philosophical complexity. In addition, critics of Anderson's politics neglect to take into account his larger view. Both Flandry and van Rijn appear at points when their respective cultures are dying. For a while what each man does makes a difference—a small individual decision can often affect the course of history—but surrounding the heroism is the conviction that nothing lasts, that all ends eventually in the Long Night. Anderson is optimistic in his faith in man, but not foolishly so.

Roald D. Tweet, "Poul Anderson," *Science Fiction Writers,* ed. E. F. Bleiler (New York: Charles Scribner's Sons, 1982), p. 261

POUL ANDERSON   I really see no excuse for sloppy workmanship. A literary genius of the first rank may, once in a while, erect a splendid edifice on foundations of sand, but literary geniuses of the first rank are few and far between. Frankly, I doubt that any are alive at this moment, in any branch of literature. Whether this is true or not, I do not see that careful construction ever does any harm; and in most cases it makes all the difference.

By this I do not mean that absolute scientific accuracy is a sine qua non of good imaginative literature. For one thing, the scientific picture is always changing. We can still enjoy C. S. Lewis' *Out of the Silent Planet,* for instance, in spite of what our space probes have since told us about Mars. Much of the cosmology in Olaf Stapledon's *Star Maker* is now obsolete, but his magnificent cosmic vision has lost nothing thereby. Yet I do invite you to note how solidly timbered these works are. ⟨. . .⟩

Besides the mutability of what we know, or believe we know, there is the fact that often a story requires a nonscientific or counterscientific assumption. Travel faster than light is an obvious example. If ever we find that this is possible after all, we will probably find it within the context of a physics totally different from any that we have any hint of today, a physics in which general relativity is just a special case. The upheaval that that implies is beyond imagination. Nevertheless, when we need to get our hero from star to star in a reasonable time, we go ahead and use "hyperspace" or whatever. This is legitimate enough in itself, provided we respect the body of well-established fact otherwise. Indeed, speculation about the nature and characteristics of, say, hyperspace can form quite an interesting element in the story.

Scientifically preposterous environments are acceptable when really necessary to the author's purpose. Bradbury's Mars comes to mind. Here, though, we border on out-and-out fantasy ⟨. . .⟩

First I would like to return to planet building. It exemplifies the literary riches to be found in science, riches almost entirely neglected by the so-called mainstream. There are other uses of hard science in science fiction, for instance in creating imaginary biologies, but planet building is closest to our topic of environments. Besides, I have spoken on it and written about it repeatedly in the past, and so can claim to know some aspects of it pretty well. I am by no means alone in this, of course, and can name Greg Bear, Greg Benford, and David Brin, all of them masters of the craft.

This is not the place to repeat myself. I simply want to skim over the subject as a way of showing that when we abide by the findings of science as best we can, we do not constrict ourselves. Rather, we get inspiration, and the tools with which to do a job that inspires and excites readers. I have sometimes called science fiction the tribal bard of science. Like a bard of old singing of the exploits of heroes, science fiction sings of wonders and possibilities revealed to us by our quest for knowledge. This is not the only thing science fiction does, of course, or even what it mostly does, but I do submit that it is something no other literary form ever really gets into.

Poul Anderson, "Nature: Laws and Surprises," *Mindscapes: The Geographies of Imagined Worlds*, ed. George E. Slusser and Eric S. Rabkin (Carbondale: Southern Illinois University Press, 1989), pp. 8–9

GERALD JONAS   Poul Anderson has been writing science fiction for over 40 years. In 1989 he published one of his most successful novels, *The Boat of a Million Years*, an adroit study of the mixed blessings of immortality. *Harvest of Stars* reads like something salvaged from a drawer of old rejects.

Anson Guthrie is the irascible but lovable founder of Fireball Enterprises, a company that dominates space travel in the solar system. Unlike all other monopolies in history, Fireball is neither inefficient nor corrupt, possibly because Guthrie, who has achieved a kind of immortality as a computer "download" after his body gives out, commands not just loyalty from his staff but a literally feudal devotion in which Fireball employees "plight troth" to their chief as he battles government baddies to win personal freedom and humanity's passage to the stars.

If this is Mr. Anderson's attempt to re-create the simple pleasures of the pulp magazines of the 1950's, he has only succeeded in proving that you can't go home again. *Harvest of Stars* is overwritten, underimagined and fatally flawed with self-satisfied musings of life-according-to-Guthrie that read suspiciously like the author's own self-justifications: "Back then, I too did my share of reading. It wasn't the fashionable stuff, no. Shakespeare, Homer, Cervantes, they might be acceptable, if outmoded, but Kipling, Conrad, MacDonald, Heinlein, that ilk, they were insensitive reactionaries. Or racists or sexists or whatever the current swear word was. You see, they dealt with things that mattered."

Gerald Jonas, [Review of Harvest of Stars], New York Times Book Review, 12 September 1993, p. 36

◈ *Bibliography*

Vault of the Ages. 1952.

Brain Wave. 1954.

The Broken Sword. 1954, 1971.

No World of Their Own (with *The 1,000 Year Plan* by Isaac Asimov). 1955, 1978 (as *The Long Way Home*).

Star Ways (*Peregrine*). 1956.

Planet of No Return (with *Star Guard* by Andre Norton). 1957, 1978 (as *Question and Answer*).

Earthman's Burden (with Gordon R. Dickson). 1957.

War of the Wing-Men (with *The Snows of Ganymede*). 1958.

Virgin Planet. 1959.

The War of Two Worlds. 1959.

We Claim These Stars! 1959.

Perish by the Sword. 1959.

The Enemy Stars. 1959.

The High Crusade. 1960.

Murder in Black Letter. 1960.

Earthman, Go Home! 1960.

The Golden Slave. 1960.

Guardians of Time. 1960, 1981.

Twilight World. 1961.

Mayday Orbit. 1961.

Strangers from Earth. 1961.

Orbit Unlimited: A Science-Fiction Adventure. 1961.

Three Hearts and Three Lions. 1961.

After Doomsday. 1962.

Murder Bound. 1962.

Un-Man and Other Novellas. 1962.

The Makeshift Rocket. 1962.

Let the Spacemen Beware! ⟨*The Night Face*⟩. 1963.

Is There Life on Other Worlds? 1963.

Shield. 1963.

Thermonuclear Warfare. 1963.

Three Worlds to Conquer. 1964.

Time and Stars. 1964.

Trader to the Stars. 1964.

Agent of the Terran Empire. 1965.

West by One and by One (editor). 1965.

The Corridors of Time. 1965.

Flandry of Terra. 1965.

The Star Fox. 1965.

Ensign Flandry. 1966.

The Trouble Twisters. 1966.

The Fox, the Dog, and the Griffin: A Folk Tale Adapted from the Danish of C. Molbech. 1966.

World without Stars. 1966.

The Horn of Time. 1968.

The Rebel Worlds. 1969.

Beyond the Beyond. 1969.

Satan's World. 1969.

Nebula Award Stories 4 (editor). 1969.

The Infinite Voyage: Man's Future in Space. 1969.

Seven Conquests: An Adventure in Science Fiction. 1969.

A Circus of Hells. 1970.

Tau Zero. 1970.

Tales of the Flying Mountains. 1970.

The Byworlder. 1971.

The Dancer from Atlantis. 1971.

Operation Chaos. 1971.

There Will Be Time. 1972.

Hrolf Kraki's Saga. 1973.

The Queen of Air and Darkness and Other Stories. 1973.

The People of the Wind. 1973.

The Day of Their Return. 1973.

Inheritors of Earth (with Gordon Eklund). 1974.

Fire Time. 1974.

A Midsummer Tempest. 1974.

The Many Worlds of Poul Anderson ⟨*The Book of Poul Anderson*⟩. Ed. Roger
    Elwood. 1974.

The Worlds of Poul Anderson ⟨*Planet of No Return, The War of Two Worlds,
    World without Stars*⟩. 1974.

A Knight of Ghosts and Shadows. 1974.

Star Prince Charlie (with Gordon R. Dickson). 1975.

The Winter of the World. 1975.

Homeward and Beyond. 1975.

Homebrew. 1976.

The Best of Poul Anderson. 1976.

Mirkheim. 1977.

Avatar. 1978.

The Earth Book of Stormgate. 1978.

The Night Face and Other Stories. 1978.

Two Worlds ⟨*Planet of No Return, World without Stars*⟩. 1978.

The Merman's Children. 1979.

A Stone in Heaven. 1979.

The Demon of Scattery (with Mildred Downey Broxon). 1979.

The Devil's Game. 1980.

Conan the Rebel. 1980.

The Last Viking (*The Golden Horn*, Book 1). 1980.

The Method of Holding the Three Ones: A Taoist Manual of Meditation of the Fourth Century A.D. (translator; with Don Wagner). 1980.

The Road of the Sea Horse. 1980.

Sign of the Raven. 1980.

The Psychotechnic League. 1981.

The Dark between the Stars. 1981.

Fantasy. 1981.

Explorations. 1981.

Winners. 1981.

Maurai and Kith. 1982.

The Winter of the World and The Queen of Air and Darkness and Other Stories. 1982.

The Gods Laughed. 1982.

The People of the Wind and The Day of Their Return. 1982.

The Psychotechnic League: Cold Victory. 1982.

Starship. 1982.

New America. 1982.

There Will Be Time and The Dancer from Atlantis. 1982.

Time Patrolman. 1983.

Hoka! (with Gordon R. Dickson). 1983.

The Long Night. 1983.

Agent of Vega. 1983.

Conflict. 1983.

Orion Shall Rise. 1983.

Annals of the Time Patrol: The Guardians of Time and The Time Patrolman. 1984.

The Unicorn Trade (with Karen Anderson). 1984.

Past Times. 1984.

The Game of Empire. 1985.

Dialogue with Darkness. 1985.

The King of Ys: Roma Mater (with Karen Anderson). 1986.

Gallicenae (with Karen Anderson). 1987.

The Enemy Stars. 1987.

The Year of the Ransom. 1988.

Dahut (with Karen Anderson). 1988.

The King of Ys (with Karen Anderson). 1988. 2 vols.

The Dog and the Wolf (with Karen Anderson). 1988.

The Boat of a Million Years. 1989.

No Truce with Kings ⟨with *Ship of Shadows* by Fritz Leiber⟩. 1989.

The Saturn Game ⟨with *Iceborn* by Gregory Benford and Paul A. Carter⟩.
    1989.

Space Folk. 1989.

The Shield of Time. 1990.

Alight in the Void. 1991.

Inconstant Star. 1991.

Kinship with the Stars. 1991.

The Longest Voyage ⟨with *Slow Lightning* by Steven Popkes⟩. 1991.

Losers' Night. 1991.

Time Patrol ⟨*The Guardians of Time*, *Time Patrolman*, *The Year of the Ransom*,
    "Star of the Sea"⟩. 1991.

Harvest of Stars. 1993.

⊠ ⊠ ⊠

Isaac Asimov
1920–1992

ISAAC ASIMOV was born on January 2, 1920, in Petrovichi, Russia. In 1923 his family emigrated to the United States. Asimov grew up in Brooklyn, New York, where his family ran a candy and magazine store; it was while working in the store that he acquired the addiction to print and habits of self-discipline that made him one of the most prolific writers of his time.

Captivated by the early science fiction magazines on the racks of the family store, Asimov's earliest writings were in the literary form for which he is known best. In 1939, the same year he graduated from Columbia University, his first published story, "Marooned Off Vesta," appeared in *Amazing Stories*. Later that year he sold "Trends" to *Astounding Science-Fiction*, beginning a long and fruitful relationship with that magazine's editor, John W. Campbell, Jr. It was Campbell who published the bulk of Asimov's output throughout the 1940s: the *Foundation* stories (1942–53), later collected as the *Foundation Trilogy* (1963), the early robot stories, from which were distilled the now famous "Three Laws of Robotics" that determined what robots could and could not do in much science fiction written afterward; and the celebrated "Nightfall" (1953). In these stories, Asimov first presented the themes that were to color all his subsequent science fiction: the colossal Galactic Empire whose politics are nonetheless much the same as politics everywhere, the idea of robots as rational, programmable human beings, and an overall affirmation of humanistic, rational inquiry as the only valid route to whatever opportunities for transcendence there may be.

Despite his prolific output throughout the 1940s, Asimov continued to view writing as a sideline and worked toward the Ph.D. in biochemistry he obtained from Columbia in 1948. In 1949 he joined the medical faculty of Boston University, where he remained until 1958, when he finally decided to write full time. By then he had published several science fiction novels in book form, most notably *Pebble in the Sky* (1950) and *The End of Eternity* (1955), as well as numerous collections including *I, Robot* (1950) and *The Martian Way and Other Stories* (1955). In the late fifties his emphasis shifted

17

to nonfiction, resulting in a steady stream on all aspects of science, plus other subjects as diverse as geology, *Paradise Lost,* set theory, the Bible, and Sherlockian limericks.

Asimov returned to writing science fiction in 1972 with the Hugo and Nebula Award–winning *The Gods Themselves.* He suffered a heart attack in 1977, but subsequent bouts with angina did little to diminish his literary output. He published several collections of science fiction and mystery short stories in the late 1970s, continued writing science columns for a number of magazines, and in 1980 lent his imprimatur to *Isaac Asimov's Science Fiction Magazine,* which is still published today. He began writing science fiction novels on a regular basis again with *Foundation's Edge* (1982), the "fourth novel in the Foundation Trilogy" and winner of the 1983 Hugo Award for best science fiction novel. It was in this novel that Asimov first suggested a merging of his *Foundation* and robots series, a promise he made good on over the course of his final science fiction novels: *The Robots of Dawn* (1983), *Robots and Empire* (1985), *Prelude to Foundation* (1988), and *Forward the Foundation* (1993).

Asimov's last decades were spent in New York City, where he lived with his second wife, Janet Opal Jeppson, whom he married in 1973. At the time of his death from complications of heart disease on April 6, 1992, he had produced nearly four hundred books, including novels, story collections, popular science, anthologies, and many works of fiction and nonfiction for juveniles. *I, Asimov* (1994), a posthumous collection of personal reminiscences, extends his two autobiographical memoirs, *In Memory Yet Green* (1979) and *In Joy Still Felt* (1980).

▨ *Critical Extracts*

FRITZ LEIBER   Here ⟨*The Stars, Like Dust*⟩ is a science fiction novel of spies and counter-spies set in a far future when man's spaceships have explored distant stars and man's culture has spread to many planets of this galaxy. First serialized in a magazine, *The Stars, Like Dust* tells of a time when empires hold sway in space and man's little home planet is almost forgotten. Yet it turns out that poor old Earth still has a most important message for the future.

Genial is the word for Isaac Asimov's writing. His characters are not all-conquering supermen [with the wisdom of Solon, the nobility of Sir Galahad and the instincts and manners of a bumptious brat] but simple human beings.

However, by having future men revert to feudalism, Asimov makes them even more naive than they are today. As a result, his characters, tho warm, are shallow.

Fritz Leiber, "Science-Fiction Novels of Spies in Far Future," *Chicago Sunday Tribune Magazine of Books*, 10 June 1951, p. 2

ISAAC ASIMOV   Science fiction is an undefined term in the sense that there is no generally agreed-upon definition of it. To be sure, there are probably hundreds of individual definitions but that is as bad as none at all. Worse, perhaps, since one's own definition gets in the way of an understanding of the next man's viewpoint. In this book, for instance, we have eleven different essayists on the subject, no two of whom, probably, would agree exactly on what it was they were discussing.

Under the circumstances, I think it best to make a personal definition here. As I am writing this without having read the other contributions, there is the chance of possible duplication. I'll risk that.

I should stress that my own definition is not necessarily better than the next man's or more valid or more inclusive or more precise. It simply expresses my way of thinking and will serve to lend a framework to this chapter.

About a year ago, I wrote an article for *The Writer* which I called "Other Worlds to Conquer." In it, I defined science fiction as follows: *Science fiction is that branch of literature which is concerned with the impact of scientific advance upon human beings.*

I intend to stick to that definition here, with a single slight modification which I will come to in a moment. I find intellectual satisfaction in the definition because it places the emphasis not upon science but upon human beings. After all, science (and everything else as well) is important to us only as it affects human beings.

The modification I wish to make in the definition is made necessary by the fact that it narrows the boundaries of science fiction to a greater extent than most people are willing to see it narrowed. For that reason, I would like to say that my definition applies not to "science fiction" but to a subdivision of the field which I find it convenient to speak of as "social science fiction."

It is my opinion that social science fiction is the only branch of science fiction that is sociologically significant, and that those stories, which are generally accepted as science fiction (at least to the point where skilled editors accept them for inclusion in their science-fiction magazines) but do not fall within the definition I have given above, are *not* significant, however amusing they may be and however excellent as pieces of fiction.

Isaac Asimov, "Social Science Fiction," *Modern Science Fiction: Its Meaning and Future*, ed. Reginald Bretnor (New York: Coward-McCann, 1953), pp. 158–59

P. SCHUYLER MILLER   These Foundation stories ⟨*Foundation and Empire*⟩ are well worth having between hard covers. They represent a great sweep of the imagination, and they may well come as close to the social forces controlling and directing human culture as do Toynbee's or Spengler's cycles of rise and fall. The force which protects the Foundation against Bel Riose is one which we hope may save the Free World from Soviet communism. But it is the structure, not the people of the Foundation or any of its worlds, that matters. The Asimov humor, too, is sadly missing. These are books for the devotee—not for the convert or the to-be-converted.

P. Schuyler Miller, [Review of *Foundation and Empire*], *Astounding Science-Fiction* 51, No. 2 (April 1953): 156–57

DAMON KNIGHT   Isaac Asimov's second novel about Lije Baley and R. (for Robot) Daneel Olivaw ⟨*The Naked Sun*⟩ is again a detective story set in a science fiction background. It is also something much more unusual in science fiction, and perhaps not wholly relevant to it: a love story. ⟨. . .⟩

As science fiction, I think most readers will find the book a little thin, although ingenious and funny in places. As a detective story, it is downright disappointing: the solution to the missing weapon problem, after all the foofarow, turns out to be over-elaborate to the point of silliness. But the shy, unstated romance between Lije and Gladia is a really delightful thing, and absolutely unexpected in a work of this kind. Ike, if you can do this, why are you bothering to write science fiction at all?

Damon Knight, [Review of *The Naked Sun*], *Infinity Science Fiction* 2, No. 5 (September 1957): 98–99

ROBERT SILVERBERG   This bulky new volume ⟨*The Rest of the Robots*⟩ comprises the companion to Asimov's *I, Robot*, which Doubleday reissued last year after the customary parade of editions. That book included nine linked stories dealing with the evolution of positronic robots; it set forth Asimov's famous Three Laws of Robotics, and developed them in every imaginable way, resulting in what amounted to a textbook demonstration of how to write stimulating science-fiction. ⟨. . .⟩

Asimov's stories go into these multiple editions for one reason above all others. They are marvellously interesting, wonderfully readable, intellectually provoking—good stories, that is. They get re-re-reprinted because they find an eager readership. Pinning down the qualities that make his work so good is a curiously difficult job, though. His prose does not sing like Ted Sturgeon's; his characters, while they are no stereotypes, do not attain the depth of the people in a Budrys novel; his imagination does not soar like that of Arthur C. Clarke; he buckles no swashes in the Poul Anderson manner. The stories are quiet, methodical, deliberate. The style is precise and unobtrusive, at least in the novels. There is a lot of talking, remarkably little action.

What's the secret? Internal consistency is part of it; an Asimov story always makes sense from start to finish, because its author obviously is in complete technical control throughout. Dexterity of plotting is another factor; the twists and turns and bypasses are superbly managed. Asimov is a storyteller in the classic tradition, with long grey beard and glittering eye, and when he begins to speak we cannot choose but listen.

Robert Silverberg, [Review of *The Rest of the Robots*], *Amazing Stories* 39, No. 3 (March 1965): 125–26

DAVID N. SAMUELSON   Asimov's prose style is superior to that of many writers of pulp fiction, but here too he seems to be aiming at a mass audience. Aside from the few dozen terms describing future technology, most of which are quickly explained, his vocabulary is simple and familiar, even trite. His sentences are relatively uncomplicated and generally cast in the active voice, resulting in a breathless, but not staccato, narrative pace. His language is relatively full of imagery and analogies, making the most unfamiliar science fictional conventions immediately accessible. The apparent impersonality of his style, a common feature of much science fiction, is modified by a serious, earnest, and optimistic tone which is characteristic of Asimov's fiction. 〈. . .〉

As a writer of science fiction as well as a scientist, Asimov is also concerned with communicating the missionary gospel of progress to a non-scientific and non-science-fictional audience beyond the science fiction community. To this end, I believe, not merely because such a *tour de force* was a challenge to the craftsman in him, Asimov attempted 〈in *The Caves of Steel*〉 to amalgamate the detective story with the science fiction novel. In addition, the combination of reservations about over-reliance on scientism with the optimistic anticipation of perfect communication and man-machine progress, while it may well represent the author's personal sense of balance between the sciences and the humanities, also seems calculated as a message of caution to the zealous prophets of science, and as an attempt to show both the masses and the literati that science fiction isn't quite as wild and radical as they may believe.

David N. Samuelson, Visions of Tomorrow: Six Journeys from Outer to Inner Space (New York: Arno Press, 1974), pp. 157–58, 161

JOSEPH F. PATROUCH, JR.   What is "Nightfall" about, and where does its compelling power lie? In his essay "Social Science Fiction" Asimov distinguishes between two kinds of fictional reactions to the French and Industrial revolutions: "Social fiction is that branch of literature which moralizes about a current society through the device of dealing with a fictitious society," and "science fiction is that branch of literature which deals with a fictitious society, differing from our own chiefly in the nature or extent of its technological development." In the context of the essay it is clear that Asimov views social fiction as presenting an alternate society with the intent of criticizing contemporary society, whereas science fiction creates an alternate society for its own sake, to show us that things could (not *should* or *ought to*) be different, to accustom us to change. Elsewhere he distinguishes between science fiction and what he calls tomorrow fiction, in which the writer simply tries to show what life will actually be like in a few years. The point in both distinctions is that science fiction must present an alternate society for its own sake rather than comment on contemporary society or attempt to show accurately where we are going.

"Nightfall" presents an alternate society for its own sake. It obviously is not an attempt to show what life will be like a few years from now, so it is not tomorrow fiction. And though it contains a few satirical touches directed at commonly held contemporary assumptions—for example, Beenay's notion that life as we know it could not exist on a planet revolving about a single sun—still it does not attempt to make us feel in our guts that air pollution is evil or that violent hoodlums have a right to their own identities. "Nightfall" is not social fiction. ⟨. . .⟩

"Nightfall" has the powerful effect it does because it convinces us that that's the way we would be under those different circumstances. "Nightfall" embodies a cosmic conception: what we are and the way we think are determined by the accident of the environment into which we are born. It figures forth an alternate world and society for its own sake. But that world is not totally irrelevant to our own. It has lessons for us, too. Consciousness, regardless of the environment that shapes it, is sacred. The people of Lagash are our brothers. When they are destroyed, we are destroyed, because we share consciousness. John Donne wrote, "No man is an island, entire of itself; every man is a piece of the continent. . . . Any man's death diminishes me, because I am involved in mankind." "Nightfall" expresses the same sentiments, only on a universal rather than a planetary scale. The sacredness and dignity of life is the message of Donne's Seventeenth Meditation, Asimov's "Nightfall," and science fiction.

Joseph F. Patrouch, Jr., *The Science Fiction of Isaac Asimov* (Garden City, NY: Doubleday, 1974), pp. 27–29

CHARLES ELKINS   What Asimov accepted as the "underlying concept" of the *Foundation* trilogy is the vulgar, mechanical, debased version of Marxism promulgated in the Thirties—and still accepted by many today. Indeed he takes *this* brand of Marxism to its logical end; human actions and the history they create become as predictable as physical events in nature. Just as those scientific elites in our world who comprehend nature's laws manipulate nature to their advantage, so, too, the guardians and the First Speaker, who alone understand Seldon's Plan, manipulate individuals and control the course of history. "Psycho-history is," as ⟨Donald A.⟩ Wollheim quaintly puts it, "the science that Marxism never became" ⟨. . .⟩ With the proviso that neither Wollheim nor Asimov has understood Marxism (and that one should substitute "mechanical pseudo-Marxism" for their mentions of it), it is precisely this treatment of history as a "science" above men which accounts for the *Foundation* trilogy's ideological fascination and evocativeness as well as for its ultimate intellectual and artistic bankruptcy.

Reading the *Foundation* novels, one experiences an overriding sense of the inevitable, of a pervading fatalism. Everything in the universe is predetermined. Unable to change the preordained course of events, man becomes, instead of the agent of history, an object, a "pawn" (using Asimov's chess metaphor) in the grip of historical necessity—i.e., of the actualization of Hari Seldon's calculations. ⟨. . .⟩

The sense of fatality and futility evoked in the *Foundation* novels is a consequence of the reader's recognition that not only will Seldon's Plan remain hidden but even those who preserve it are almost overwhelmed by its complexity. A few will be free; the rest will be under the thumb of those who can understand the Plan. The First Speaker (and clearly Asimov himself, along with many other science fiction writers such as Robert Heinlein) envisions a society organized not according to the principles of equality but according to a hierarchy of merit. It is a society similar to the one urged by Saint-Simon, the French utopian thinker; he also argued for a society governed by *savants* (mathematicians, chemists, engineers, painters, writers, etc.), who would form a Council of Newton and, because they were men of genius, would have the right to determine human destiny. In the *Foundation* trilogy the masses merely follow. Unable either to discover or to comprehend the Plan's "synthesis of the calculus of n-variables and n-dimensional geometry," the great majority of mankind is at the mercy of complex forces which they can neither understand nor control, and surrender their freedom to a techno-bureaucratic elite. Asimov thus expresses a modern version of Saint-Simon's ideology, namely, the necessity of society's being governed by a technocratic elite.

Charles Elkins, "Asimov's *Foundation* Novels: Historical Materialism Distorted into Cyclical Psychohistory," *Isaac Asimov*, ed. Joseph D. Olander and Martin H. Greenberg (New York: Taplinger, 1977), pp. 104–5

ALESSANDRO PORTELLI   The analogy between Blacks and robots is obvious in most of Asimov's work, though he makes half-hearted attempts at covering it up (for instance, both in "Strikebreaker" and in *The Naked Sun* [1956] he compares the social system to that of ancient Sparta, rather than contemporary Alabama). The fear that the Earth may be surreptitiously integrated by an infiltration of humanoid robots hints at miscegenation, and reproduces the obsession with light-skinned Blacks "passing" into the white race. The question of "passing" is at the root of Asimov's finest robot character, R. Daneel Olivaw. He knows he cannot be accepted as an equal among humans but cannot understand why, since he feels in no way their inferior. He takes a special pleasure in passing for human in front of his human detective colleague, an expert in robotics, a fanatic anti-robot extremist. "Passing" is also the theme of "Evidence," a story about a robot who manages to get elected mayor in an anti-robot community (and then again, he may not have been a robot after all: as in Faulkner's *Light in August*, it is not the *fact* so much as the *doubt* of passing which makes it so dreadful).

Olivaw's plea is presented in such a way as to induce the reader to sympathize with him. He is one of the few Asimov characters endowed with more than a rudimentary psychology, including a sort of straight-faced, Buster-Keaton humor each time he takes seriously human contradictions and nonsense. But he is entitled to sympathy, after all, because he is so much like us—like Eliza in *Uncle Tom's Cabin*, who is so much like white folks it's a shame she's Black. Indeed, the double nature of robots—as machines and as a metaphor for Blacks—involves Asimov in an intricate contradiction: thanks to the fiction he has set up, he cannot support the comparatively respectable cause of racial integration without at the same time supporting the more controversial cause of automation and unemployment. According to the solution he works out in his more recent stories, he seems to be in favor of stressing the racial over the industrial metaphor. In the stories collected in *The Bicentennial Man* (1976), the parallel between robots and Blacks, far from being covered up, is emphasized and made all the more obvious. The book's title story is remarkable for its skillful treatment of miscegenation: man and robot become more organic. The story may indeed be read as the SF counter-version of Alex Haley's Bicentennial bestseller, *Roots*: it tells of the robot's fidelity to his owner's family through several generations, and of his final acceptance as a human being (on the point of death and as a unique, exceptional case) once he has successfully rid himself of all traces of what made him different from the ruling race. Taken together, the three stories collected in this book deal with the blurring of man-machine differences for the sake of assimilation. Yet beneath the egalitarian surface runs a detectable preoccupation that, once differences are abolished, robots will—peacefully—"take over" (after all, aren't they, in Susan Calvin's words, "a cleaner, better breed than we are"?). Thus, "The Life and Times of Multivac" finally reverses the Frankenstein complex by having humans rebel against robots.

The role of the Three Laws in the parallel between Blacks and robots is made explicit in *The Naked Sun*. Here, on a planet much reminiscent of Southern plantations, a murder occurs in which all evidence shows robots to have been at least instrumental. But, like Richard Wright's Bigger Thomas in *Native Sun*, robots ought to be below suspicion. The idea that they may concur in the killing of a man is enough to throw the entire planet into a panic: its entire social structure is based on the certainty that robots "cannot revolt," on the existence of "good, healthy slave complexes" in the machines.

Alessandro Portelli, "The Three Laws of Robotics: Laws of the Text, Laws of Production, Laws of Society," *Science-Fiction Studies* 7, No. 2 (July 1980): 152–53

JAMES GUNN   The theme of *The End of Eternity* is as significant as anything Asimov ever touched. Since it was virtually Asimov's last extended thought about science fiction until unusual circumstances produced *The Gods Themselves*, the 1955 novel may define the values Asimov was upholding after nearly twenty years of writing science fiction. It may also provide clues to his decision to leave the fantasy world of fiction writing for the real world of science writing.

The End of Eternity shares with other Asimov fiction his basic concern for intelligent choice. Although Harlan begins as a cold and withdrawn Eternal, apparently moved only by intellectual concerns and sharing the values of a group that can change other people's Realities and lives at will, and although Harlan changes only because of his love for Noys, reason still wins out over emotion. In the final chapter, Harlan is persuaded by Noys's rational arguments, not by his love for her. Out of resentment that his love has been manipulated, Harlan has made up his mind to kill Noys, but when he matches his own experience with Noys's accusations, he is persuaded.

In another sense, perhaps, Asimov's old science-fiction enthusiasms may have emerged victorious over his rationality. After her comments on Eternity's choosing safety and mediocrity, Noys says, "The real solutions . . . come from conquering difficulty, not avoiding it." Carried to their ultimate conclusion, these statements, which Asimov implicitly accepts for the sake of the novel, imply that humanity cannot improve its lot by rational choice. Or perhaps, if Asimov is given credit for dealing with a special case, they mean only that humanity cannot change the past.

If one wished to personalize the message of the novel, one might speculate that Asimov, looking back over his own past, has concluded that no amount of tinkering will change it for the better. This is, indeed, one of the messages of his autobiographical writings. Everything happened for the best: Campbell's early rejections, Sam Merwin's rejection of "Grow Old with Me," the change of administration at the Boston University School of Medicine that led to his full-time writing (which still awaited him). . . . If he had had the opportunity to make things happen differently, he would have made the wrong choice, he might be saying, would have chosen safety and mediocrity over risk and greatness. In *The End of Eternity*, at least, Asimov chose, as rationally as he could, uncertainty over certainty and infinity over not eternity but Eternity, that is, over the limitation of man's possibilities by too much tinkering with them. Asimov is not denying humanity's potential for rationality or the need for considering choices rationally but humanity's capacity to play God. Humanity will not consciously choose the uncertainty of adventure, or the adventure of uncertainty.

James Gunn, *Isaac Asimov: The Foundations of Science Fiction* (New York: Oxford University Press, 1982), pp. 182–84.

C. N. MANLOVE   ⟨. . .⟩ *Foundation's Edge* draws on the cosmogony first used in Asimov's *The End of Eternity* (1955), which predicates a group of Eternals, who chose from a myriad of possibles (also acutalised) one universe in which man would be the sole intelligent lifeform—and in which, no doubt, a man called Hari Seldon would eventually arise to make all events in that universe no longer random but rational. There, indeed, is a larger Plan, a wheel governing wheels within wheels. It mirrors the process of expanding discovery that the novel follows—an expansion which widens out not to an infinite, but curiously to a benign 'enclosure', a circumscribing, that folds the universe back on itself; and back on its centre in the Seldon Plan. In parallel with this, one may note, Asimov himself has reached out to incorporate much of his literary output in the history of this galaxy, placing his novels *The Stars, Like Dust, The Currents of Space* and *Pebble in the Sky* during the period of the growth of the First Empire, and his 'robotic' novels and short stories during a period in which the galaxy was colonised by robots. His own separate works, like the temporally separated acts within the trilogy, are thus caught up in a larger Plan, devoured as it were by the very fiction they create. Nothing could more surely testify to the dominant urge behind Asimov's work being the need to make life coherent. Yet ⟨. . .⟩ he does not enforce coherence in any desperate way: he lets it find itself almost by chance and certainly as much by choice as by imposition.

> C. N. Manlove, "Isaac Asimov, the *Foundation* Trilogy (1951–53; serialized 1942–49)," *Science Fiction: Ten Explorations* (Kent, OH: Kent State University Press, 1986), pp. 33–34

CLYDE WILCOX   Four changes in Asimov's future worlds have been traced to changes in the political and social culture. First, the growing awareness of diversity within worldwide communism and the decline of cold war tensions produced a change in Asimov's vision of future galactic politics. While the early novels portrayed clashing blocs of planets, the later novels allowed for the possibility of detente.

Second, the increased politicization of the 1960s seems to have led to a greater emphasis on domestic politics. Although the early novels generally ignored political struggles between domestic factions, the later books portrayed these political processes with greater detail.

Third, the counterculture cry for increased participatory democracy is echoed in a discussion of democratic political systems in the later books, replacing the corrupt empires and theocratic, plutocratic, and oligarchic governments of the early works. In addition to discussions of legislatures and elected executives, Asimov produces in these latest books the ultimate participatory democracy: a vision of the universe in which all matter is intelligent and participates in decisions which affect its future.

Finally, the enormous changes in the role of women over the past 30 years are reflected in the greater role given to women in the later novels. Women in the early Asimov novels are principally daughters or wives of important actors; in the later novels they are central figures—and often are important political or scientific figures. In the early novels they are naive, frivolous, and often simpleminded, but in the later novels they are ambitious, intelligent, and strong. Indeed, the progressive liberation of Gladia in the later Robot novels seems to mirror the progress of feminist organizations in American politics.

> Clyde Wilcox, "The Greening of Isaac Asimov: Cultural Change and Political Futures," *Extrapolation* 31, No. 1 (Spring 1990): 61–62

DONALD HASSLER   Rather than just "gee whiz" wonder at expansion into space or sentimental nostalgia over lost youth, both of which are simpler effects for which Asimov in the typical science-fiction tradition might have settled, paradox and the continual deepening and complication of the big themes mark each of ⟨his⟩ late fictions. It seems to be the philosophic puzzle of causation and purpose that drives these books—and that may have driven Asimov back to fiction. There is, in fact, nearly a surfeit of images to express this puzzle. One big word for the notion is "orthogenesis." Though Asimov does not burden the stories with the word itself, every turn of image, plot, and characterization is haunted by the question of the nature of purposeful evolution. In *Foundation's Edge*, the gestalt-planet Gaia, which will grow to the organically unified and gestalt-galaxy called Galaxia, represents the ordained and general "law." However, the decision, or choice, to move Galactic expansion in that direction is given to one individual human, Trevize. The final novel, then, will puzzle over how the hero *knew* to follow the correct hunch and to make the right decision. No law could tell him to follow the law. In other words, decision or choice may be grounded more on hunch and on individuality than on law and generality.

In the Robot novels, the puzzle emerges again in the differences between Spacers and Earthmen as well as in the extent and nature of robot control. Asimov wrings out an addition to the Three Laws: the Zeroth Law is used to abstract the purposeful direction of humanity in general. He has telepathic robots designed by Spacer technology derive this Fourth Law. He links such benevolent despotism to psychohistory and ultimately to the total control of Gaia and Galaxia. Still he retains the need for individual human choice, not to mention that someone had to make the machines who derive the laws. Long before Golan Trevize's role as the hero who makes a choice, the hero robots Daneel and Giskard puzzle over the question of how direction and "newness" can ever be inserted into a system of Law:

> "You gave a perfect answer, friend Giskard . . ."
> "It was the best answer within the compass of the Three Laws. It was not the best answer possible."
> "What was the best answer possible?"
> "I do not know, since I cannot put it into words or even concepts as long as I am bound by the Laws."
> "There is nothing beyond the Laws," said Daneel.

The problem, then, is the question of from where, eventually, the Fourth Law comes. A related problem is that if Law is done away with, allowing for random "newness," nothing in the way of historical development can be sure. Reading Asimov brings to mind such questions.

Donald Hassler, *Isaac Asimov* (Mercer Island, WA: Starmont House, 1991), pp. 100–102

WILLIAM TOUPONCE   Asimov does not systematically present the scientific concepts underlying the new science ⟨of robotics⟩. Instead, he works out the inherent verbal and situational ambiguities in the Three Laws, which provide him with the conflicts and uncertainties required for new stories. To Asimov's great relief, "it always seemed possible to think up a new angle out of the sixty-one words of the Three Laws." As ⟨Thomas⟩ Kuhn has demonstrated, the paradigm that provides the basis for a new tradition of scientific research never completely resolves all of its problems. In fact, resolving these puzzles and problems becomes the primary activity of scientists working within the paradigm. For Kuhn, as for Asimov, paradigms are constitutive elements of science, and the object of normal science is to solve a puzzle or problem whose very existence is assumed to confirm the validity of the paradigm. Normal science is, then, an enterprise that aims to refine, extend, and articulate a paradigm already in existence. According to Kuhn, one of the most important foci for research in normal science is empirical work (which may include the "instrumentation" of a theory in the field testing of scientific equipment) undertaken "to articulate the paradigm theory, resolving some of its residual ambiguities and permitting the solution of problems to which it had previously only drawn attention."

Hence, that most of Asimov's robots take the narrative form of a puzzle or problem is no accident. With these stories, Asimov is trying to represent a period of normal science in which robotics has already been established. He seeks to convey to the reader the intellectual pleasures of using ingenuity in the puzzle solving that occurs within a new scientific paradigm.

William Touponce, *Isaac Asimov* (Boston: Twayne, 1991), pp. 34–35

Bibliography

Pebble in the Sky. 1950.

I, Robot. 1950.

The Stars, Like Dust. 1951.

Foundation ⟨*The 1,000 Year Plan*⟩. 1951.

David Starr, Space Ranger. 1952.

Foundation and Empire. 1952.

The Currents of Space. 1952.

Biochemistry and Human Metabolism (with Burnham S. Walker and William C. Boyd). 1952, 1954, 1957.

Second Foundation. 1953.

Lucky Starr and the Pirates of the Asteroids. 1953.

The Caves of Steel. 1954.

Lucky Starr and the Oceans of Venus. 1954.

The Chemicals of Life: Enzymes, Vitamins, Hormones. 1954.

The Martian Way and Other Stories. 1955.

The End of Eternity. 1955.

Races and People (with William C. Boyd). 1955.

Lucky Starr and the Big Sun of Mercury. 1956.

Chemistry and Human Health (with Burnham S. Walker and M. Kolaya Nicholas). 1956.

Inside the Atom. 1956, 1958, 1961, 1966, 1974.

The Naked Sun. 1957.

Lucky Starr and the Moons of Jupiter. 1957.

Building Blocks of the Universe. 1957, 1972.

Earth Is Room Enough: Science Fiction Tales for Our Own Planet. 1957.

Only a Trillion. 1957, 1976.

The World of Carbon. 1958.

Lucky Starr and the Rings of Saturn. 1958.

The World of Nitrogen. 1958.

The Death Dealers. 1958.

Nine Tomorrows: Tales of the Near Future. 1959.

The Clock We Live On. 1959, 1965.

Words of Science and the History Behind Them. 1959.

Realm of Numbers. 1959.

The Living River. 1960.

The Kingdom of the Sun. 1960, 1962.

Realm of Measure. 1960.

Breakthroughs in Science. 1960.

Satellites in Other Space. 1960, 1973.

The Wellsprings of Life. 1960.

The Intelligent Man's Guide to Science. 1960 (2 vols.), 1965 (as The New
    Intelligent Man's Guide to Science), 1972 (as Asimov's Guide to Science),
    1984 (as Asimov's New Guide to Science).

The Double Planet. 1960.

Triangle ⟨The Currents of Space, Pebble in the Sky, The Stars, Like Dust⟩. 1961.

Words from the Myths. 1961.

Realm of Algebra. 1961.

Life and Energy. 1962.

Words in Genesis. 1962.

Fact and Fancy. 1962.

Words on the Map. 1962.

The Hugo Winners (editor). 1962–86. 5 vols.

The Search for the Elements. 1962.

The Genetic Code. 1962.

The Foundation Trilogy ⟨Foundation, Foundation and Empire, Second Founda-
    tion⟩. 1963.

Words from the Exodus. 1963.

The Human Body: Its Structure and Operation. 1963.

Fifty Short Science Fiction Tales (editor; with Groff Conklin). 1963.

View from a Height. 1963.

The Kite That Won the Revolution. 1963.

The Human Brain: Its Capacities and Functions. 1964.

A Short History of Biology. 1964.

Quick and Easy Math. 1964.

Adding a Dimension: Seventeen Essays on the History of Science. 1964.

Planets for Man (with Stephen H. Dole). 1964.

The Rest of the Robots. 1964.

Asimov's Biographical Encyclopedia of Science and Technology. 1964, 1972, 1976, 1982.

A Short History of Chemistry. 1965.

The Greeks: A Great Adventure. 1965.

Of Time and Space and Other Things. 1965.

An Easy Introduction to the Slide Rule. 1965.

Fantastic Voyage. 1966.

From Earth to Heaven. 1966.

The Noble Gases. 1966.

The Neutrino: Ghost Particle of the Atom. 1966.

The Roman Republic. 1966.

Understanding Physics. 1966. 3 vols.

The Genetic Effects of Radiation (with Theodosius Dobzhansky). 1966.

Tomorrow's Children: 18 Tales of Fantasy and Science Fiction (editor). 1966.

The Universe: From Flat Earth to Quasar. 1966, 1971, 1983.

The Moon. 1966.

Environments Out There. 1967.

The Roman Empire. 1967.

Through a Glass, Clearly. 1967.

Is Anyone There? 1967.

To the Ends of the Universe. 1967.

Mars. 1967.

The Egyptians. 1967.

Asimov's Mysteries. 1968.

Science, Numbers, and I. 1968.

Stars. 1968.

Galaxies. 1968.

The Near East: 10,000 Years of History. 1968.

The Dark Ages. 1968.

Asimov's Guide to the Bible. 1968–69. 2 vols.

Words from History. 1968.

Photosynthesis. 1968.

The Shaping of England. 1969.

20th Century Discovery: The Planets. 1969, 1976.

Nightfall and Other Stories. 1969.

Opus 100. 1969.

ABC's of Space. 1969.

Great Ideas of Science. 1969.

The Solar System and Back. 1970.

Asimov's Guide to Shakespeare. 1970. 2 vols.

Constantinople: The Forgotten Empire. 1970.

ABC's of the Ocean. 1970.

Light. 1970.

The Stars in Their Courses. 1971.

Where Do We Go from Here? (editor). 1971.

What Makes the Sun Shine? 1971.

The Sensuous Dirty Old Man. 1971.

The Best New Thing. 1971.

Isaac Asimov's Treasury of Humor (editor). 1971.

The Land of Canaan. 1971.

ABC's of the Earth. 1971.

The Left Hand of the Electron. 1972.

An Isaac Asimov Double: Space Ranger; Pirates of the Asteroids. 1972.

The Gods Themselves. 1972.

More Words of Science. 1972.

Electricity and Man. 1972.

ABC's of Ecology. 1972.

The Early Asimov; or, Eleven Years of Trying. 1972.

The Shaping of France. 1972.

The Story of Ruth. 1972.

Ginn Science Program: Intermediate Level A (with Roy A. Gallant). 1972.

Ginn Science Program: Intermediate Level C (with Roy A. Gallant). 1972.

Asimov's Annotated Don Juan (editor). 1972.

Comets and Meteors. 1972.

The Sun. 1972.

Worlds within Worlds: The Story of Nuclear Energy. 1972. 3 vols.

How Did We Find Out the Earth Is Round? 1973.

How Did We Find Out about Electricity? 1973.

A Second Isaac Asimov Double: The Big Sun of Mercury; The Oceans of Venus. 1973.

The Shaping of North America from the Earliest Times to 1763. 1973.

Today and Tomorrow and . . . 1973.

Jupiter, the Largest Planet. 1973.

Ginn Science Program: Advanced Level A (with Roy A. Gallant). 1973.

Ginn Science Program: Advanced Level B (with Roy A. Gallant). 1973.

How Did We Find Out about Numbers? 1973.

Please Explain. 1973.

The Tragedy of the Moon. 1973.

Dar Tellum: Stranger from a Distant Planet by James R. Berry (editor). 1973.

How Did We Find Out about Dinosaurs? 1973.

Nebula Award Stories 8 (editor). 1973.

The Best of Isaac Asimov. 1974.

Asimov on Astronomy. 1974.

The Birth of the United States 1763–1816. 1974.

Have You Seen These? 1974.

Before the Golden Age: A Science Fiction Anthology of the 1930's (editor). 1974.

Our World in Space (with Robert McCall). 1974.

How Did We Find Out about Germs? 1974.

Asimov's Annotated Paradise Lost (editor). 1974.

Tales of the Black Widowers. 1974.

Asimov on Chemistry. 1974.

Earth, Our Crowded Spaceship. 1974.

How Did We Find Out about Vitamins? 1974.

The Third Isaac Asimov Double: The Rings of Saturn; The Moons of Jupiter. 1974.

Of Matters Great and Small. 1975.

The Solar System. 1975.

Our Federal Union: The United States from 1816 to 1865. 1975.

How Did We Find Out about Comets? 1975.

Science Past, Science Future. 1975.

Buy Jupiter and Other Stories. 1975.

Eyes on the Universe: A History of the Telescope. 1975.

The Heavenly Host. 1975.

Lecherous Limericks. 1975.

The Ends of the Earth: The Polar Regions of the World. 1975.

How Did We Find Out about Energy? 1975.

The Dream, Benjamin's Dream, and Benjamin's Bicentennial Blast. 1976.

Asimov on Physics. 1976.

Murder at the ABA: A Puzzle in Four Days and Sixty Scenes. 1976.

How Did We Find Out about Atoms? 1976.

Good Taste: A Story. 1976.

The Planet That Wasn't. 1976.

The Bicentennial Man and Other Stories. 1976.

More Lecherous Limericks. 1976.

More Tales of the Black Widowers. 1976.

Alpha Centauri, the Nearest Star. 1976.

How Did We Find Out about Nuclear Power? 1976.

Familiar Poems, Annotated (editor). 1976.

The Collapsing Universe. 1977.

Asimov on Numbers. 1977.

How Did We Find Out about Outer Space? 1977.

Still More Lecherous Limericks. 1977.

The Beginning and the End. 1977.

Mars, the Red Planet. 1977.

The Golden Door: The United States from 1865 to 1918. 1977.

The Key Word and Other Mysteries. 1977.

Asimov's Sherlockian Limericks. 1978.

100 Great Science Fiction Short Short Stories (editor; with Martin H. Greenberg
      and Joseph D. Olander). 1978.

Quasar, Quasar, Burning Bright. 1978.

How Did We Find Out about Earthquakes? 1978.

Animals of the Bible. 1978.

Life and Time. 1978.

Limericks, Too Gross (with John Ciardi). 1978.

How Did We Find Out about Black Holes? 1978.

The Far Ends of Time and Earth. 1979.

Saturn and Beyond. 1979.

Prisoners of the Stars ⟨*The Stars, Like Dust, The Martian Way and Other Stories,
      The Currents of Space*⟩. 1979.

In Memory Yet Green: Autobiography 1920–1954. 1979.

Opus 200. 1979.

Isaac Asimov Presents the Great SF Stories: 1939–1963 (editor; with Martin
      H. Greenberg). 1979–92. 25 vols.

Extraterrestrial Civilizations. 1979.

How Did We Find Out about Our Human Roots? 1979.

The Road to Infinity. 1979.

A Choice of Catastrophes: The Disasters That Threaten Our World. 1979.

The Science Fictional Solar System (editor; with Martin H. Greenberg and
      Charles G. Waugh). 1979.

The 13 Crimes of Science Fiction (editor; with Martin H. Greenberg and Charles G. Waugh). 1979.

Isaac Asimov's Book of Facts (with others). 1979.

How Did We Find Out about Antarctica? 1979.

Casebook of the Black Widowers. 1980.

The Future in Question (editor; with Martin H. Greenberg and Joseph D. Olander). 1980.

How Did We Find Out about Oil? 1980.

In Joy Still Felt: Autobiography 1954–1978. 1980.

Who Done It? (editor; with Alice Laurence). 1980.

Space Mail (editor; with Martin H. Greenberg and Joseph D. Olander). 1980–81. 2 vols.

Microcosmic Tales: 100 Wondrous Science Fiction Short-Short Stories (editor; with Martin H. Greenberg and Joseph D. Olander). 1980.

The Seven Deadly Sins of Science Fiction (editor; with Martin H. Greenberg and Charles G. Waugh). 1980.

The Annotated Gulliver's Travels (editor). 1980.

How Did We Find Out about Coal? 1980.

The Future I (editor; with Martin H. Greenberg and Joseph D. Olander). 1981.

In the Beginning. 1981.

Wild Inventions (editor; with Martin H. Greenberg and Charles Waugh). 1981.

Asimov on Science Fiction. 1981.

Venus, Near Neighbor of the Sun. 1981.

3 by Asimov: Three Science Fiction Tales. 1981.

How Did We Find Out about Solar Power? 1981.

How Did We Find Out about Volcanoes? 1981.

Vision of the Universe (with Kazuaki Iwasaki). 1981.

Catastrophes! (editor; with Martin H. Greenberg and Charles G. Waugh). 1981.

Isaac Asimov Presents the Best Science Fiction of the 19th Century (editor; with Martin H. Greenberg and Charles G. Waugh). 1981.

The Seven Cardinal Virtues of Science Fiction (editor; with Martin H. Greenberg and Charles G. Waugh). 1981.

Fantastic Creatures (editor; with Martin H. Greenberg and Charles G. Waugh). 1981.

The Sun Shines Bright. 1981.

Travels through Time (editor; with Martin H. Greenberg and Charles Waugh). 1981.

Change! Seventy-one Glimpses of the Future. 1981.

Raintree Reading Series (editor; with Martin H. Greenberg and Charles G. Waugh). 1981–84. 3 vols.

After the End (editor; with Martin H. Greenberg and Charles Waugh). 1981.

A Grossery of Limericks (with John Ciardi). 1981.

Miniature Mysteries: 100 Malicious Little Mystery Stories (editor; with Martin H. Greenberg and Charles G. Waugh). 1981.

The Twelve Crimes of Christmas (editor; with Martin H. Greenberg and Carol-Lynn Rossel Waugh). 1981.

Tantalizing Locked Room Mysteries (editor; with Martin H. Greenberg and Charles G. Waugh). 1982.

TV: 2000 (editor; with Martin H. Greenberg and Charles G. Waugh). 1982.

Laughing Space: An Anthology of Science Fiction Humor (editor; with J. O. Jeppson). 1982.

How Did We Find Out about Life in the Deep Sea? 1982.

The Complete Robot. 1982.

Speculations (editor; with Alice Laurence). 1982.

Flying Saucers (editor; with Martin H. Greenberg and Charles G. Waugh). 1982.

Exploring the Earth and the Cosmos: The Growth and Future of Human Knowledge. 1982.

How Did We Find Out about the Beginning of Life? 1982.

Dragon Tales (editor; with Martin H. Greenberg and Charles G. Waugh). 1982.

Earth Invaded (editor; with Martin H. Greenberg and Charles Waugh). 1982.

The Big Apple Mysteries (editor; with Martin H. Greenberg and Carol-Lynn Rossel Waugh). 1982.

Mad Scientists (editor; with Martin H. Greenberg and Charles Waugh). 1982.

Isaac Asimov Presents Superquiz (with Ken Fisher). 1982–89. 4 vols.

The Last Man on Earth (editor; with Martin H. Greenberg and Charles G. Waugh). 1982.

Science Fiction A to Z: A Dictionary of the Great Themes of Science Fiction (editor; with Martin H. Greenberg and Charles G. Waugh). 1982.

Foundation's Edge. 1982.

Isaac Asimov Presents the Best Fantasy of the 19th Century (editor; with Martin H. Greenberg and Charles G. Waugh). 1982.

How Did We Find Out about the Universe? 1983.

Counting the Eons. 1983.

The Winds of Change and Other Stories. 1983.

Show Business Is Murder (editor; with Martin H. Greenberg and Carol-Lynn Rossel Waugh). 1983.

Hallucination Orbit: Psychology in Science Fiction (editor; with Martin H. Greenberg and Charles G. Waugh). 1983.

Caught in the Organ Draft: Biology in Science Fiction (editor; with Martin H. Greenberg and Charles G. Waugh). 1983.

The Roving Mind. 1983.

The Science Fiction Weight-Loss Book (editor; with Martin H. Greenberg and George R. R. Martin). 1983.

The Measure of the Universe. 1983.

Isaac Asimov Presents the Best Horror & Supernatural of the 19th Century (editor; with Martin H. Greenberg and Charles G. Waugh). 1983.

Starships (editor; with Martin H. Greenberg and Charles G. Waugh). 1983.

The Union Club Mysteries. 1983.

Norby, the Mixed-Up Robot (with Janet Asimov). 1983.

How Did We Find Out about Genes? 1983.

The Robots of Dawn. 1983.

13 Horrors of Halloween (editor; with Martin H. Greenberg and Carol-Lynn Rossel Waugh). 1983.

The Robot Collection ⟨The Caves of Steel, The Naked Sun, The Complete Robot⟩. 1983.

Creations: The Quest for Origins in Story and Science (editor; with George Zebrowski and Martin H. Greenberg). 1983.

Wizards (editor; with Martin H. Greenberg and Charles G. Waugh). 1983.

Those Amazing Electronic Thinking Machines (editor; with Martin H. Greenberg and Charles G. Waugh). 1983.

Computer Crimes and Capers (editor; with Martin H. Greenberg and Charles G. Waugh). 1983.

Intergalactic Empires (editor; with Martin H. Greenberg and Charles G. Waugh). 1983.

Machines That Think: The Best Science Fiction Stories about Robots and Computers (editor; with Patricia S. Warrick and Martin H. Greenberg). 1983.

"X" Stands for the Unknown. 1984.

100 Great Fantasy Short Short Stories (editor; with Martin H. Greenberg and Terry Carr). 1984.

Witches (editor; with Martin H. Greenberg and Charles G. Waugh). 1984.

Murder on the Menu (editor; with Martin H. Greenberg and Carol-Lynn Rossel Waugh). 1984.

Young Mutants (editor; with Martin H. Greenberg and Charles G. Waugh). 1984.

Isaac Asimov Presents the Best Science Fiction Firsts (editor; with Martin H. Greenberg and Charles G. Waugh). 1984.

Norby's Other Secret (with Janet Asimov). 1984.

How Did We Find Out about Computers? 1984.

Opus 300. 1984.

The Science Fictional Olympics (editor; with Martin H. Greenberg and Charles G. Waugh). 1984.

Living in the Future (editor). 1984.

Fantastic Reading (editor; with Martin H. Greenberg and David Clark Yeager). 1984.

Banquets of the Black Widowers. 1984.

Election Day 2084: A Science Fiction Anthology on the Politics of the Future (editor; with Martin H. Greenberg). 1984.

Limericks for Children. 1984.

Young Extraterrestrials (editor; with Martin H. Greenberg and Charles G. Waugh). 1984.

Sherlock Holmes through Time and Space (editor; with Martin H. Greenberg and Charles G. Waugh). 1984.

Supermen (editor; with Martin H. Greenberg and Charles G. Waugh). 1984.

Baker's Dozen: Thirteen Short Fantasy Novels (editor; with Martin H. Greenberg and Charles G. Waugh). 1984.

How Did We Find Out about Robots? 1984.

Asimov's Guide to Halley's Comet. 1985.

Cosmic Knights (editor; with Martin H. Greenberg and Charles G. Waugh). 1985.

Young Monsters (editor; with Martin H. Greenberg and Charles G. Waugh). 1985.

The Exploding Suns: The Secrets of the Supernovas. 1985.

Norby and the Lost Princess (with Janet Asimov). 1985.

Spells (editor; with Martin H. Greenberg and Charles G. Waugh). 1985.

How Did We Find Out about the Atmosphere? 1985.

Robots: Machines in Man's Image (editor; with Karen A. Frenkel). 1985.

The Edge of Tomorrow. 1985.

Great Science Fiction Stories by the World's Great Scientists (editor; with Martin
    H. Greenberg and Charles G. Waugh). 1985.

The Subatomic Monster. 1985.

The Disappearing Man and Other Mysteries. 1985.

Robots and Empire. 1985.

Amazing Stories: 60 Years of the Best Science Fiction (editor; with Martin H.
    Greenberg). 1985.

Young Ghosts (editor; with Martin H. Greenberg and Charles G. Waugh).
    1985.

Thirteen Short Science Fiction Novels (editor; with Martin H. Greenberg and
    Charles G. Waugh). 1985.

It's Such a Beautiful Day. 1985.

Norby and the Invaders (with Janet Asimov). 1985.

Giants (editor; with Martin H. Greenberg and Charles G. Waugh). 1985.

The Adventures of Lucky Starr ⟨*Lucky Starr: Space Ranger, Lucky Starr and the
    Pirates of the Asteroids, Lucky Starr and the Oceans of Venus*⟩. 1985.

How Did We Find Out about DNA? 1985.

The Further Adventures of Lucky Starr ⟨*Lucky Starr and the Big Sun of Mercury,
    Lucky Starr and the Moons of Jupiter, Lucky Starr and the Rings of Saturn*⟩.
    1985.

The Alternate Asimovs. 1986.

Comets (editor; with Martin H. Greenberg and Charles G. Waugh). 1986.

Young Star Travelers (editor; with Martin H. Greenberg and Charles G.
    Waugh). 1986.

The Dangers of Intelligence and Other Science Essays. 1986.

Mythical Beasties (editor; with Martin H. Greenberg and Charles G. Waugh).
    1986.

How Did We Find Out about Blood? 1986.

How Did We Find Out about the Speed of Light? 1986.

Future Days: A Nineteenth-Century Vision of the Year 2000. 1986.

Tin Stars (editor; with Martin H. Greenberg and Charles G. Waugh). 1986.

The Best Science Fiction of Isaac Asimov. 1986.

The Best Mysteries of Isaac Asimov. 1986.

Foundation and Earth. 1986.

Robot Dreams. 1986.

Norby and the Queen's Necklace (with Janet Asimov). 1986.

Magical Wishes (editor; with Martin H. Greenberg and Charles G. Waugh).
    1986.

Far as Human Eye Could See. 1987.

Space Shuttles (editor; with Martin H. Greenberg and Charles G. Waugh). 1987.

Atlantis (editor; with Martin H. Greenberg and Charles G. Waugh). 1987.

Norby Finds a Villain (with Janet Asimov). 1987.

How Did We Find Out about the Brain? 1987.

Past, Present, and Future. 1987.

How Did We Find Out about Sunshine? 1987.

Other Worlds of Isaac Asimov. Ed. Martin H. Greenberg. 1987.

How to Enjoy Writing: A Book of Aid and Comfort (with Janet Asimov). 1987.

Bare Bones Dinosaur (with David Hawcock). 1987.

Young Witches and Warlocks (editor; with Martin H. Greenberg and Charles G. Waugh). 1987.

Fantastic Voyage II: Destination Brain. 1987.

Beginnings: The Story of Origins—of Mankind, Life, the Earth, the Universe. 1987.

Prelude to Foundation. 1988.

Encounters (editor; with Martin H. Greenberg and Charles Waugh). 1988.

Little Brothers. 1988.

The Relativity of Wrong. 1988.

Our Solar System. 1988.

The Sun. 1988.

The Earth's Moon. 1988.

Mars, Our Mysterious Neighbor. 1988.

The Asteroids. 1988.

Saturn, the Ringed Beauty. 1988.

Uranus, the Sideways Planet. 1988.

Our Milky Way and Other Galaxies. 1988.

Did Comets Kill the Dinosaurs? 1988.

Rockets, Probes, and Satellites. 1988.

Quasars, Pulsars, and Black Holes. 1988.

Isaac Asimov's Book of Science and Nature Quotations (editor; with Jason A. Shulman). 1988.

Monsters (editor; with Charles G. Waugh and Martin H. Greenberg). 1988.

Isaac Asimov Presents the Best Crime Stories of the 19th Century (editor; with Martin H. Greenberg and Charles G. Waugh). 1988.

Hound Dunnit (editor; with Martin H. Greenberg and Carol-Lynn Rossel Waugh). 1988.

How Did We Find Out about Superconductivity? 1988.

Intergalactic Empires (editor; with Charles G. Waugh and Martin H. Greenberg). 1988.

Azazel. 1988.

Unidentified Flying Objects. 1988.

Asimov's Annotated Gilbert and Sullivan (editor). 1988.

Pluto: A Double Planet. 1989.

Asimov's Chronology of Science and Discovery. 1989.

Ghosts (editor; with Martin H. Greenberg and Charles G. Waugh). 1989.

Norby Down to Earth (with Janet Asimov). 1989.

The Birth and Death of Stars. 1989.

How Did We Find Out about Microwaves? 1989.

The Mammoth Book of Golden Age Science Fiction: Short Novels of the 1940s (editor; with Charles G. Waugh and Martin H. Greenberg). 1989.

Space Garbage. 1989.

Asimov on Science: A 30-Year Retrospective. 1989.

Science Fiction, Science Fact. 1989.

Is There Life on Other Planets? 1989.

Ancient Astronomy. 1989.

Astronomy Today. 1989.

Jupiter, the Spotted Giant. 1989.

Visions of Fantasy: Tales from the Masters (editor; with Martin H. Greenberg). 1989.

Frontiers: New Discoveries about Man and His Planet, Outer Space, and the Universe. 1989.

Little Treasury of Dinosaurs. 1989.

Think about Space: Where Have We Been and Where Are We Going? (with Frank White). 1989.

Earth: Our Home Base. 1989.

How Did We Find Out about Photosynthesis? 1989.

Nemesis. 1989.

Asimov's Galaxy: Reflections on Science Fiction. 1989.

Tales of the Occult (editor; with Martin H. Greenberg and Charles G. Waugh). 1989.

Norby and Yobo's Great Adventure (with Janet Asimov). 1989.

Space Spotter's Guide. 1989.

Curses (editor; with Martin H. Greenberg and Charles G. Waugh). 1989.

Mercury, the Quick Planet. 1989.

The Tyrannosaurus Prescription and Other Essays. 1989.

Senior Sleuths (editor; with Martin H. Greenberg and Carol-Lynn Rossel Waugh). 1989.

How Was the Universe Born? 1989.

Invasions (editor; with Martin H. Greenberg and Charles G. Waugh). 1990.

The Mammoth Book of Vintage Science Fiction (editor; with Charles G. Waugh and Martin H. Greenberg). 1990.

Great Tales of Classic Science Fiction (editor; with Charles G. Waugh and Martin H. Greenberg). 1990.

Nightfall (with Robert Silverberg). 1990.

The World's Space Programs. 1990.

Out of the Everywhere. 1990.

Puzzles of the Black Widowers. 1990.

The Complete Science Fair Handbook (with Anthony D. Fredericks). 1990.

Norby and the Oldest Dragon (editor; with Janet Asimov). 1990.

Mythology and the Universe. 1990.

Projects in Astronomy. 1990.

How Did We Find Out about Neptune? 1990.

How Did We Find Out about Lasers? 1990.

Colonizing the Planets and Stars. 1990.

Mythology and the Universe. 1990.

Comets and Meteors. 1990.

Cosmic Critiques: How and Why Ten Science Fiction Stories Work (editor; with Martin H. Greenberg). 1990.

The Birth and Death of Stars. 1990.

Piloted Space Flights. 1990.

Venus: A Shrouded Mystery. 1990.

Neptune: The Farthest Giant. 1990.

Robot Visions. 1990.

The Complete Stories. 1990–92. 2 vols.

The Asimov Chronicles: Fifty Years of Isaac Asimov. Ed. Martin H. Greenberg. 1991.

The Mammoth Book of New World Science Fiction: Short Novels of the 1960s (editor; with Charles G. Waugh and Martin H. Greenberg). 1991.

Norby and the Court Jester (with Janet Asimov). 1991.

How Did We Find Out about Pluto? 1991.

The New Hugo Winners (editor). 1991.

Ferdinand Magellan: Opening the Door to World Exploration. 1991.

The Secret of the Universe. 1991.

Asimov's Guide to Earth and Space. 1991.

Faeries (editor; with Martin H. Greenberg and Charles G. Waugh). 1991.

The March of the Millennia: A Key to Looking at History (with Frank White). 1991.

What Is an Eclipse? 1991.

Why Do We Have Different Seasons? 1991.

What Is a Shooting Star? 1991.

Why Do Stars Twinkle? 1991.

Christopher Columbus: Navigator to the New World. 1991.

Why Does the Moon Change Shape? 1991.

Henry Hudson: Arctic Explorer and North American Adventurer (with Elizabeth Kaplan). 1991.

Our Angry Earth (with Frederik Pohl). 1991.

Asimov's Chronology of the World. 1991.

Atom: Journey across the Subatomic Cosmos. 1991.

Child of Time (with Robert Silverberg). 1991.

The Positronic Man (with Robert Silverberg). 1992.

The Mammoth Book of Fantastic Science Fiction (editor; with Charles G. Waugh and Martin H. Greenberg). 1992.

Asimov Laughs Again: More Than 700 Favorite Jokes, Limericks and Anecdotes. 1992.

The Ugly Little Boy (with Robert Silverberg). 1992.

Why Does Litter Cause Problems? 1992.

Why Are Whales Vanishing? 1992.

Why Are the Rain Forests Vanishing? 1992.

Why Are Some Beaches Oily? 1992.

What's Happening to the Ozone Layer? 1992.

Why Are Animals Endangered? 1992.

Where Does Garbage Go? 1992.

Why Is the Air Dirty? 1992.

What Causes Acid Rain? 1992.

Is Our Planet Warming Up? 1992.

The Mammoth Book of Modern Scence Fiction (editor; with Martin H. Greenberg and Charles G. Waugh). 1993.

Forward the Foundation. 1993.

Why Do People Come in Different Colors? (with Carrie Dierks). 1993.

Why Do Some People Wear Glasses? (with Carrie Dierks). 1993.

Why Do We Need to Brush Our Teeth? (with Carrie Dierks). 1993.

Why Do We Need Sleep? (with Carrie Dierks). 1993.

How Does a Cut Heal? (with Carrie Dierks). 1993.

Frontiers II: More Recent Discoveries about Life, Earth, Space, and the Universe
        (with Janet Asimov). 1993.

The Future in Space (with Robert Giraud). 1993.

How Is Paper Made? (with Elizabeth Kaplan). 1993.

What Happens When I Flush the Toilet? (with Elizabeth Kaplan). 1993.

How Does a TV Work? (with Elizabeth Kaplan). 1993.

How Do Airplanes Fly? (with Elizabeth Kaplan). 1993.

How Do Ships Float? (with Elizabeth Kaplan). 1993.

I, Robot: The Illustrated Screenplay (with Harlan Ellison). 1994.

I, Asimov: A Memoir. 1994.

⬙ ⬙ ⬙

Alfred Bester
1913–1987

ALFRED BESTER was born in Manhattan on December 18, 1913, to James J. and Belle Silverman Bester. Although his mother was a Christian Scientist, Bester was raised as a middle-class Jew. He attended the University of Pennsylvania in Philadelphia where, he recalls in his autobiographical essay, "My Affair with Science Fiction" (1975), he tried to be a renaissance man and only distinguished himself on the fencing team. Years before Bester attended college, he had discovered Hugo Gernsback's science fiction magazines, which inaugurated his love-hate relationship with the field.

Upon graduation in 1935 Bester enrolled in law school. The following year he married Rolly Goulko, an actress. Unsure about pursuing a career in law, he tried his hand at writing science fiction. He submitted his first effort, "Diaz-X," to *Thrilling Wonder Stories* in 1939. With the guidance of editors Mort Weisinger and Jack Schiff, Bester polished the story and entered it in the magazine's contest for best story by an amateur under the title "The Broken Axiom." It won, over Robert A. Heinlein's "Lifeline" (which would later become Heinlein's first professional sale at *Astounding Science-Fiction*), and proved the first of fourteen stories Bester would publish in such science fiction pulps as *Thrilling Wonder Stories, Astonishing Stories, Amazing*, and ultimately *Astounding* over the next three years.

In 1942 Bester followed the lead of Weisinger, Schiff, and many science fiction authors and turned to plotting and writing scenarios for *Superman, Batman*, and other comic books before moving on to the scripting of science fiction radio shows. Although he virtually disappeared from science fiction, he acknowledged the lessons he learned about action and pacing during these years as among the reasons for the tremendous success of his first novel, *The Demolished Man*, when it was published in 1953. A detective-cum-science fiction story about a murder committed in a future society where extrasensory perception has rendered crime nearly impossible, it was remarkable for its depiction of an entire culture shaped by the benefits of ESP and its handling of Freudian insights into the motivations of its characters.

However, it was the breathless pacing and pyrotechnic effects of the story that earned it the first Hugo Award for best novel.

Bester's second science fiction novel, *Tiger! Tiger!* (1956; published in the United States as *The Stars My Destination*), written during a sojourn in Italy, also poured on the pyrotechnics in its account of a wronged everyman transformed into a superman by his megalomaniacal desire for revenge (a plot Bester later admitted to having cribbed from Dumas's *The Count of Monte Cristo*). Both novels crystallized cynical attitudes about the future of human civilization and the impact of environment upon character that Bester had expressed in his earlier short stories, and captured the dark mood of much postwar science fiction. At the same time that his stories were winning science fiction's highest awards, Bester wrote several blistering essays and addresses that attacked the genre for pandering to juvenile tastes.

Notice for his novel *"Who He?"* (1953; later retitled *The Rat Race*), a critique of the advertising business, landed Bester a job as an entertainment writer for *Holiday* magazine, which he held until 1970. He returned to science fiction with the novel *The Computer Connection* in 1975, but this and two later novels, *Golem*[100] (1980) and *The Deceivers* (1981), failed to live up to the promise of his incandescent earlier work. Bester died after a lengthy period of illness in 1987. His mainstream novel *Tender Loving Rage* was published posthumously in 1991, nearly twenty years after it was written.

❖ *Critical Extracts*

ALFRED BESTER   Intellectually, science-fiction is guilty of the naïveté of the child and the over-simplification of the child. Its naïveté leads it to adopt fads, believe in nostrums, and discuss disciplines of which it has only the most superficial understanding. I need mention no names. The followers of the "Bacon Wrote Shakespeare" cult and the interpreters of the Great Cipher have their blood brothers in science-fiction, as have the lunatic members of Gulliver's Grand Academy of Lagado.

The political and sociological theorizing in science-fiction is puerile. Philosophic thought is absurdly commonplace. Serious discussions are generally on the level of a bull session of high school sophomores who are all rather pleased with themselves and snobbish toward the rest of the world—

toward "The Mere," as Ste. Daisy Ashford put it. There have been many exceptions to this, of course; and there will be many exceptions to the rest of my analysis; but I am discussing the average.

It's true that you will occasionally find fragments of good sense in science-fiction, but at best they are only parts of a whole which is not understood—tags and tatters of learning like the Latin aphorisms that every schoolboy remembers with ease but translates with difficulty. One result is that science-fiction makes no attempt to use the disciplines as tools. It cannot. It does not know how to handle them professionally. It peers through the microscope and dreams. Another result is distortion of idea development leading to false conclusions. The most serious result is a childish tendency to generalize. Lacking detailed knowledge and understanding of its subjects, failing to realize that speculation is not for amateurs, science-fiction takes refuge in simplification. ⟨. . .⟩

The morality play simplification of science-fiction is ⟨. . .⟩ revealed in its plots, and I wonder how many people have noticed that most science-fiction stories end at exactly the point where they should begin. This is a deadly sin in the arts and one of the standards by which you separate the men from the boys. What the stories amount to, as a rule, is an artificially masked exposition of a situation. When the situation is finally revealed, the story ends. The great classics of science-fiction have been the exceptions to this rule—stories which have courageously and imaginatively tackled problems, no matter how difficult. But in general, science-fiction is afraid to come to grips with its situations. It is afraid of complexities.

This reflects the childish yearning for a simple world. It reflects the immature desire to find simple yes-no solutions for complicated problems. Let me cite one more example of this over-simplification. The story in which the protagonist solves a complex problem which has been baffling experts by turning up one simple factor which has been overlooked or ignored. In part this is merely the Dreams of Glory of our youth, but more importantly, it is a childish refusal to accept the complexity of reality and the complex response demanded by reality. And out of this refusal arises the emotional immaturity of science-fiction.

Alfred Bester, "The Trematode: A Critique of Modern Science-Fiction," *The Best Science Fiction Stories: 1953*, ed. Everett F. Bleiler and T. E. Dikty (New York: Frederick Fell, 1953), pp. 12–14

MARK REINSBERG   The story ⟨*The Demolished Man*⟩ has a breath-catching pace. The telling is tremendously dramatic. The conclusion is an extraordinary mixture of dread and joy.

Alfred Bester is a successful radio and television writer. *The Demolished Man* is his first novel. It originally appeared as a serial in a science fiction magazine.

Perhaps only two books of its kind are in the same class of entertainment—Aldous Huxley's *Brave New World* and George Orwell's *1984*. Tho Bester's novel may be less significant from a political or philosophical point of view, as imaginative writing it has greater impact than either of these classics.

The Demolished Man is a science fiction masterpiece.

> Mark Reinsberg, "A 'Future' of Breath Catching Pace; Life of Dread and Joy in 24th Century," *Chicago Sunday Tribune Magazine of Books*, 22 March 1953, p. 3

ANTHONY BOUCHER and J. FRANCIS McCOMAS   Since 1940, when Robert A. Heinlein's first serial was published, no work of fiction has caused as much pleasurable excitement among readers of science fiction as the serialization of Alfred Bester's *The Demolished Man*. Such excitement should be renewed and intensified to an even headier pitch by the appearance of that novel, extensively revised and rewritten, in hardcovers (Shasta). A taut, surrealistic melodrama, the story is a masterful compounding of science and detective fiction.

But it is no routine puzzle of *who*; reader and detective know the killer's identity from the beginning. The suspense lies in the chase, in the murderer's magnificent—one can't help but admire him!—effort to match his mind against the better endowed telepathic detective. And the puzzle—most brilliantly conceived and fairly clued—is *why*; not even the murderer is consciously aware of the real motive for his crime!

Just as fascinating is Mr. Bester's setting of this criminological problem in a society, ruthless and money-mad on the surface, that is dominated and being subtly reshaped by telepaths. While his picture of that future civilization is not a perfect whole, tending at times to be a sort of piecemeal report, he does state the problem of such a culture in no uncertain terms and clearly delineates its one inevitable answer. Oddly, his telepaths emerge as more convincing people than do his "normal" characters; very likely this is due to his concentration on the unassailable argument that ESP man is always, in the ultimate analysis, a *man* . . . and must live as such.

But these science and detective fictional enlargements, however perceptively done, are asides; Mr. Bester never forgets that his main job is to tell a story. The riches of his imagination are ever disciplined to his prime purpose, to carry the reader headlong from a savage, useless killing to the inescapable, curious fate of the killer.

> Anthony Boucher and J. Francis McComas, [Review of *The Demolished Man*], *Magazine of Fantasy and Science Fiction* 5, No. 1 (July 1953): 84

LESLIE FLOOD   If asked to name the enfant terrible among science fiction authors my choice would be Alfred Bester, narrowly ousting Ray Bradbury, the only other possible candidate for this role. *The Demolished Man* established his reputation as a writer of great power and ingenuity, but it is now clear that this was only a taste of this man's talents, and far better books were yet to come. For some time Bester's new novel has been waiting to see print. I believe it is due, after some postponement, as a serial "The Burning Spear" in the *Magazine of Fantasy and Science Fiction,* or will it be as "The Stars My Destination" announced as *Galaxy*'s new serial? But, to their eternal credit, an English publishing house has been brave enough, or shall I say astute enough, to present in first hard-cover publication Alfred Bester's *Tiger! Tiger!* In my opinion it is a slightly tarnished masterpiece. It is a furiously paced story which can bludgeon the unwary reader into accepting it on first impression as one of the most significant and spectacular novels ever written in the genre. When the first shock of wonder has worn off, and the pulse has quieted down, it might seem that Mr. Bester, perhaps with tongue in cheek, had resolved to write *the* science-fiction novel to end all such novels. Clearly it was intended that anything new based on psi powers after this would be an anti-climax. ⟨. . .⟩

⟨. . .⟩ It is as though Olaf Stapledon had finished a manuscript by Heinlein and Kornbluth and Spillane. But this is rather unfair, because *Tiger! Tiger!* is pure Bester, and as such must surely take its place among the top ten science-fiction novels of all time.

> Leslie Flood, [Review of *Tiger! Tiger!*], *New Worlds* No. 50 (August 1956): 126–28

ROBERT SILVERBERG   Bester can do things with words that don't seem possible until he does them. His stories are constructed with awesome skill. He deftly lets the air out of not only every cliché of science fiction but out of our entire culture. This ⟨Starburst⟩ is a book for fans to devour and for writers to study with care.

> Robert Silverberg, [Review of Starburst], Infinity Science Fiction 4, No. 2 (November 1958): 95

DAMON KNIGHT   The formula for Alfred Bester's writing is given on page 71 of his collection, Starburst. It appears in "Oddy and Id": " 'We need a short-cut.' . . . 'What do you suggest?' 'Dazzlement,' Migg spat. 'Enchantment.' "

Dazzlement and enchantment are Bester's methods. His stories never stand still a moment; they're forever tilting into motion, veering, doubling back, firing off rockets to distract you. The repetition of the key phrase in "Fondly Fahrenheit," the endless reappearances of Mr. Aquila in "The Starcomber" are offered mockingly: try to grab at them for stability, and you find they mean something new each time. Bester's science is all wrong, his characters are not characters but funny hats; but you never notice: he fires off a smoke-bomb, climbs a ladder, leaps from a trapeze, plays three bars of "God Save the King," swallows a sword and dives into three inches of water. Good heavens, what more do you want?

> Damon Knight, "Decadents," In Search of Wonder: Essays on Modern Science Fiction (1956; rev. ed. Chicago: Advent, 1967), p. 234

SAMUEL R. DELANY   Alfred Bester's The Stars My Destination ⟨. . .⟩ is considered by many readers and writers, both in and outside the field, to be the greatest single s-f novel. In this book, man, both intensely human yet more than human, becomes, through greater acceptance of his humanity, something even more. It chronicles a social education, but within a society which, from our point of view, has gone mad. In the climactic scene, the protagonist, burning in the ruins of a collapsing cathedral, has his senses confused by synesthesia. Terrified, he begins to oscillate insanely in time and space. Through this experience, with the help of his worst enemy transformed by time into his savior, he saves himself and attains a state of innocence and rebirth.

This is the stuff of mysticism.

It is also a very powerful dramatization of Rimbaud's theory of the systematic derangement of the senses to achieve the unknown. And the Rimbaud reference is as conscious as the book's earlier references to Joyce, Blake, and Swift. ⟨. . .⟩ To recapitulate: whatever the inspiration or vision, whether it arrives in a flash or has been meticulously worked out over years, the only way a writer can present it is by what he can make happen in the reader's mind between one word and another, by the way he can maneuver the existing tensions between words and associated images.

> Samuel R. Delany, "About Five Thousand One Hundred and Seventy Five Words" (1969), *The Jewel-Hinged Jaw: Notes on the Language of Science Fiction* (Elizabethtown, NY: Dragon Press, 1977), p. 47

JEFF RIGGENBACH   ⟨Bester's⟩ intense literary preoccupation with fire, heat, and passion generally is fully realized in "Fondly Fahrenheit." References to fire, furnaces, burning, red, orange, and smoke litter every page of this story ⟨. . .⟩ "Fondly Fahrenheit" is narrated by James Vandaleur, a psychotic who projects his murderous desires onto the personality of his android, creating a "killer android" from whose crimes he must continually flee. His narration is a first person of mixed singulars and plurals that shifts occasionally to a third person. The point of view appears to flutter among Vandaleur, his android, and some emphatic observer. This technique makes a first reading of the story somewhat confusing, but it is a necessary (and brilliant) device, for "Fondly Fahrenheit" is a *Doppelgänger* story of a highly original kind. Vandaleur is the evil side of the narrator; his android is the good, unable *by nature* to endanger life or property. Through projection, evil overcomes sanity and morality to set loose murder and destruction.

As in *The Demolished Man*, there are sufficient clues planted in the story for the reader to figure this out long before Bester tells him in the last paragraph. Why doesn't Vandaleur sell his android? He continually threatens to, but never does. Even if he took a loss on the sale, he could buy a less expensive model and live more modestly, something he is forced to do anyway when he bruises the android's head and hires it out as a common labourer. There is no rational purpose in keeping the android—except that it is Vandaleur's alter-ego, the objective form which the good side of his character has taken. As the story progresses, Vandaleur begins killing people himself (Blenheim, Nan Webb) and even humming the android's song, "All Reet!"—Vandaleur, who had been shocked by the murders that his android had committed and who had no reason for committing murder himself, except to protect the android whom he had no reason to protect. Most important of all: at the opening of the story we are told that androids *cannot* kill; this fact is repeatedly emphasized as the narrative develops, yet we are induced to disbelieve it, to attribute the merging identities to the *android's* psychotic projection, to pity Vandaleur. Bester works very skilfully to induce all this wrongheadedness in his readers, but he succeeds only if they disregard the evidence before them. *Why* should we not accept the facts as stated—androids can't kill—and look for an explanation of this android's impossible behavior, instead of accepting the specious explanation that ". . . looks like one android was made wrong." If we do this at the outset, every other clue in the story, the theory of psychotic projection, the heat, Vandaleur's irrational desire to keep the android, takes on new meaning and points to the truth: the evil, the impulse to murder and destroy, comes from Vandaleur to his android and not the other way around. On this view, also, the heat, the fire, the astronomical temperatures that seem so to affect the android's behavior, are merely the objective forms taken by Vandaleur's projected passions and compulsions. He not only projects his psychosis onto the android, but he also projects his splintered personality onto the world to create the heat, the fire, the smoke, the burnt orange sky that pursues him wherever he runs. All these things—the android, the furnaces, the heat—are *real*, that is, have objective evidence, but their *cause* is Vandaleur's insane *will*.

Jeff Riggenbach, "Science Fiction as Will and Idea: The World of Alfred Bester," *Riverside Quarterly* 5, No. 3 (August 1972): 170–71

PAUL WILLIAMS   The most obvious stylistic antecedent to Bester's novels are the novels of A. E. Van Vogt, science fiction master of ingeniously complex plots and universe-wrecking superheroes. Perhaps the most interesting insight into how *The Demolished Man* and *The Stars My Destination* were created is Bester's own contention that he read no science fiction at all between about 1942 and 1950 . . . thus missing out on a critical transition period in the development of science fiction, and arriving back on the scene in the 1950s to find a greatly matured field but with no personal experience, as writer or reader, of that maturation process. As a result, his science fiction in the early 1950s reflected his extensive background in the pre-1942 concept of science fiction, plus his own maturation as a person and as a (non-science fiction) professional writer; but at the same time he came in fresh without any of the built-in assumptions about what science fiction in the 1950s *should* be that other science fiction writers shared.

Bester's deep love for science fiction has always existed in him side by side with a kind of contempt for science fiction as escape fiction, a feeling of condescension. ("It [science fiction] is a special art-form, only indirectly related to reality. I would class it with the *cliches-verres*, the glass prints with which the Barbizon artists amused themselves in the middle 19th century. They achieved some spectacular effects, but after a brief vogue, glass prints died out.") Although he is unquestionably a science fiction insider, a fan for almost fifty years and a professional writer for thirty-five of them, he sees himself as an outsider; and this brings a valuable freshness to his science fiction writing.

> Paul Williams, "Introduction," *The Stars My Destination* by Alfred Bester (Boston: Gregg Press, 1975), p. xiii

---

JOHN CLUTE   His view of man is autumnal, and much of Twentieth century literature shares with him a point-of-view that is technically ironic, technically "superior" to its subject matter. Out of this common material and common import, however, Bester makes sf stories through a kind of sleight-of-hand: The worlds in which his characters operate are *themselves* radically shaped by his hagridden Gully Foyles and Oddys and the rest of them; dominating and coercing and obsessing the real worlds about them, they engender sf situations by the binding extravagance of their natures. Simple enough, but heady in its implications, for this transforming of the internal into the external comes close to defining the deep structure of all genre creations. Understandably enough, most sf writers remain content with the vivid, entertaining, kinetic world of externalized dreams, where schizoid ex-marines remember their superpowers just in time to save the galaxy, and we're all American Pals together beneath the skin, jawing away. But Alfred Bester's peak novels and stories (most of the 50s batch in these collections) are different. They are passable excursions into the demonology of the self; and they are fine adventures in the light of day, Technicolor, torrential. More important than that, however, their pyrotechnics work as an explanatory dialogue between the inner and the after worlds. For that reason—and because the man can write so well when he's not being a chum, or a posh journalist—they are about the best sf ever published. They define the genre they inhabit.

> John Clute, [Review of *The Light Fantastic* and *Star Light, Star Bright*], *Magazine of Fantasy and Science Fiction* 52, No. 2 (February 1977): 47–48

ROBERT SCHOLES and ERIC S. RABKIN   In two books first serialized in *Galaxy* during the early fifties, Bester made his reputation and then fell silent for almost twenty years, but those two books are still very much alive, and have been influential on a younger generation of writers. *The Demolished Man* appeared as a book in 1953, *The Stars My Destination* in 1956. Both have been admired, but the second made the greatest impact. It tells the story of Gully Foyle, "the stereotype common man," who is inspired by revenge to become a great man. The world in which this happens is the medium-distant future: "All the habitable worlds of the solar system were occupied. Three planets and eight satellites and eleven billion people swarmed in one of the most exciting ages ever known" (Prologue).

"Exciting" is the key word here. Bester has taken a plot like that of *The Count of Monte Cristo* and updated it. In this world people have mastered teleportation but all the old divisions between rich and poor, and the old compulsion to make war have remained unchanged by the new technology. But Bester is not concerned with extrapolating the future. He is telling a fairy tale, a moral fable, using his exotic future world as a dazzling backdrop for a picaresque adventure story that becomes a novel of education, which is really a reshaping of an old myth. Gully Foyle starts out looking for revenge on a space ship that left him stranded as an outcast in space. In the course of this revenge he develops his own intelligence and imagination, so that when he gains the power for revenge his goals have shifted. He finishes by trying to spread his power around, to awaken other dead souls, to give men a choice between death and greatness. All this is narrated in a style of great energy and playfulness. ⟨. . .⟩

This playfulness is mixed with a high degree of literary awareness. The novel abounds with allusions to Blake and Rimbaud, carefully worked into context so that they will not trouble the untutored reader. And though the moral fable is serious, the spirit of play in the whole work indicates a kind of self-consciousness new to science fiction. This is not the clumsy earnestness of Doc Smith writing a genuinely "popular" fiction. This is a literate author deliberately choosing to work in a popular mode of fiction because of the opportunities it affords him. It is not easy to do this kind of thing without the inverted snobbery showing awkwardly, but Bester brings it off. He gives us a high-powered adventure, following a character who moves through society and space with great rapidity, whose experiences call for a bravura display of writing to describe them, climaxing in an extended passage of synesthetic derangement and cosmic displacement. Bester brought the Gosh-Wow! back into science fiction, but accompanied by a knowing wink, and he almost started an American New Wave all by himself. It is not surprising that his third novel, *The Computer Connection* (1975), which appeared in *Analog* as *The Indian Giver* in 1974, fits in beautifully with what is presently going on in science fiction—since a lot of what is going on is what Bester started in the early fifties.

Robert Scholes and Eric S. Rabkin, *Science Fiction: History, Science, Vision* (New York: Oxford University Press, 1977), pp. 67–69

ALGIS BUDRYS   *Golem*[100] is a bad book. It will infuriate you particularly if you become involved with the characters and their problems, which you may easily do. Three-quarters of the way through, Bester throws overboard everything he has built to that point, lapses into incoherence rather than pyrotechnics, kills off characters he had promised to shepherd safely through genuine troubles, and just generally bushes up his performance.

I can't understand this. In an alternate draft of this column, I spent five pages detailing how I think a writer as capable and charming as Alfred Bester could in effect repudiate everything he has ever shown us about storytelling. I spent another few pages looking for signs that he is actually producing something even more satisfactory in the way of craftsmanship or art. It isn't there. The final fourth of this book is a collection of words and images thrown at you to make you think the book is still going on, and that's what it is, and all it is.

Algis Budrys, [Review of Golem[100]], *Magazine of Fantasy and Science Fiction* 60, No. 1 (January 1981): 40–41

CAROLYN WENDELL   Bester is generally unconcerned with science, accurate or inaccurate. In a question-answer session at Seacon, 1979, Bester said: "I *hate* hard science fiction" and went on to explain that he is not even faintly interested in science fact and formula and will happily make it up as he goes along; his concern is people, and the science, valid or invalid, is a mere convenience to place people into stress situations.

And this is, without doubt, Bester's towering strength in science fiction where idea or plot usually takes precedence over character. For Bester, character is first. And the memorable aspects of Bester's work are seldom ideas or even plotting, but the people. How, exactly, Ben Reich (*The Demolished Man*) murders and is captured may be of far less significance than Ben himself, battling with all his wits to escape from his own deranged self. What Gully Foyle (*The Stars My Destination*) does to exact revenge stands out less than Gully himself, the mad, driven beast. Blaise Skiaki and Gretchen Nunn ("The Four-Hour Fugue") are involved in a peculiar mystery, but what fascinates is their characters, not the mystery. For most, or at least too much, science fiction, plot is all, and discussions of works often disintegrate into synopses. This is simply and emphatically not true of Bester's works—a plot summary would not enlighten (it might even confuse) without analysis of the people in the plot.

One of Bester's favorite character types is the obsessive, the person driven by internal needs not even the character himself understands. Ben Reich and Gully Foyle are obvious examples of this type. Aldiss, paraphrased earlier, calls Bester mad—so are Bester's characters. In the novel and short stories, insanity, or an insane aberration, is often the motivation, as evidenced by James Vandaleur ("Fondly Fahrenheit"); Blaise Skiaki ("The Four-Hour Fugue"); Peter Marko ("The Pi Man"); Jeffrey Halsyon ("5,271,009"); and John Strapp ("Time Is the Traitor"). Even those who lack the obvious symptoms of lunacy are not quite normal—often because they wish for something they can't have, like Addyer, the mousey statistician in "Hobson's Choice," or Henry Hassel, the brilliant scientist in "The Men

Who Murdered Mohammed." Bester's people learn to behave rationally (or are forced to by others, like Ben Reich or Jeffrey Halsyon), and perhaps there is hope in this—few manage to destroy themselves or their world (Odysseus Gaul in "Oddy and Id" is an obvious exception). But surely, no contemporary besides Sturgeon has shown the concern for the human predicament that Bester has. Younger writers, like Malzberg with his mad astronauts or Dick with his demented future citizens, may well have learned from Bester.

Carolyn Wendell, *Alfred Bester* (Mercer Island, WA: Starmont House, 1982), pp. 16–17

PATRICK A. McCARTHY   *The Stars My Destination* is quintessentially a Romantic novel, not only in its adaptation of specific elements from Blake but in its vision and design. To a lesser extent the same can be said of many other SF novels; the difference is not only that Bester multiplies the Romantic elements in his novel to a degree beyond what we are likely to encounter in works by any other SF author, but that he self-reflexively converts the idea of Romanticism into an important theme of his fiction. Near the beginning of his Prologue, Bester refers to the "Romantics" who, in the 25th century, "cry 'Where are the new frontiers?' . . . unaware that the frontier of the mind" has already been opened through the discovery of jaunting. At the end of the Prologue he outlines the context in which we are to interpret Gully Foyle's eventual discovery of the power to space-jaunte:

> It was an age of freaks, monsters, and grotesques. All the world
> was misshapen in marvelous and malevolent ways. The Classicists
> and Romanticists who hated it were unaware of the potential
> greatness of the twenty-fifth century. They were blind to a cold
> fact of evolution . . . that progress stems from the clashing merger
> of antagonistic extremes, out of the marriage of pinnacle freaks.
> Classicists and Romantics alike were unaware that the Solar
> System was trembling on the verge of a human explosion that
> would transform man and make him the master of the universe.

In the novel, the "marriage of pinnacle freaks" takes the form of the imaginative union of reason and passion. Here, Bester seems to be adopting

Blake's dictum, in *The Marriage of Heaven and Hell*, that "Without Contraries [there] is no progression. Attraction and Repulsion, Reason and Energy, Love and Hate, are necessary to Human existence." Such a "marriage" of opposites does not result, either for Blake or for Bester, in Classical balance and reconciliation, but in the dynamic tension of the Romantic myth. Thus it is a mistake to expect, say, the polished ironies of a Jane Austen novel from an author like Bester, whose vision leads him to something closer to the cruder yet more powerful ironies of *Frankenstein* or *Wuthering Heights*. Similarly, if we find it difficult to evaluate Gully Foyle at the end of the novel, it is because Bester's concept of irony here is so thoroughly Romantic that we can arrive only at a paradox: to the extent that Foyle is a figure of redemption, we owe that redemption not to his virtues but to his viciousness. Thus his ultimate insight into the nature of social responsibility is made possible only by the complete selfishness and egocentrism of his life, qualities that have forced him deeply enough into himself to enable him to see other people for the first time.

The difficulty in arriving at a moral judgment may be even greater here than in *Frankenstein*, the grandfather of all SF novels about Promethean figures. Like other types of Prometheus, Foyle is both destroyer and redeemer, Satan and Christ—not alternately but at the same time. His decision to distribute PyrE across the world and to force upon everyone the responsibility for using it safely will of course be interpreted by many readers as something like a decision to give every man his own hydrogen bomb. There is no evading the charge that, in the end, the decision is supremely irresponsible— or so it seems when considered in isolation. In the context of the novel, however, Foyle is telling us that we cannot have the keys to heaven (space-jaunting) without the keys to hell (PyrE). And if PyrE is deadly—it is "Pronounced 'pyre' as in 'funeral pyre,'" and Gully Foyle himself calls it "the road to hell"—it is also potentially creative, for it is believed to be "the equivalent of the primordial protomatter which exploded into the Universe." Walking a tightrope between the poles of destruction and resurrection, both of which are implicit in visions of the apocalypse, Bester's conclusion is ironic in its refusal to resolve the book's paradoxes.

Patrick A. McCarthy, "Science Fiction as Creative Revisionism: The Example of Alfred Bester's *The Stars My Destination*," *Science-Fiction Studies* 10, No. 1 (March 1983): 66–67

TIM BLACKMORE Bester's sweeping style coupled with the stunning ingenuity and thoroughness of his world-building in *The Demolished Man* (hereafter referred to as *Demolished*) earned him the attention of the science fiction world, as well as its top honor—the Hugo award. Bester's 1951 masterpiece remains a textbook case for the creation of a different world. Bester fashioned a new society, its implicit and explicit laws, and its modes of operation; in short, a whole culture. This kind of convincing "world design" is now taken for granted (Ursula Le Guin, Frank Herbert, and Larry Niven are three who followed Bester's lead, if not his style). Bester describes the special passion he must feel if he is to create characters for such a world: "I can't start a story until I can hear the characters talking, and by that time they've got will and ideas of their own and have gone into business for themselves." Nearly twenty years before the above comment was made, Bester described the process in *Demolished* where creation originates in "the never-ending make-and-break synapses contribut[ing] a crackling hail of complex rhythms. Packed in the changing interstices were broken images, half-symbols, partial references . . . the ionized nuclei of thought" (*Demolished*). Bester must understand the totality of his construct if he is to write about it. He must hear the characters, see them play, use all his senses to understand them. Beneath the senses is the war between the head and the heart. Heavily influenced by Freud (Bester comments that his "habit is to look at characters from the Freudian point of view first—other points of view receive equal time later"), Bester champions man's reason but often shows the id triumphant. This accounts for the dark, often desperate tone of his stories. Like his character the Pi Man, Bester strives for a balance between rationality and unreason, between hate and love. Bester's respect for the id's forces doesn't prevent him from generating mindscapes, incredible (rational) worlds created by the ego and superego. Each major novel is based on a simple "what-if": what if . . . (1) an elite group of telepaths ran society (*Demolished*),—(2) everyone had powers of teleportation—some more than others (*The Stars My Destination* hereafter *Destination*), or (3) humanity can gain immortality—under special conditions (*The Computer Connection*). Telepathy, teleportation, and immortality are all seen by Bester to be powers of the mind that hint at its potential—Lincoln Powell sums up: "You are what you think" (*Demolished*). ⟨. . .⟩

Bester's true music is the language he uses. The seemingly doomed Gully Foyle, trapped in a burning slag heap in *Destination*, finds his senses overloading so that "he saw the sound of his shouted name in vivid rhythms. . . .

Motions came as sounds to him. He heard the writhing of the flames, he heard the swirls of smoke . . . the flickering, jeering shadows . . . all speaking deafeningly in strange tongues. Color was pain to him . . . Touch was taste to him . . . feel of wood was acrid and chalky in his mouth, metal was salt, stone tasted sour-sweet to the touch of his fingers, and the feel of glass cloyed his palate like over-rich pastry." This powerful description of synesthesia demonstrates Bester's ability to pull the reader into a world that transcends words. ⟨Jeff⟩ Riggenbach noticed this pattern, commenting that "Bester's sentences are full of verbs and exclamation points. They are sentence-fragments as often as they are sentences. Scenes and times change abruptly as they do in motion pictures and comic books, media in which action and dialogue are frequently the only methods of narration." His typographical games bring in vision but by trapping the reader "In the kaleidoscope of his own cross-senses" (*Destination*), Bester makes sound and motion come from the page.

Tim Blackmore, "The Bester/Chaykin Connection: An Examination of Substance Assisted by Style," *Extrapolation* 31, No. 2 (Summer 1990): 102–3, 105–6

▧ *Bibliography*

The Demolished Man. 1953.

"Who He?" ⟨*The Rat Race*⟩. 1953.

Tiger! Tiger! ⟨*The Stars My Destination*⟩. 1956.

Starburst. 1958.

The Dark Side of the Earth. 1964.

The Life and Death of a Satellite. 1966.

An Alfred Bester Omnibus ⟨*The Dark Side of the Earth, Tiger! Tiger!, The Demolished Man*⟩. 1967.

The Computer Connection ⟨*Extro*⟩. 1975.

The Great Short Fiction of Alfred Bester. 1976. 2 vols.

Golem[100]. 1980.

The Deceivers. 1981.

Experiment Perilous: Three Essays on Science Fiction (with Marion Zimmer Bradley and Norman Spinrad). 1983.

Tender Loving Rage. 1991.

⊠ ◈ ⊠

James Blish
1921–1975

JAMES BENJAMIN BLISH was born on May 23, 1921, in East Orange, New Jersey, the only child of Asa Rhodes Blish and Dorothea Schneewind Blish. Blish's parents divorced in 1927 and his mother took him to Chicago; there Blish cultivated a youthful interest in chemistry and music, which in 1931 was augmented by an interest in science fiction triggered by his reading of *Astounding Stories*. In 1934 Blish and his mother returned to East Orange, and he graduated from East Orange High School in 1938. By this time he had discovered the world of science fiction fandom: he engaged in a brief correspondence with H. P. Lovecraft, issued a short-lived fanzine entitled *The Planeteer*, and contributed to *Tesseract*, the journal of the Science Fiction Advancement Association.

In September 1938 Blish attended the first meeting of the Futurian Society of New York, along with Isaac Asimov, Frederik Pohl, Donald A. Wollheim, and others who would later become prominent in science fiction. The next year he began studies at Rutgers University, from which he received a B.Sc. in Education in 1942. Blish's first professionally published work was a story in *Super Science Stories* (edited by Pohl) in 1940, and he published several other stories before being drafted in the U.S. army in 1942. Blish, disliking military discipline, remained a private during his two years in the army, although his scientific training allowed him to become a laboratory medical technician. Blish then attended graduate school at Columbia for two years, but failed to receive a degree. In 1947 he married Virginia Kidd, with whom he had three children (one died in infancy). In the early 1950s he moved his family out of Manhattan to the small town of Milford, Pennsylvania.

While editing various trade journals in the drug and food industries, Blish published voluminously in the science fiction pulps, including such celebrated stories as "Surface Tension" (1952) and "A Case of Conscience" (1953; later to be expanded into a novel). After publishing several minor novels, Blish wrote the first novel in the "Cities in Flight" tetralogy, *Earth-man, Come Home* (1955), which was followed by *They Shall Have Stars*

63

(1956), *The Triumph of Time* (1958), and *A Life for the Stars* (1962). This series reveals the profound influence of Oswald Spengler and his theories on the successive rise and fall of civilizations. *A Case of Conscience* (1958), a novel combining science fiction and religion, won for Blish the Hugo Award.

Blish worked for Charles Pfizer & Co. (a drug company), Hill & Knowlton (a public relations firm), and the Tobacco Institute between 1955 and 1968 while continuing to write. Aside from fiction, Blish became one of the pioneering critics in the science fiction field, and he collected his essays and reviews in two volumes, *The Issue at Hand* (1964) and *More Issues at Hand* (1970), under the pseudonym William Atheling, Jr. Blish chafed at what he perceived to be the limited range of science fiction, and in 1964 he published *Doctor Mirabilis* (1964), a scintillating historical novel about Roger Bacon.

In 1964 Blish's wife obtained a divorce, and later that year he married Judith Ann Lawrence. In 1965 Blish took his first trip to England, and he moved there permanently in 1967. In order to support himself as a full-time writer, Blish published twelve adaptations of "Star Trek" episodes between 1967 and 1977, although the last several were written solely by Judith Blish and her mother, Muriel Lawrence. Blish's later novels, *Black Easter* (1968), *Anywhen* (1970), and *The Day After Judgment* (1971), are challenging and cerebral works that are as much philosophy as science fiction; while being admired by critics, they were not well received by fans. Although Blish had earlier declared himself an atheist or agnostic, he had by now developed an interest in the theological work of C. S. Lewis.

Blish's last years were marred by illness—cancer, ulcers, arthritis, and other ailments. A heavy smoker and drinker, Blish was diagnosed with lung cancer; he died on July 30, 1975, at his home outside Oxford. *The Best of James Blish* was edited by his longtime friend Robert A. W. Lowndes in 1979, and a final volume of his critical work, *The Tale That Wags the God*, appeared in 1987.

▩ *Critical Extracts*

DAMON KNIGHT   One of Blish's most engaging traits is the habit he has of examining the most moth-eaten and idiotic kind of plot, with an interested expression, like an open-minded watchmaker inspecting a Rube Goldberg, and then carefully rearranging it so that, by hook or crook, it actually makes sense. For example, we have here ⟨in "Beanstalk"⟩ Villain kidnaping Heroine, and Hero chasing off through black forest to the lonely mountain cabin where she is pent, guided by Faithful Dog.

This is pure nonsense from beginning to end, as nobody realizes better than Blish; so he has given the villain an odd but perfectly sensible reason (which, pardon me, I am not going to reveal) for snatching the girl, and he has made the dog a mutated specimen with more intelligence than a chimpanzee.

I haven't finished yet. I'll say once more, just to make it perfectly clear, that all these unlikely patchwork pieces have been totally absorbed; not a scrap is still Western, or murder, or love story; it's all science fiction.

As if this were not unlikely enough, Blish has proceeded to make the science fiction itself a synthesis of nearly every major period in the history of the literature, from gadgeteering to sociological, and to match the masters of each on their own grounds; and again there are no seams; the whole is one. ⟨. . .⟩

Plateaus of learning, commonly noticed in the early training of children, seem to occur in later ages and other fields as well; I was in one myself, as a writer, for ten years, and I like to suppose that I am in another now. If Jim Blish has just jumped to a new plateau, meaning that this story is not a brilliant exception but the starting-point for another slow, steady advance, I suggest that the incumbent Mr. Science Fiction get ready to move over.

Damon Knight, "The Jagged Edge: James Blish," *In Search of Wonder: Essays on Modern Science Fiction* (1956; rev. ed. Chicago: Advent, 1967), pp. 151–52

ROBERT SILVERBERG   This complex, fascinating, uneven, difficult book ⟨*A Case of Conscience*⟩ is probably the most adult novel yet to appear in this era of "adult" science fiction. It is adult in the sense that Blish has made no concessions to his readers' intelligence, or lack thereof, in writing the book; only a reader who can see the power and excitement inherent in an abstract theological argument is apt to enjoy this book. Others are likely to regard it as a thundering bore. The kind of reader who finds the writings of, say, Aquinas or Kierkegaard stimulating and challenging will find much to admire and relish in *A Case of Conscience*—but such readers are in a minority, and admirers of Blish's new book will probably be likewise. ⟨. . .⟩

The core of Blish's novel is the conflict within Father Ruiz-Sanches, and its ultimate spectacular resolution. That such a plot element could serve as the basis for an entire sf novel—or even a short story—would have been incomprehensible twenty or ten years ago. Even today it is a distinctly uncommercial concept, and it's hard to see hundreds of thousands of paperback novel-readers deriving much satisfaction from A Case of Conscience; the book will simply be over many heads. ⟨. . .⟩

⟨. . .⟩ In A Case of Conscience Blish has written that rarest of books, the intellectually exciting science-fiction novel. Captain Future fans take heed, and purchase only at your own risk. This book will give your mind a workout.

> Robert Silverberg, [Review of A Case of Conscience], Infinity Science Fiction 4, No. 1 (October 1958): 109–11

SAMUEL R. DELANY   The book ⟨Black Easter⟩ is basically a study of three characters, the white magician Father Francis Xavier Domenico Bruno Garelli, the black magician Theron Ware, and the millionaire lawyer Baines who tries to enlist the help of both for the most diabolical purposes.

The portraits of the magicians are superb; and the descriptions of the conjuring are the best I've encountered, including those in Eddison's The Worm Ouroboros. Theron Ware, the black magician, is cerebral, witty, the expert sophist. The bumbling, barefoot white magician Father Domenico is the quintessence of all I find delightful in Tolkien (though Mr. Blish might not consider this a compliment, I certainly do). The only character who remains vague for me is Baines. Perhaps if the lust of Ginsberg and the seeking-after-knowledge of Hess (Ginsberg and Hess are Baines' two human henchmen) had all been given to Baines himself, he would have been able to support his tercet of the flaming brazier. Even so, including A Case of Conscience and "Surface Tension," this is the most enjoyable Blish I've read yet.

> Samuel R. Delany, [Review of Black Easter], Amazing Stories 42, No. 4 (November 1968): 75

LESTER DEL REY   He is an atheist in the sense that he feels logic provides no answer to the problems of divine creation nor to the need for divinity. Yet he is very deeply a mystic; a man who has vigorously opposed the rash of psionics in science fiction—and has written one of the best novels on it and used everything from telepathy to lycanthropy in some of his best stories. He is one of the most vigorous proponents of science fiction as something that must be art—and yet he enjoys writing the "Star Trek" books, knowing that they are essentially hack work, no matter how well done. He loves to write, yet until recently found that he wrote more and better when working at a daily job than when having full time in which to write.

He's an extraordinarily impatient man when he confronts stupidity or lazy thinking; yet he can listen patiently to the worst kind of nonsense when he believes his listener needs his help. He is a severe critic—and a kind one. Sometimes he seems cold; yet, though he originally disliked what must have seemed arrogance and fraud on my part, he came across town to take me to his bosom at once when he discovered I had written the story he only partly liked but felt to be an honest experiment.

Jim is one of the most complex men I have known. We've spent a lot of time together in our joys and troubles. Yet I can't claim to understand him fully. (For instance, I can't understand how his magnum opus, *Dr. Mirabilis* plus *A Case of Conscience* plus *Black Easter* and its sequel form a trilogy to him. I find no central character or theme. But Jim, who demands rigor in statement and exactitude in words, insists they are a trilogy. *De gustibus semper disputandum est!*) ⟨. . .⟩

Blish has continued through the fifties and sixties to maintain both a high output of all lengths of stories and his high and deserved repute. But I think it only fair to say that he hasn't, in my opinion, gone above the general average he maintained between 1950 and 1960.

Lester del Rey, "The Hand at Issue," *Magazine of Fantasy and Science Fiction* 42, No. 4 (April 1972): 75–77

BRIAN M. STABLEFORD   The most interesting of the stories which Blish wrote during the hobbyist period of the early forties was one which did not see print until ten years later—the novelette "There Shall Be No Darkness" ⟨. . .⟩

The mechanics of the plot of "There Shall Be No Darkness" are crude in several respects—not least in the establishment of the basic situation, which is an English country-house party where the anti-social and slightly drunk Paul Foote becomes convinced (rather incredibly) that the suave foreigner playing the piano is a werewolf. He quickly discovers that his suspicions are justified, and because another member of the party is an expert on lycanthropy he acquires the means to offer the whole company convincing evidence of the fact.

In a classical fantasy or a modern horror story this could only be the prelude to a long crescendo of predatory suspense and evolving terror, with the affective qualities of the story dictating both pace and development. But that is not the way that Blish and his characters handle the situation. What is remarkable in the story is its rationality—not only the determined attempt to make the hypothesis plausible by the recruitment of a "scientific explanation" for lycanthropy, but also the logical manner in which the protagonist and his allies proceed with the task of destroying the menace. A corollary to both these aspects of the story's rationality is provided in the melodramatic (but eminently satisfactory) conclusion, where the werewolf's view of himself and his circumstances is extrapolated and displayed.

The method by which Blish constructs a rationalised account of lycanthropy (all the properties ascribed to the werewolf by legend are shown as effects or side-effects of a hormone secreted by a hyperpineal gland which allows liquid protoplasm to reconstruct its containing structures) is fairly straightforward—the science of biology is invoked in order to provide a jargon of apology rather than as a springboard for the imaginative exploration of possibility. It must be pointed out, though, that both the rigorousness and the competence of Blish's supportive argument are unusual, not only in the context of the science fiction of 1940, when the story was written, or even of 1950, when it was published, but in general. Jack Williamson's *Darker Than You Think*, published shortly after Blish wrote his story, attempts a similar rationalisation, but in a much shallower manner, invoking a rather vague hereditary process which pays no heed to Mendelian genetics. The slightness of this alternative (and more usual) jargon of apology does not detract from the novel's power as a literary work, but sets its methodology apart from that of the Blish story. In the great majority of sf stories—today as in 1940—the establishment of the basic hypothesis is little more than a ritual process, the priority being given (for very good reasons) to reasoning *forward* from the notion to its consequences. In Blish's fiction a much stronger priority is given to *backward* reasoning, in search of firmer foundations for hypotheses: greater justification in the service of a higher degree of realisation. It is to a large extent this greater degree of thoughtfulness, this more analytical approach, which gives the science fiction of James Blish its unique qualities.

Brian M. Stableford, "The Science Fiction of James Blish," *Foundation* No. 13 (May 1978): 15–16

BRIAN W. ALDISS   Jim Blish, in his wisdom, did a lot of strange things. He was a thinker, a maker, until the day of his death. Unlike so many science fiction writers—enslaved by editors, formulae and prospect of riches—he did not grow less interesting as he grew older, as he engaged in a daily fight with death and the night shapes. One of the themes that 'Common Time', 'Beep', and *A Case of Conscience* have in common is immortality: immortality of thought, immortality of material things, immortality of evil. When the city of Dis makes its dreadful apparition in the seared lands of America which Blish had by then vacated, we feel it as an eruption of a dreadful cancer—largely forgotten, yet ever-living.

In the volumes of the *Cities in Flight* series, along with the spin-dizzies go the anti-death drugs that confer extreme longevity on all. In the years when Blish was writing of Mayor Amalfi and the cities, he was carefree enough to use the idea as no more than a plot-device. But the evil days would come, and what was merely thought would be entirely felt. Reason and emotion would unite.

Like Mayor Amalfi, James Blish has made the perilous crossing into another state of being, where perhaps little survives but mathematics. In the words of Browne, he is 'by this time no Puny among the mighty Nations of the Dead; for tho' he left this World not many Days past, yet every Hour you know largely addeth unto that dark Society; and considering the incessant Mortality of Mankind, you cannot conceive that there dieth in the whole Earth so few as a thousand an Hour.'

As for the works Blish left behind, there were, as we might anticipate, several that will remain incomplete and uncompleted; for those that are complete we must be grateful. At their best, the cadences of his prose are spare, capable of keeping us alive to the unsparing intellect behind them. His originality, his unquenchable thirst for knowledge, must always ensure that we remember his name when the rolls of leading science fiction writers are called; but he would seek no finer epitaph than that which one of his

characters bestowed on mankind: 'We did not have the time to learn
everything that we wanted to know.'

Brian W. Aldiss, "James Blish and the Mathematics of Knowledge," *This World and
Nearer Ones: Essays Exploring the Familiar* (London: Weidenfeld & Nicolson, 1979),
pp. 49–50

GARY K. WOLFE   James Blish, in one of the classic treatments of
human transformation in science fiction, the stories published collectively
as *The Seedling Stars* (1957), gives some account of the lineage of this
subgenre:

> The notion of modifying the human stock genetically to live on
> the planets as they were found, rather than changing the planets
> to accommodate the people, had been old with Olaf Stapledon; it
> had been touched upon by many later writers; it went back, in
> essence, as far as Proteus, and as deep into the human mind as
> the werewolf, the vampire, the fairy changeling, the transmigrated
> soul. ⟨. . .⟩

Blish's *The Seedling Stars* contains four separate treatments of the theme
of transformation, united by the overall notion of a vast "seeding" program
undertaken to insure the continuity of the human race by genetically transforming human beings into creatures able to live in various planetary environments. One of the stories in the collection, "Surface Tension," has
become something of a science-fiction classic, but all the stories are revealing
of how science fiction thinks of humanity, of the importance of barrier
imagery to the fundamental structural antinomy of known-unknown, and,
perhaps parenthetically, of some of the stylistic problems involved in describing what might be called transhuman cultures—how to describe a society
as convincingly human when that society has no physiological or environmental resemblance to any known human culture. ⟨. . .⟩

Intelligence ⟨. . .⟩ is virtually the only defining factor of humanity in this
series of stories (although some mention is made of a common "spirit of
rebellion" in "The Thing in the Attic"). Common culture cannot be transmitted through the pantropes, nor can specific memories, though there are
apparently traces of racial memory in all the pantropic cultures. Almost as
if to make up for the destruction of human culture implicit in his concept

of a seeding program, Blish fills his prose with allusions to contemporary human culture that seem jarring in the alien contexts he has created. These allusions constantly make readers aware of their own alienation from the characters of the stories, and of the literary culture that the pantropes have abandoned: "privations of which Jack London might have made a whole novel"; "a classic example . . . of the literary device called 'the pathetic fallacy' "; "whole chapters, whole cantos, whole acts of what might have been conscious heroism . . . were thrown away"; "the old magazine clipping . . . was as yellow as *paella*"; "he had never heard of Kant and the Categorical Imperative"; and so on. It is possible that Blish is trying to give some intellectual legitimacy to stories which, when first published, were part of a genre widely regarded as pulpish and subliterate; but it is also possible that the allusions represent an intelligent author grappling with the problem of describing alien states and being in a style which, because of the nominal realism demanded by the traditions of science fiction, is limited to the familiar.

> Gary K. Wolfe, *The Known and the Unknown: The Iconography of Science Fiction* (Kent, OH: Kent State University Press, 1979), pp. 208, 210–11, 214

GREGORY FEELEY   Blish's sustained burst of creativity between 1957 and 1962, when he called in the debts of all the stories he had begun and never relinquished and exerted his major influence on science fiction, produced 11 novels, two collections and a volume of criticism. In a sense Blish was using the capital he had accumulated in the ten years following his return to science fiction after World War II, for he was never to produce work at that rate again, and even those works produced during the latter half of this period show a change in tone—a diminishing of the density and energy informing those works of the late fifties—and are not so highly regarded today. Blish's major efforts of the early and middle 1960s are *Doctor Mirabilis* (1964), a brilliant historical novel often regarded as his finest work, and *A Torrent of Faces* (with Norman L. Knight, 1967): the author's longest and most exhaustively thought-out books. During this period Blish published five brief and unimpressive juvenile novels, of which *A Life for the Stars* is probably the best. One assumes that Blish's major attentions were directed to his researches and labors on the longer works; but a look at *The Star Dwellers* (1961) shows how little Blish's temperament and talents were fitted to the teenage coming-to-maturity novel that Heinlein wrote so masterfully, and the paucity of result from the efforts of forcing his talents against the grain.

The publication of *Black Easter* in 1968 inaugurated the final period of Blish's career, when he began producing gnomic and highly dense novellas at the rate of about one slim volume a year until the onset of his final illness. These last works have received nothing like the acclaim greeting Blish's output of the late Fifties, and most are now out of print in the United States. That readers who continue to find pleasure in *The Seedling Stars* and *Cities in Flight* have not welcomed *The Day After Judgment* or *Anywhen* suggests less a waning of Blish's powers in his last years than the likelihood that readers have responded to the genre exuberance and vestigial pulp elements still present in these middle works, which are not to be found in the uncompromising, distilled stories that followed. *The Seedling Stars* remains, among other things, an enjoyable and suspenseful adventure story, which can hardly be said for the relentless intellectualism and muted external action that make up these final works. ⟨. . .⟩

If these late works are too extreme in their rarefication—or their attributes are too fitted to their specific strategies—to have had much influence upon the science fiction of its time, *The Seedling Stars* was not. Accessible in its modulation between overt intellectual optimism and covert Stoicism, provocative in its displacing of our culture's heroic (male) self-images into situations altered in frame of reference, and pleasing in the intelligence with which the individual stories are told, *The Seedling Stars* served with *A Case of Conscience* and Blish's successful short fiction of the Fifties as a model of the first several steps science fiction must take in becoming an adult fiction that aspires to artistry. So Blish was more influential in the virtuosity of his discovery of his own voice than in his period of true maturity, as Heinlein had made his own enormous impact upon modern science fiction in the early Forties yet began producing his best work a decade later. For a field that is only a few steps closer to true maturity than the milestone Blish left in *The Seedling Stars*, not necessarily farther than Blish himself finally got, this salutary point on the accessibility of influence remains valuable, and yet to be appreciated. The same can be said for much of the work of James Blish.

Gregory Feeley, "Cages of Conscience from Seedling Stories: The Development of Blish's Novels," *Foundation* No. 24 (February 1982): 66–67

DAVID KETTERER   Blish himself, using the William Atheling, Jr. persona, wrote one plausible conclusion to any account of his own work. From his hospital bed just before his death, he put the finishing touches on a dense, synoptic article with the Joycean title "Probapossible Prolegomena to Ideareal History." In this last essay he makes use of the Spenglerian "ideareal" (i.e., Platonic) notion of historical cycles that had earlier structured his *Cities in Flight* tetralogy to formulate a theory of the nature and historical place of SF. What has, to my knowledge, nowhere been observed is the way in which this essay ties in with, and provides a gloss on, what Blish is doing in *Black . . . Judgment* ⟨*Black Easter* and *The Day After Judgment*⟩. In the light of "Probapossible Prolegomena" it is apparent that *Black . . . Judgment* is to some extent a fantasy about the nature and place of science fiction, and the relationship between science fiction and fantasy. The essay and the diptych provide a culmination to the development of Blish's theoretical ideas about science fiction. An emphasis on operating (by way of extrapolation) within the parameters of science in the 1951 "Science in Science Fiction" series of articles gives way to the Kuhnian concept of breaking paradigms in "The Science in Science Fiction" article of 1971. But only in the Atheling piece, published in 1978, does Blish fully confront the fact that at best science fiction can do no more than offer the illusion of breaking paradigms and thus the inevitable element of fantasy. ⟨. . .⟩

Blish's career as an SF writer constitutes an opening of the field, an opening composed of gaps. Cy Chauvin speaks to this when he writes that Blish

> bridged many of the gaps in sf between writers in America and England . . . between the new generation of writers and the old . . . between routine commercial fiction and that which attempted to be literature . . . and, of course, between writers and critics. I know of no one else in science fiction who was a bridge between so many.

Not only, it should be added, does Blish's corpus encompass the New Wave; it also anticipates the current engulfment of SF by fantasy. What finally needs to be emphasized, then, is the bridge that Blish devised between SF and fantasy in terms of the relationship between physics and metaphysics. By putting demonology up against science and reversing the normal SF balance between the scientific and the "transcendental" in *Black . . . Judg-*

ment, he found a way of avoiding, surmounting, and transforming the controlling clichés of SF. Taking Roger Bacon and Spengler as his models, Blish
saw to it that science fiction itself participated—at least provisionally—in
the process of conceptual breakthrough. At such moments of breakthrough,
one becomes aware of the fantasy of reality and the reality of fantasy. And
that is the enigma that characterizes science fiction, the tortured *mise en
abîme* to which so much of Blish's work testifies.

> David Ketterer, *Imprisoned in a Tesseract: The Life and Work of James Blish* (Kent,
> OH: Kent State University Press, 1987), pp. 313–14, 319

GARY K. WOLFE   At the time of Blish's death in 1975 (according
to Cy Chauvin in his preface to *The Tale That Wags the God*), he had
planned on completing two additional volumes: one on SF scholarship, the
other on critical reactions to various modern art-forms (including music,
fantasy, and SF). The former volume, alas, never made it to the revision
stage, and none of it survives except in the Blish papers at Oxford. (It would
have been particularly enlightening to see first-hand what Blish had to
say about Moskowitz, Suvin, Merril, *et al.*, particularly given his habit of
uncompromising directness.) The second volume, which seems to have been
conceived in much the same spirit as Tom Wolfe's various attacks on
contemporary art-forms and critical credulity, does survive in part in this
volume—in essays on James Branch Cabell, SF, and modern music. Chauvin
has rounded out the volume with seven other essays, an interview between
Blish and Brian Aldiss, and a useful and thorough bibliography by Judith
Blish.

Blish's earlier volumes with Advent led to his deserved reputation as the
field's premier "technical" critic, commenting on everything from punctua-
tion to verb usage to narrative structure. Many of his insights, dressed up
in proper academic garb, could pass for modern deconstructionist criticism.
While Blish's concern with matters of form and technique is still much in
evidence, *The Tale That Wags the God* is generally much broader in scope
and more ruminative than the *Issues at Hand* volumes. It is as comprehensive
an overview as we are likely to get of Blish the essayist and lecturer, the
erstwhile musicologist and scholar of Joyce and Cabell.

The first five essays in this volume cover various aspects of modern SF
and its tribulations, and some of them seem a bit old hat by now. "The

Function of Science Fiction" first appeared in 1970 ⟨. . .⟩ The essay repeats the now-familiar litany of mainstream writers who have attempted SF, argues that SF can be a form of thought-experiment and a kind of modern mythology, and drags in some heavy artillery from the likes of Susanne Langer, Simon O. Lesser, and Michael Polanyi to show how the concerns of SF reflect the concerns of the best minds of our age. None of this seems at all fresh anymore, but the clarity of Blish's reasoning and his insightful side comments on the success of novels such as *Rosemary's Baby* make the piece worth reading. Two complementary essays follow, on the science in SF and the arts in SF; and here Blish's insights seem to gain value over time. "The Science in Science Fiction" rightly observes that most of what passes for "hard" SF is more technology fiction than SF, and concludes that "the most important scientific content in modern science fiction are the impossibilities." "The Arts in Science Fiction" covers territory that is still too rarely explored, and seems to derive from the difficulties Blish had in assembling stories for an anthology on this theme (*New Dreams This Morning*, 1966). Blish focusses not only on the portrayal of art and artists in SF (in the process identifying a disturbing strain of philistinism), but on the impact of various arts, including the literary, on SF narrative itself. ⟨. . .⟩

The third section of the book concerns Blish himself. The longest piece in *Tale*, "A Science Fiction Coming of Age," is a moving but unsentimental autobiographical essay which will be of great value to any student of Blish—although his tone throughout is decidedly uncomfortable. The final selection is a 1973 conversation with Brian Aldiss in which Aldiss draws out some very useful comments about the "Cities in Flight" and "After Such Knowledge" series. It provides a nice coda; each author seems genuinely fond of the other, and neither quite knows what to make of the fact that, as Aldiss says, "we're household words—in a limited number of households!" ⟨. . .⟩

In retrospect, *The Tale That Wags the God* may be of more interest to more students of SF—and particularly of Blish—than the *Issues at Hand* volumes. While it lacks the documentary excitement of those earlier essays, which chronicled SF's ongoing struggle towards coherence during a critical period, it provides us with a much clearer overview of Blish the writer and the critic—and gives us further reason (as if we needed it) to lament the things that never got said.

Gary K. Wolfe, "Writers as Critics," *Science-Fiction Studies* 17, No. 3 (November 1990): 393–95

▨ *Bibliography*

Jack of Eagles. 1952.

Witches Three ⟨*Conjure Wife* by Fritz Leiber; *There Shall Be No Darkness* by
    James Blish; *The Blue Star* by Fletcher Pratt⟩. 1952.

The Warriors of Day. 1953.

Earthman, Come Home. 1955.

They Shall Have Stars. 1956, 1957 (as *Year 2018!*).

The Frozen Year ⟨*Fallen Star*⟩. 1957.

The Seedling Stars. 1957.

The Triumph of Time ⟨*A Clash of Cymbals*⟩. 1958.

A Case of Conscience. 1958.

VOR. 1958.

The Duplicated Man (with Robert A. W. Lowndes). 1959.

Galactic Cluster. 1959.

The Star Dwellers. 1961.

So Close to Home. 1961.

Titan's Daughter. 1961.

A Life for the Stars. 1962.

The Night Shapes. 1962.

Doctor Mirabilis. 1964.

The Issue at Hand: Studies in Contemporary Magazine Science Fiction. 1964.

Mission to the Heart Stars. 1965.

Best Science Fiction Stories of James Blish. 1965, 1973, 1977 (as *The Testament
    of Andros*).

New Dreams This Morning (editor). 1966.

Paranoia and Science Fiction (with Alexei Panshin and Joanna Russ). 1967.

A Torrent of Faces (with Norman L. Knight). 1967.

Welcome to Mars. 1967.

Star Trek. 1967–77. 12 vols. (Vol. 12 with Judith A. Lawrence).

Black Easter; or, Faust Aleph-Null. 1968.

The Vanished Jet. 1968.

Spock Must Die! A Star Trek Novel. 1970.

More Issues at Hand: Critical Studies in Contemporary Science Fiction. 1970.

Cities in Flight ⟨*They Shall Have Stars, A Life for the Stars, Earthman, Come
    Home, The Triumph of Time*⟩. 1970.

Anywhen. 1970.

Nebula Award Stories 5 (editor). 1970.

Thirteen O'Clock and Other Zero Hours by C. M. Kornbluth (editor). 1970.
The Day After Judgment. 1971.
—*And All the Stars a Stage.* 1971.
Midsummer Century. 1972.
The Quincunx of Time. 1973.
The Best of James Blish. Ed. Robert A. W. Lowndes. 1979.
The Tale That Wags the God. Ed. Cy Chauvin. 1987.
The Devil's Day. 1990.
A Work of Art and Other Stories. Ed. Francis Lyall. 1993.

Ray Bradbury
b. 1920

RAYMOND DOUGLAS BRADBURY was born on August 22, 1920, in Waukegan, Illinois, the first child of Leonard Spaulding Bradbury, an electrical lineman whose family tree included an ancestor hanged as a witch during the Salem witch trials, and Esther Moberg Bradbury. Bradbury lived a happy childhood soaking up the sights and atmosphere of his rural midwestern town. His love of fantasy began with a viewing of *The Hunchback of Notre Dame* with Lon Chaney in 1923 and was reinforced by his discovery of the science fiction magazine *Amazing Stories* in 1929. His interest in writing was stimulated by family members reading the works of L. Frank Baum and Edgar Allan Poe to him, and later by his acquaintance with the work of Thomas Wolfe.

In 1934 Bradbury moved with his family to Los Angeles, where he was introduced to science fiction fandom through new friends Leigh Brackett and Henry Kuttner. Upon graduating from high school he supported himself selling newspapers and wrote prodigiously. His first professional fiction sale, a collaboration with Henry Hasse entitled "Pendulum," appeared in *Super Science Stories* in 1941. Shortly thereafter Bradbury became a regular contributor to *Weird Tales*, where his evocative tales of the dark side of small-town life were hailed as a turning point in weird fiction, hitherto dominated by excesses of the Gothic style. The best of these stories were collected in his first book, *Dark Carnival* (1947), the contents of which were modified and reprinted as *The October Country* (1955). In 1947 he married Marguerite McClure, with whom he would have four children.

In the late 1940s Bradbury began sending to *Planet Stories*, *Thrilling Wonder Stories*, and other pulp science fiction magazines interplanetary adventures more concerned with human conflict than the scientific extrapolation by which the genre was defined. In 1950 he assembled many of these stories into *The Martian Chronicles*, an episodic first novel about mankind's colonization of Mars that helped to bring science fiction to the attention of the literary mainstream. Although Bradbury's collections *The Illustrated Man* (1951) and *The Golden Apples of the Sun* (1953) and his dystopic novel

Fahrenheit 451 (1953) were reviewed enthusiastically in the leading periodicals of the day, they were often scorned by science fiction purists.

Bradbury continued to branch out in his writing, adapting his stories for comic books, editing the contemporary fantasy anthologies *Timeless Stories for Today and Tomorrow* (1952) and *The Circus of Dr. Lao and Other Improbable Stories* (1956), producing a children's book, *Switch On the Night* (1955), and writing the screenplay for John Huston's film of *Moby Dick* (1956). In 1957 he turned a number of his nonfantastic stories into the novel *Dandelion Wine*, a nostalgic paean to childish innocence and imagination. *Something Wicked This Way Comes* (1962), about a sinister traveling carnival that almost steals the souls of two young boys on the brink of manhood, further explored many of the themes addressed in *Dandelion Wine*. With the later novels *Death Is a Lonely Business* (1985), *A Graveyard for Lunatics* (1990), and *Green Shadows, White Whale* (1992), these books constitute a fictional autobiography in which Bradbury traces the persistence of youthful imagination into adulthood.

Since the 1960s, Bradbury has concentrated increasingly on poetry and drama. His many adaptations of his stories to the stage have been collected as *Ray Bradbury on Stage: A Chrestomathy of His Plays* (1991) and his poetry has been published in several volumes, beginning with *When Elephants Last in the Dooryard Bloomed* (1973) and culminating in *Complete Poems* (1982). His screenplays include *It Came from Outer Space* (1963) and the Oscar-nominated *Icarus Montgolfier Wright* (1962); screen adaptations of Bradbury's work by others include François Truffaut's 1966 film of *Fahrenheit 451*, several episodes of Rod Serling's "The Twilight Zone," and the 1980 television miniseries based on *The Martian Chronicles*. Bradbury is a recipient of numerous awards, including the Science Fiction Writers of America's Nebula Grand Master Award and the World Fantasy Award for lifetime achievement. His literary influence can be found in the writing of Richard Matheson, William F. Nolan, Charles Beaumont, Dennis Etchison, and many other leading fantasists of the day.

◈ *Critical Extracts*

CHRISTOPHER ISHERWOOD   The best of this new generation of science-fiction writers are highly sensitive and intelligent. They are under no illusions about the prospective blessings of a machine-age utopia. They do not gape at gadgets with adoring wonder. Their approach to the inhabitants of other worlds is anthropological and nonviolent. They owe more to Aldous Huxley than to Jules Verne or H. G. Wells. Insofar as the reading public is turning to them and forsaking the cops and the cowboys, the public is growing up.

This is not to suggest, however, that Ray Bradbury can be classified simply as a science-fiction writer, even a superlatively good one. *Dark Carnival*, his earlier book of stories, showed that his talents can function equally well within comparatively realistic settings. If one must attach labels, I suppose he might be called a writer of fantasy, and his stories "tales of the grotesque and the arabesque" in the sense in which those words are used by Poe. Poe's name comes up almost inevitably, in any discussion of Mr. Bradbury's work; not because Mr. Bradbury is an imitator (though he is certainly a disciple) but because he already deserves to be measured against the greater master of his particular genre.

It may even be argued that *The Martian Chronicles* are not, strictly speaking, science fiction at all. The most firmly established convention of science fiction is that its writers shall use all their art to convince us that their stories *could* happen. The extraordinary must grow from roots in the ordinary. The scientific "explanations" must have an authoritative air. (There are, as a matter of fact, some science-fiction writers whose work is so full of abstruse technicalities that only connoisseurs can read it.) Such is not Mr. Bradbury's practice. His brilliant, shameless fantasy makes, and needs, no excuses for its wild jumps from the possible to the impossible. His interest in machines seems to be limited to their symbolic and aesthetic aspects. I doubt if he could pilot a rocketship, much less design one.

Christopher Isherwood, [Review of *The Martian Chronicles*], *Tomorrow* 10, No. 2 (October 1950): 56–57

ISAAC ASIMOV   Bradbury has written scores of stories about Mars. He gives Mars an Earthlike temperature, an Earthlike atmosphere and Earthlike people, sometimes down to tuxedoes and pocket-handkerchiefs. His stories reek with scientific incongruity. But he gets away with it. Not only does he get away with it, but, among the general population, he is by far the most popular science-fiction writer and regularly appears in such magazines as the *Saturday Evening Post*.

In my opinion, Bradbury gets away with it because he does not really write science fiction. He is a writer of social fiction. His "Mars" is but the mirror held up to Earth. His stories do not depict possible futures; they are warnings and moral lessons aimed at the present. Because Bradbury believes that our present society is headed for chaos and barbarism unless it changes its present course (he may well be right), his warnings are jeremiads. This has led some critics to the superficial belief that the man is simply "morbid" or that he has a "death wish." Nonsense! He is simply writing social fiction.

Isaac Asimov, "Social Science Fiction," *Modern Science Fiction: Its Meaning and Future*, ed. Reginald Bretnor (New York: Coward-McCann, 1953), p. 175

RAY BRADBURY   ⟨. . .⟩ I very much enjoy, I *relish*, writing science fiction.

There is great serious fun for the writer in asking himself: when does an invention stop being a reasonable escape mechanism—for we must all evade the world and its crushing responsibilities at times—and start being a paranoiacally dangerous device? How much of any one such invention is good for a person, bad for a person, fine for this man, fatal to the next?

So much depends, of course, on what the individual *hears* when he gives himself over to the electronic tides breaking on the shore of his Seashell. The voice of conscience and reason? An echo of morality? A new thought? A fresh idea? A morsel of philosophy? Or bias, hatred, fear, prejudice, nightmare, lies, half-truths, and suspicions? Or, perhaps even worse, the sound of one emptiness striking hollowly against yet another and another emptiness; broken at two-minute intervals by a jolly commercial, preferably in rhymed quatrains or couplets?

In writing a science-fiction story around such an idea, the author must consider many things. Is there, for instance, a delicate interplay where the society does not crush the individual but where the individual realizes that without his cooperation society would fly to pieces through the centrifugal force of anarchy? Is the programming on such an ear-button receiver of a caliber to enable a man to be a gyroscope, both taking from and giving to society: beautifully balanced? Does it tell him what to do *every* hour and *every* minute of *every* day? Or, fearing knowledge of any sort, tell him nothing, and spoon-feed him mush? The challenge and the fun come in handling all the above ideas and materials in such a way as to predict how perversely or how well man will use himself, and therefore his mechanical extensions, in the coming time of our lives.

It is both exciting and disconcerting for a writer to discover that man's machines are *indeed* symbols of his own most secret cravings and desires, extra hands put out to touch and reinterpret the world. The machines themselves are empty gloves into which a hand, either cold and excessively bony, or warm, full-fleshed, and gentle, can be inserted. The hand is always the hand of man, and the hand of man can be good or evil, while the gloves themselves remain amoral.

The problem of good and evil fascinates, then, especially when it is to be found externalized and purified in the thousands of semi-robots we are using and will use in the coming century. Our atomic knowledge destroys cancer or men. Our airplanes carry passengers or jellied gasoline bombs. The hairline, the human, choice is there. Before us today we see the aluminum and steel and uranium chess pieces which the interested science-fiction writer can hope to move about, trying to guess how man will play out the game. ⟨. . .⟩

Over and above everything, the writer in this field has a sense of being confronted by dozens of paths that move among the thousand mirrors of a carnival maze, seeing his society imaged and re-imaged and distorted by the light thrown back at him. Without moving anything but his typewriter, that immensely dependable Time Machine, the writer can take those paths and examine those billion images. Where are we going? Well, first let us see where we've *been*. And let us ask ourselves what we *are* at this very hour. Fortified with this knowledge, nebulous at most, the writer's imagination selects the first path.

> Ray Bradbury, "Day After Tomorrow: Why Science Fiction?," *Nation*, 2 May 1953, pp. 364–65

J. B. PRIESTLEY   His stories use the familiar properties of science fiction—fabulous travel in space and time, wars between planets, weird beings from beyond the solar system—but not in the usual routine fashion. He is concerned not with gadgets but with men's feelings. He creates imaginatively; and it may be assumed that he is not merely turning out stuff for a new and flourishing market but is trying to express some of his own deepest feelings. It is significant that he lives in Southern California, that advance post of our civilisation, with its huge aircraft factories, TV and film studios, automobile way of life (you can eat and drink, watch films, make love, without ever getting out of your car), its flavourless cosmopolitanism, its charlatan philosophies and bogus religions, its lack of anything old and well-tried, rooted in tradition and character. Here, on this signpost to the Future, sits Mr. Bradbury, telling us his dreams.

They are very sinister. When they impose themselves on us, they fill us with a sense of desolation and horror. Compared with these glimpses of the future, most of the old hells seem companionable and cosy. This is a world, we feel, to get out of soon as we can. An excellent covering title for these tales of tomorrow would be *Better Dead*. The price our descendants will pay for our present idiocies is terrible. After us—not the deluge but the universal nightmare. One of Mr. Bradbury's favourite devices, not without its symbolism, is the sudden transformation of the familiar and friendly into something appallingly menacing, so that just when you think all is well, you are trapped—these are not the people who will help your time-travelling escape but the police from the nightmare future; this is not your long-lost brother but a Martian who has assumed his appearance. The physicist, the astronomer, the biologist, may smile at the liberties such fantasies take, or dismiss their obvious impossibilities with a shrug. But can we afford those smiles and shrugs? I think not.

J. B. Priestley, "Thoughts in the Wilderness: They Come from Inner Space," *New Statesman and Nation*, 5 December 1953, p. 712

STEPHEN HUGH-JONES   Why is Ray Bradbury so good? It is not—the conventional science fiction criterion—that his ideas are so striking. They tend to be no better than average; indeed many of these stories, as usual, are not SF at all and don't claim to be. It is partly a remarkable economy and delicacy of style; there aren't many people writing today who can say so easily exactly what they want to say. It is partly pure sentiment, that dogrose and cornflower sweetness common to so many American writers. This can be unspeakable corn, or not: Mr Bradbury sometimes teeters toward the borderline. This collection ⟨*The Machineries of Joy*⟩ gave me a lot of pleasure, as must be evident, but also some unease. One story—the explorers

of a new planet are promptly possessed by a resident intelligence—stands
out: it is also the only one which is almost pure SF. Others, particularly
those where a setting such as Mexico replaces an idea, are less impressive.

Stephen Hugh-Jones, "Bradburies," *New Statesman*, 18 September 1964, p. 406

MARTIN GARDNER   I do not know whether Bradbury has read
much of ⟨G. K.⟩ Chesterton, but *The Martian Chronicles*, like all of Bradbury's
writing, glows with a Chestertonian mix of wonder, hilarity, exhilaration
(and thankfulness?) at finding oneself miraculously alive in an endlessly
fascinating universe. It cannot be said too often that Bradbury is not particularly interested in science. The scientific content of the *Chronicles*—what
point is there in denying it?—is quite low. We learn very little about the
actual Mars, and what we learn is ⟨. . .⟩ mostly wrong. We do learn a great
deal about the colors and mysteries of *tellurian* experience. Going to Mars,
like going anywhere, helps us take fresh looks at the too-familiar scenery
of Green Town, Illinois. "Space travel," says Bradbury's unnamed philoso-
pher in the book's epigraph, "has again made children of us all."

The descriptive touches in the *Chronicles* delight and startle the reader
the way a rainbow, seen for the first time, startles and delights a child.
Martian children play with toy spiders made of gold, spiders that spin filmy
webs and scurry up their legs. Martian books are raised hieroglyphics on
silver pages (aluminum in earlier printings of the stories) that speak and
sing when fingertips brush over them. Martian airships are white canopies
drawn by thousands of flame-birds. Blue-sailed sand-ships carry Martians
over the sandy beds of dead seas, like the sand-ship that Johnny Doit built
for Dorothy and Shaggy Man to use in crossing the Deadly Desert that
surrounds Oz. At night, Martians sleep suspended in a blue mist that in the
morning lowers them gently to the floor. Martian guns shoot streams of
deadly bees. The canals, cutting through mountains of moonstone and
emerald, flow with green and lavender wine. Silver ringfish float on the
rippling water, "undulating and closing like an iris, instantly, around food
particles."

Bradbury is in love with the sights and sounds and smells of the world,
and (like all true poets) he prefers to describe them with those simple,
elemental words that are part of a child's vocabulary. Colors on Mars are
red, blue, green, black, gold, silver—no fancy synonyms, just the old familiar

color words. And the pages of the *Chronicles* are splattered with simple weather words: heat, cold, summer, winter, sun, stars, fire, ice, fog, rain, snow, wind.

Martin Gardner, *"The Martian Chronicles"* (1974), *Gardner's Whys & Wherefores* (Chicago: University of Chicago Press, 1989), pp. 41–42

WILLIS E. McNELLY   Essentially a romantic, Bradbury belongs to the great frontier tradition. He is an exemplar of the ⟨Frederick Jackson⟩ Turner thesis, and the blunt opposition between a traditionbound Eastern establishment and Western vitality finds itself mirrored in his writing. The metaphors may change, but the conflict in Bradbury is ultimately between human vitality and the machine, between the expanding individual and the confining group, between the capacity for wonder and the stultification of conformity. These tensions are a continual source for him, whether the collection is named *The Golden Apples of the Sun, Dandelion Wine,* or *The Martian Chronicles.* Thus, to use his own terminology, nostalgia for either the past or future is a basic metaphor utilized to express these tensions. Science fiction is the vehicle.

Ironic detachment combined with emotional involvement—these are the recurring tones in Bradbury's work, and they find their expression in the metaphor of "wilderness." To Bradbury, America is a wilderness country and hers a wilderness people. There was first the wilderness of the sea, he maintains. Man conquered that when he discovered this country and is still conquering it today. Then came the wilderness of the land. He quotes, with obvious approval, Fitzgerald's evocation at the end of *The Great Gatsby:* ". . . the fresh, green breast of the new world . . . for a transitory enchanted moment man must have held his breath in the presence of this continent . . . face to face for the last time in history with something commensurate to his capacity for wonder."

For Bradbury the final, inexhaustible wilderness is the wilderness of space. In that wilderness, man will find himself, renew himself. There, in space, as atoms of God, mankind will live forever. Ultimately, then, the conquest of space becomes a religious quest. The religious theme in his writing is sounded directly only on occasion, in such stories as "The Fire Balloons," where two priests try to decide if some blue fire-balls on Mars have souls, or "The Man," where Christ leaves a far planet the day before an Earth rocket lands. Ultimately the religious theme is the end product of Bradbury's vision of man; the theme is implicit in man's nature.

Willis E. McNelly, "Two Views" (1976), *Ray Bradbury*, ed. Joseph D. Olander and Martin Harry Greenberg (New York: Taplinger, 1980), p. 20

WAYNE L. JOHNSON   Bradbury seems to regard man's survival in the atomic age as pretty much of an all-or-nothing proposition. He devotes little attention to the day after the end of the world. "The Vacation" ⟨. . .⟩ is an exception—though, of course, in that story the end of the world is the result of a wish, not a war. Another exception is "The Smile." In a setting reminiscent of that in Shirley Jackson's "The Lottery," a group of townfolk gather to engage in a primitive celebration. Jackson's story is set in an indeterminate time, but Bradbury's is set in a world still in the aftershock of atomic war. As in Jackson's story, the festivity the townspeople indulge in is one of destruction. But Bradbury's characters do not pursue human sacrifice, they seek instead to ritually obliterate all remnants of the previous "civilization," which they blame for the shambles the world has become. On this particular day, the people have chosen to destroy Da Vinci's *Mona Lisa*. This destruction of works of imagination as a means of cleansing mankind of dangerous passions is a theme underlying several of Bradbury's stories, among them *Fahrenheit 451*, "Pillar of Fire," "The Exiles," and "Usher II," from *The Martian Chronicles*. In each of these stories, the main character endeavors in his own way to preserve what his fellows would destroy. In "The Smile," Bradbury's protagonist, a young boy named Tom, cannot save the whole painting but is at least able to retrieve the fragment of canvas containing the famous smile. The little piece of canvas becomes, in effect, another of Bradbury's magic objects. It is a symbol, for the boy and for us, of art itself, and for its value in human society. But it also generates nostalgia for the past and recreates for Tom some of the emotions generated by the whole painting. It serves as talisman and fetish, linking Tom with the past he never knew, and with the future he must live in. The scrap of canvas has changed Tom; the story implies that he will work to create a new "civilized" world, utilizing the better things the past has to offer.

Wayne L. Johnson, *Ray Bradbury* (New York: Frederick Ungar Publishing Co., 1980), pp. 65–66

JOHN HUNTINGTON   In *Fahrenheit 451* the future is bad because people, denied the rich traditional culture contained in books and imaged by nature, have become unstimulated and unstimulating. The dystopian world is in large part conveyed in terms of the denial of positives. Firechief Beatty's defense of the bookless future is essentially that of the Grand Inquisitor, with the important change that the mass's fear of freedom is seen to be a historical phenomenon, a failure of education. In the past, so the ironic argument goes, people were capable of freedom, but because of technology and the triumph of a debased mass culture they have lost their ability to choose and their joy in freedom. Beatty's argument seems to be the author's; in Montag's wife we see heavily done exactly the mindlessness, the need for booklessness that Beatty defends. Beatty argues that mass culture is necessarily simple and, therefore, inevitably a decline from our own élite culture based on books, and in much of its satire the novel supports him. Where the novel makes Beatty clearly an ironic spokesman to be refuted is not in his characterization of the masses and what they want, but in his inadequate appreciation of the sensitive few who are capable of freedom.

The novel expresses this vision of freedom with images of sentimentalized nature (Clarisse rhapsodizes about the smell of leaves, the sight of the man in the moon), the recollection of the small, mid-western town (the front porch and the rocking chair become symbols of freedom), some tag ends of 1930s' romanticizing of Depression survival, and an unquestioning admiration for books. This cluster poses an absolute pole around which accrues all good and in relation to which all movement away is bad. The dystopian and utopian possibilities in the novel are thus represented by separate clusters of images and ideas that the novel finds unambiguous and leaves unchallenged.

What needs emphasis here is the extent to which Bradbury's novel preserves the dystopian-utopian structure by ignoring the implications of its own imagery. The author advises his audience that they must preserve books to prevent the horror he imagines, but he never questions the values implicit in the books. When the new age is accused of serious flaws—unhappiness, fear, war, and wasted lives—there is no sense that the age of books may have also suffered from such problems. At the end, in his vision of a wandering group of book-people Bradbury invokes an idealized hobo mystique, but with little sense of the limits and tragedy of such a life.

John Huntington, "Utopian and Anti-Utopian Logic: H. G. Wells and His Successors," *Science-Fiction Studies* 9, No. 2 (July 1982): 136–37

DAVID MOGEN   Though Bradbury has written passionately of space exploration throughout his career, he has also produced a large body of science fiction focusing on technological and social issues. Because he associates space travel with the American frontier myth, his space-travel fiction, however ironic, tends ultimately to celebrate our destiny in the cosmos, which he identifies with immortality. His images of earthbound futures tend to be more unrelievedly grim. Partially because Bradbury's implicit mythology identifies earthbound futures with death, his science-fiction stories set on earth tend to be warnings, projecting futures in which unresolved contemporary problems have become monstrous in scope. Yet some of the later stories especially celebrate the potential benefits of technology and progress. The title of Marvin E. Mengeling's excellent essay, "The Machineries of Joy and Despair: Bradbury's Attitude toward Science and Technology," accurately describes the range of possibilities projected in these fictions, which metaphorically express Bradbury's deepest loves and fears.

Bradbury himself has never despaired that we are doomed to inherit his "machineries of despair," for he has always regarded such warnings as part of science fiction's healthy functions—to dramatize current problems with crazy mirrors, designed to help us avoid the potential dangers they reflect. Indeed, in *Fahrenheit 451* the most ominous threat of the future is our tendency fatuously to ignore problems. Thus, Bradbury's reputation as a "technophobe," blindly opposed to technology and progress, was never deserved, even during the period when he wrote his bleakest fiction. And his science fiction has changed in emphasis over the years, increasingly adopting a tone of celebration rather than of warning.

In a general sense, Bradbury's early shift in attitudes about the fruits of technology parallels the disillusionment of many in his generation. As an adolescent, he was an enthusiastic member of Technocracy, Inc., an organization devoted to the Wellsian faith that science and social engineering could create utopia. His disillusionment at discovering that Technocracy, Inc. was linked to fascism only anticipated the impact of the Second World War and the Bomb, experiences that gave the Frankenstein myth new meaning, whose impact inspired some of Bradbury's most powerful science-fiction imagery in the forties and fifties. Yet by the sixties he was becoming predominantly celebratory in tone, both about the impact of technology and about the future. ⟨. . .⟩

The final irony, perhaps, is that Bradbury's early ironic fiction seems to have made greater imaginative impact than his later celebrations. Though he has continued to express his enthusiasm for the future in numerous formats, most notably in his three volumes of poetry, his early "warning" fiction expressing his distaste for the most ominous aspects of mid-century American culture still is central to his literary reputation. His most sustained work in this vein, *Fahrenheit 451*, provides an earthbound nightmare alternative to the ironic space romance of *The Martian Chronicles*. If mankind does not fulfill its destiny in space, Bradbury's mythos suggests, the best we can hope for is to survive the coming apocalypse with some of our cultural heritage intact.

David Mogen, *Ray Bradbury* (Boston: Twayne, 1986), pp. 94–95

SUSAN SPENCER   In *Fahrenheit 451* the reader has the feeling of moving backward in time to a preliterate society, and the content of the society's "literature," although here it is for political ends, strengthens this impression.

The last phase of Beatty's pronouncement, "That way lies melancholy," with its literary overtones—very different from the plainer common speech of his subordinates—is not unusual for Beatty. In keeping with the idea that knowledge is power, Bradbury gives us several hints that the fire chief has had frequent access to the forbidden texts and that this is either a cause or a result of his being made chief (just which is unclear). Like Kurt Vonnegut, Jr.'s short story "Harrison Bergeron," set in another disturbing dystopia where "everybody [is] finally equal," some people are seen clearly to be more equal than others and thus enabled to wield power over their fellows. In Vonnegut's story, the ascendancy is physical: Diana Moon Glampers, the "Handicapper General," is the only citizen who isn't decked out in distorting glasses, distracting ear transmitters, and bags of birdshot to weaken her to the level of society's lowest common denominator. In *Fahrenheit 451*, the ascendancy is purely textual, but that is enough. Beatty's obnoxious confidence and habit of quoting famous works strikes the reader immediately and leads to a question that Bradbury never answers: why is this highly literate person permitted to survive, let alone hold a position of high authority, in an aggressively oral society? Something is rotten in the whole system. Evidently someone higher up, Beatty's shadowy superior, feels that there is some inherent value in a well-read man, in spite of all the political rhetoric. This probability is directly opposed to Beatty's frequent depreciation of texts (a protection of his own monopoly?) and claim that the eventual ban of almost all books was not a political coup accomplished by a power-hungry elite at one fell swoop. Beatty's explanation, which we are never called upon to doubt, is that an outraged people seeking complete equality called for more and more censorship as texts became more widely available to interest groups that might be offended by them: "It didn't come from the Government down. There was no dictim, no declaration, no censorship, to start with, no! Technology, mass exploitation, and minority pressure carried the trick." As Plato warned thousands of years earlier, well-read man had become an offensive "burden to his fellows."

Bradbury closes the novel, however, with an optimistic view: the text *will* prevail, and man will be the better for it. This is shown symbolically in the escape from the city by Montag and Faber, the only two literate men in the story besides Beatty—who, also symbolically, perishes in the same manner as the many books he has burned. The ignorant oral-culture citizens, radios tamped securely in their ears, remain in the city to be blown up by an enemy they could easily have escaped, if it weren't for the fact that their monolithic media preferred to keep them ignorant and happy. Having taken up with a group of itinerant professors, haltingly trying to remember the text of Ecclesiastes, Montag takes the first steps toward realizing the dream he had as he blindly fled the government's persecution: "Somewhere the saving and the putting away had to begin again and someone had to do the saving and keeping, one way or another, in books, in records, in people's heads, any way at all so long as it was safe, free from moths, silverfish, rust and dry-rot, and men with matches."

The idea that it is safe only when locked away in memory is almost a startling one in this book that so privileges the literary text; it seems as if the author has come full circle to an oral culture and the need to circumvent the shortcomings of Theuth's invention. Yet Bradbury makes it clear that they will write everything down as soon as possible and will try to reconstruct a fully literate society again. This should not take long, and is certainly desirable. The concept of text is a progressive thing, not a cyclical, and as long as any remnants remain there is always a base, however small, on which to build a better and wiser world.

Susan Spencer, "The Post-Apocalyptic Library: Oral and Literate Culture in *Fahrenheit 451* and *A Canticle for Leibowitz*," *Extrapolation* 32, No. 4 (Winter 1991): 334–35

🔲 *Bibliography*

Dark Carnival. 1947.

The Martian Chronicles. 1950.

The Illustrated Man. 1951.

Timeless Stories for Today and Tomorrow (editor). 1952.

No Man Is an Island. 1952.

The Golden Apples of the Sun. 1953.

Fahrenheit 451. 1953.

Switch On the Night. 1955.

The October Country. 1955.

The Circus of Dr. Lao and Other Improbable Stories (editor). 1956.

Sun and Shadow. 1957.

Dandelion Wine. 1957.

A Medicine for Melancholy. 1959.

The Essence of Creative Writing. 1962.

Something Wicked This Way Comes. 1962.

R Is for Rocket. 1962.

The Anthem Sprinters and Other Antics. 1963.

The Machineries of Joy. 1964.

The Pedestrian. 1964.

The Vintage Bradbury: Ray Bradbury's Own Selection of His Best Stories. 1965.

Twice Twenty-two ⟨*The Golden Apples of the Sun, A Medicine for Melancholy*⟩.
    1966.

The Day It Rained Forever. 1966.

The Pedestrian (drama). 1966.

S Is for Space. 1966.

Teacher's Guide: Science Fiction (with Lewy Olfson). 1968.

I Sing the Body Electric! 1969.

Bloch and Bradbury (with Robert Bloch). Ed. Kurt Singer. 1969.

Old Ahab's Friend, and Friend to Noah, Speaks His Peace: A Celebration. 1971.

The Wonderful Ice-Cream Suit and Other Plays. 1972.

The Halloween Tree. 1972.

Zen and the Art of Writing and The Joy of Writing: Two Essays. 1973.

When Elephants Last in the Dooryard Bloomed: Celebrations for Almost Any Day
    in the Year. 1973.

That Son of Richard III: A Birth Announcement. 1974.

Ray Bradbury. Ed. Anthony Adams. 1975.

Kaleidoscope. 1975.

Pillar of Fire and Other Plays for Today, Tomorrow, and Beyond Tomorrow.
     1975.

1984 Will Not Arrive: A Prediction for the Greening of Scripps. 1975.

Long After Midnight. 1976.

That Ghost, That Bride of Time: Excerpts from a Play-in-Progress Based on the
     Moby Dick Mythology and Dedicated to Herman Melville. 1976.

Something Wicked This Way Comes: Second Draft Screenplay. 1976.

Where Robot Mice and Robot Men Run Round in Robot Towns: New Poems,
     Both Light and Dark. 1977.

Man Dead? Then God Is Slain! A Celebration. 1977.

The God in Science Fiction. c. 1977.

The Bike Repairman. 1978.

Twin Hieroglyphs That Swim the River Dust. 1978.

The Mummies of Guanajuato. 1978.

The Poet Considers His Resources. 1979.

Beyond 1984: A Remembrance of Things Future. 1979.

To Sing Strange Songs. 1979.

About Norman Corwin. 1979.

This Attic Where the Meadow Greens. 1979.

The Aqueduct: A Martian Chronicle. 1979.

The Stories of Ray Bradbury. 1980.

The Last Circus and The Electrocution. 1980.

Imagine. 1981.

The Haunted Computer and the Android Pope. 1981.

The Ghosts of Forever. 1981.

The Flying Machine. 1981.

Complete Poems. 1982.

The Love Affair: A Short Story; and Two Poems. 1982.

Dinosaur Tales. 1983.

October. 1983.

Forever and the Earth. 1984.

A Memory of Murder. 1984.

The Last Good Kiss. 1984.

Novels (Fahrenheit 451, Dandelion Wine, Something Wicked This Way Comes).
     1984.

Death Is a Lonely Business. 1985.

A Device out of Time. 1986.

Death Has Lost Its Charm for Me. 1987.
Fever Dream. 1987.
The Other Foot. 1987.
The Veldt. 1987.
The April Witch. 1988.
The Toynbee Convector. 1988.
The Fog Horn. 1988.
The Dragon. 1988.
The Fog Horn and Other Stories. 1989.
Classic Stories. 1990. 2 vols.
A Graveyard for Lunatics: Another Tale of Two Cities. 1990.
Zen in the Art of Writing. 1990.
Ray Bradbury on Stage: A Chrestomathy of His Plays. 1991.
The Smile. 1991.
Yestermorrow: Obvious Answers to Impossible Futures. 1991.
Green Shadows, White Whale. 1992.
The Stars. 1993.

Arthur C. Clarke
b. 1917

ARTHUR CHARLES CLARKE was born on December 16, 1917, in Minehead, Somerset, England, the son of Charles Wright Clarke, a farmer, and Nora Willis Clarke. In 1936 he moved to London to work in the British Civil Service as an auditor for His Majesty's Exchequer and Audit Department. During World War II he served as a radar instructor with the R.A.F. After the war he studied at Kings College, London, graduating with first-class honors in physics and mathematics in 1948. From 1949 to 1950 he worked as associate editor of *Science Abstracts* magazine; since 1951 he has written full-time.

Clarke's first published story, "Rescue Party," appeared in John W. Campbell's *Astounding* in 1946. In 1948 his first novel, *Against the Fall of Night*, was published in *Startling Stories*; it appeared as a book in 1953 and in 1956 was revised under the title *The City and the Stars*. Although Clarke continued to write and publish novels and short stories throughout the 1950s, probably his best-known works from that period are "The Sentinel" (1951) and *Childhood's End* (1953), the latter being considered by many to be a groundbreaking novel about contact with aliens and human transcendence.

By the 1960s Clarke had begun to focus more heavily on nonfiction. In 1962 he received UNESCO's Kalinga Prize for writing on scientific topics; in that same year he was honored by the Franklin Institute for having been the first to propose the concept of the communication satellite in a technical paper published in 1945. Meanwhile, Clarke moved to Ceylon (later Sri Lanka) in 1956 in order to pursue his interest in underwater research, and much of his writing—fiction and nonfiction—came to focus on this other frontier of human exploration.

Nonetheless, Clarke is best known for his science fiction. In 1968 he and Stanley Kubrick developed *2001: A Space Odyssey* from the short story "The Sentinel," with Clarke writing the novel of that title at the same time Kubrick wrote the screenplay and directed the film. In 1972 Clarke won the Science Fiction Writers of America's Nebula Award for "A Meeting with Medusa" (1971), and two years later he won another Nebula along with the Hugo Award for *Rendezvous with Rama* (1973). Other novels of this period include *Imperial Earth* (1975) and *The Fountains of Paradise* (1979).

Clarke has continued writing up to the present day. Among his more recent works are two sequels to *2001* (*2010: Odyssey Two*, 1982; *2061: Odyssey Three*, 1987) along with four collaborations with NASA scientist Gentry Lee: *Cradle* (1988) and a trilogy based upon *Rendezvous with Rama* (*Rama II*, 1989; *The Garden of Rama*, 1991; *Rama Revealed*, 1993). Several of these novels have not been well received and appear largely the work of Lee. Clarke has also compiled a collection of his scientific papers, *Ascent to Orbit* (1984), and an autobiography of his life as a science fiction writer, *Astounding Days* (1989), which supplements an earlier autobiography, *The View from Serendip* (1977).

Clarke married Marilyn Mayfield in 1953; they divorced in 1964. Clarke continues to live in Sri Lanka.

Critical Extracts

PETER J. HENNIKER-HEATON   Arthur C. Clarke has been for some years chairman of the British Interplanetary Society and has written high quality straight works such as *The Exploration of Space*. He may therefore be expected to have the necessary knowledge of natural science for writing space fiction. The four volumes of space fiction he has so far written justify this expectation.

Of these volumes, this reviewer finds *The Sands of Mars* easiest to recommend for the general reader. The construction there put on facts is, except for the part dealing with the discovery of life on Mars, highly convincing. The storytelling, when covering actual space-journeys, daily living on Mars, and the attitude of Earth's government to its colony on Mars, is effective. Handling of human characterization and personal relationships is less happy.

Childhood's End is a more ambitious book. It flies higher and falls farther. To many, as to this reviewer, its final conclusion will be unacceptable. Its value lies in the new possibilities which it opens for space fiction. ⟨. . .⟩

The answer of this novel is not necessarily Mr. Clarke's own; it is offered by him as a possibility. Perhaps on a future occasion he will explore a more promising possibility—how each individual may find that he is already related to a larger unity and that relationship, when understood, both preserves and enhances individuality.

Space fiction of this type is not just for adolescents. It may have far to go before fully establishing its place in serious literature, but it is already meat for adult readers.

> Peter J. Henniker-Heaton, "Space Fiction Can Be Literature," *Christian Science Monitor*, 10 September 1953, p. 7

JEREMY BERNSTEIN   Science fiction is not for everyone. But the Clarke genre is something else again. By standing the universe on its head, he makes us see the ordinary universe in a different light; the things that are accessible to our experience become illuminated by the light cast on them by our imagination. *2001* began as a short story about the moon, and then, in the four years Kubrick and Clarke worked on it, it became a complex allegory about the history of the world. Fiction it is, but in our time the line between fact and fiction is often as nebulous as the matter in outer space. In his foreword to *2001*, Clarke cautions, "But please remember: this is only a work of fiction. The truth, as always, will be far stranger."

> Jeremy Bernstein, "Chain Reaction," *New Yorker*, 21 September 1968, p. 184

DAVID N. SAMUELSON   Arthur C. Clarke's *Childhood's End* is one of the classics of modern SF, and perhaps justifiably so. It incorporates into some 75,000 words a large measure of the virtues and vices distinctive to SF as a literary art form. Technological extrapolation, the enthronement of reason, the "cosmic viewpoint," alien contact, and a "sense of wonder" achieved largely through the manipulation of mythic symbolism are all important elements in this visionary novel. Unfortunately, and this is symptomatic of Clarke's work and of much SF, its vision is far from perfectly realized. The literate reader, especially, may be put off by an imbalance between abstract theme and concrete illustration, by a persistent banality of style, in short, by what may seem a curious inattention to the means by which the author communicates his vision. The experience of the whole may be saved by its general unity of tone, of imagery, and of theme, but not without some strain being put on the contract implicit between author and reader to collaborate in the "willing suspension of disbelief." ⟨. . .⟩

From the moon-bound rockets of the "Prologue" to the last stage of the racial metamorphosis of mankind, familiar science fictions guide us gradually if jerkily through *Childhood's End*. Besides futuristic technological hardware, we are shown three rational utopian societies and mysterious glimpses of extrasensory powers. Reducing all of these, however, practically to the status of leitmotifs, the theme of alien contact is expanded to include something close enough to the infinite, eternal, and unknowable that it could be called God; yet even this being, called the Overmind, is rationalized, and assumed to be subject to natural laws. ⟨. . .⟩

Technology accounts in part for the utopian social organizations projected in this book, and also for their failings. Technologically enforced law and order, technology-conferred freedom of movement and sexuality, help to establish a worldwide "Golden Age," but the elimination of real suffering and anguish, combined with the humans' sense of inferiority, results in mild anxiety, resentment, and lethargy. To make utopia really utopian, an artists' colony is established, on the traditionally utopian locale of an island, but the colonists don't regard their creations as having any real value. Whether Clarke could imagine predictable great art is irrelevant, since their futility underscores the insignificance of New Athens in the larger context: for the Overlords, the island is a gathering-point for them to observe the most gifted human children in the first stages of metamorphosis. Besides being unimportant, however, utopia is unreachable; just as technology can not make everyone happy on Earth, so is it insufficient for the supremely rational and scientific Overlords. Their placid orderliness, their long lives, may excite our envy, but they in turn envy those species which can become part of the Overmind.

Thus *Childhood's End* is not really utopian, as Mark Hillegas contends, so much as it is a critique of utopian goals. Whatever the social machinery, and Clarke is extremely sketchy about how this society is run, peace and prosperity are inadequate; the people of New Athens need something more to strive for. This particular "utopia" is only a temporary stage in man's development. Theoretically, he could go in the direction of enlarging his storehouse of empirical knowledge; this is the way of the Overlords, without whom man could not have defused his own self-destructive tendencies. Yet, paradoxically, the Overlords are present in order to cut man off from entering their "evolutionary *cul de sac*," to insure that he takes the other road, paralleling the mystical return of the soul to God.

> David N. Samuelson, "*Childhood's End:* A Median Stage of Adolescence" (1973), *Arthur C. Clarke*, ed. Joseph D. Olander and Martin Harry Greenberg (New York: Taplinger, 1977), pp. 196–98

ERIC S. RABKIN   Clarke provides us handily with but one of countless examples of powerful science fiction based on older literary and cultural forms. *The Lion of Comarre* is the first of a number of his books in which the hero must break down the separation between a self-contained city and a more pastoral area surrounding it. In this novel the dwellers in the city are lulled by artificially created dreams fed them through surgical connections with their nerves. Clarke uses the term "Lotus Eaters," reminding us of Homer and Tennyson perhaps; his surgical motif had already been used by Fletcher Pratt and Laurence Manning in "City of the Living Dead" (1930). This pleasure-dome image of the dangerously deadening allurements of technology and self-indulgence is worked out again by Clarke in the story "Patent Pending" (1954) ⟨. . .⟩ The protagonist of *The Lion of Comarre* has a typically central position, "no longer a man, but a symbol, one of the keys to the future of the world." His solution to the stagnation of Comarre rests on the active egocentrism we associate with the immature, a perfect carelessness that the Gallant Tailor would approve: "First he would disconnect the circuits, then he would sabotage the projectors so that they could never again be used. The spell that Comarre had cast over so many minds would be broken forever." Although he does need some help from the superlion he had earlier fed, Richard Peyton III manages to save the world.

Clarke's most notable later versions of this story are *Against the Fall of Night* (1953) and its revision, *The City and the Stars* (1956). The latter begins with this description so clearly dependent upon the style we have associated with fairy tales:

> Like a glowing jewel, the city lay upon the breast of the desert.
> Once it had known change and alteration, but now Time passed
> it by. Night and day fled across the desert's face, but in the streets
> of Diaspar it was always afternoon, and darkness never came. The

long winter nights must dust the desert with frost, as the last
moisture left in the thin air of Earth congealed—but the city
knew neither heat nor cold. It had no contact with the outer
world; it was a universe itself.

The city of Diaspar, like the castle of "Sleeping Beauty," hovers in the
near-dead "always afternoon." A world sealed off from the wider world, the
city awaits renewed contact. Just as the enchanted castle existed "long, long
ago," Diaspar exists in that far future when the very atmosphere of Earth
has thinned. "Sleeping Beauty" is a story about a girl who at fifteen pricks
her finger on a spindle and swoons back into a bed, not to awaken until
kissed by her proper mate one hundred years later. The whole of her world
falls asleep with her. In Clarke's novel the hero, Alvin, occupies a similarly
central position: through no fault of his own he is, as it says in *Against the
Fall of Night*, "the only child to be born . . . for seven thousand years." To
make this point clearer, the later *The City and the Stars* calls Alvin "the
first child to be born . . . for at least ten million years." "Sleeping Beauty"
defines its own happy ending as the reawakening of the Princess and her
marriage to the Prince; Clarke's novels define their happy endings as the
release of the people of the city and the people of the country from their
respective isolation. Alvin, like the sexually successful Prince, is the agent
of this change: he must break out of the city and into the country to cross-
fertilize the cultures and start progress up again. As in the fairy tale, the
ending is happy.

Eric S. Rabkin, "Fairy Tales and Science Fiction," *Bridges to Fantasy*, ed. George E.
Slusser, George R. Guffey, and Mark Rose (Carbondale: Southern Illinois University
Press, 1980), pp. 88–89

NICHOLAS RUDDICK   From the unprecedented number of
awards that *Rendezvous with Rama* received on its publication in 1973, we
might suppose that the book would be, in the words of William H. Hardesty,
"one of those novels obviously destined to become instant classics." However, the first flush of enthusiasm quickly faded, so that in John Hollow's
recent book-length study of Clarke's fiction, *Rama* receives about as much
attention as the early *Sands of Mars* (1951) and the undistinguished *Glide
Path* (1963). The novel has not been neglected, but it has never been given
the sort of attention it deserves. It is not hard to see why: *Rama* fails to

offer, it seems, a vision that has proved so appealing that it has led to what
Hardesty has called the "almost cult status of Clarke's other works about
aliens" (in particular *Childhood's End* [1953], *2001: A Space Odyssey* [1968],
and *2010: Odyssey Two* [1982]). Instead, the alien artifact Rama, indifferent
to the stir it has caused among the United Planets, departs the Solar System
and leaves the reader with a sense of bathos and frustration as a result of
all the enigmas left unsolved. We may praise Clarke's sophisticated techniques of estrangement based on rigid extrapolation, and feel awe at his
vision of an insignificant human race, still crudely homocentric, suddenly
gaining a glimpse of the unknowability of the cosmos, but we still feel let
down. Awe is all very well, and won the novel its prizes; but in the long
term we want solutions to the riddle of Rama, and there Clarke seems to
fail us.

Yet while *Rendezvous with Rama* is full of enigmas, they are of human
manufacture and so have human solutions. If we forget that the alien artifact
is the product of a human imagination, we are in danger of missing the
point of the novel. Clarke's strategy in *Rama* is different in kind from, and
far more daring than, the more characteristically Clarkeian alien encounters
in *Childhood's End* and the *Odysseys*. We note, first of all, that there are
no aliens in *Rendezvous with Rama*. This hardly seems an insight; yet if we
combine this idea with the now well-accepted one that there are no such
things as aliens in good SF, we may watch as the apparent difficulties
caused by the unresolved elements in the novel all but evaporate. We must,
therefore, either attempt to decode Rama or merely seek consolation, like
Eric S. Rabkin, in the idea that because the Ramans seem to do everything
in threes, there may perhaps be another chance to explore Rama and that
next time (perhaps) we will be readier.

What Roland Barthes calls the hermeneutic code dominates the text of
Rama. The novel's energy lies not in plot or character, but in the posing
of a riddle, followed by the discovery of an apparent solution, followed by
the realization that a deeper riddle is implied by this solution—and so on
until the very structure of the universe seems to founder ("There goes
Newton's Third Law"). After Rama's departure, everything is changed for
mankind in the 22nd century, but nothing is understood. Some critics
have confessed to a disappointment similar to that suffered by Commander
Norton, leader of the explorers of Rama: "a sense of anticlimax and the
knowledge of opportunities missed." E. Michael Thron, for example, speaks
of his own "sense of emptiness at the end of the book," a result of "the gap

between satisfying plot and the closure of an idea." George Slusser finds the bathetic ending to be part of Clarke's rather unattractive satiric intent: the "tongue-in-cheek transcendence" is merely the last of the "deflating moments" whereby mankind is mocked as a "stupid tourist before the mysteries of the universe." But while Norton does indeed approach despair at Rama's inscrutability, Clarke is continuously urging the reader to distinguish between those enigmas which are capable of being solved and those which are not. The former lead to important truths; the latter are merely irrelevant. If we do so distinguish, we find that Clarke does offer us a transcendent vision in Rama, but one far less reliant on supernatural intervention and so more accessible than is to be found elsewhere in his oeuvre. We find, too, a work comic without satiric bitterness, and one full of its creator's delight in having constructed an artifact awesome not in its strangeness, but in the uncanny sense of familiarity with which it is haunted.

Nicholas Ruddick, "The World Turned Inside Out: Decoding Clarke's *Rendezvous with Rama*," *Science-Fiction Studies* 12, No. 1 (March 1985): 42–43

JOHN HOLLOW   ⟨. . .⟩ the final difference between Clarke's *2001* and Kubrick's is that Clarke hopes that, whatever the future may hold, the race will not have lived in vain. He does not know what a Star-Child would do, but he hopes that the evolution thus suggested, the evolution beyond the bomb, will happen. He hopes that the descendants of Moon-Watcher and his cousins will not pass as meaninglessly as the dinosaurs seem to have done. We may not have any more understanding of the Star-Child than Moon-Watcher would have of us, but our having had to have been in order for the Star-Child to be is terribly important to the novel. The design is that evolution goes from flesh to machine to spirit, and each of the steps is both necessary and legitimized by the result. The machine step, which is the surprising one, is justified by exactly what Kubrick fears in such a change: Clarke's Bowman becomes as emotionless as a robot as he journeys on alone. As Kubrick's Bowman gets further and further from the family of humans, he confronts the universe on a more and more individual basis. He is the young man growing up, discovering that the universe and himself are more and better than he had been taught. Clarke's Bowman, on the other hand, is able to hurry through the machine stage of evolution because the distance from other humans brings him closer to a universal perspective.

He gives up listening to recordings of plays because the problems they deal with seem "so remote," "so easily resolved with a little common sense." ⟨. . .⟩ He becomes, without having had to identify completely with a machine, as free of human emotions as a creature of the universe ought to be. ⟨. . .⟩

The Bowman of the novel re-establishes ⟨. . .⟩ contact with Earth after he disconnects Hal. He broadcasts back everything that happens to him right up to the point when he enters the Star Gate. Clarke does not want even that much of human experience to be lost. He wants somehow to compensate for the "thirty ghosts" that stand behind "every man now alive" (for that is the "ratio," he explains in the novel's Foreword, "by which the dead outnumber the living"). He is even careful to use the popular idea that one's life flashes before one's eyes at the moment of death to insist that "nothing" of Bowman's life is "being lost; all that he had ever been, at every moment of his life, was being transferred to safer keeping. Even as one David Bowman ceased to exist, another became immortal."

2001 the novel, in other words, is not about the revolt of the machines, but about the two things Clarke seems to think we mortals would most like to know in a universe in which we can only hope that the odds are in favor of the race's survival: that we are not alone and that we have not lived in vain.

> John Hollow, *Against the Night, the Stars: The Science Fiction of Arthur C. Clarke* (1983; rev. ed. Athens: Ohio University Press, 1987), pp. 146–48

ARTHUR C. CLARKE   I would not like anyone to think that my boyhood reading consisted entirely of pulp magazines, so perhaps it's time to back away a little from *Astounding*. I devoured "real" books as well; but I must confess that they, too, were almost all science fiction.

My first encounter with the master, H. G. Wells, was slightly discreditable. Browsing through the shelves of W. H. Smith's Taunton branch during my lunch hour I discovered *The War of the Worlds*—but its price was several shillings beyond me.

No problem: I was (as you may have gathered) a fast reader. Day after day I returned to the shelf, and after a week or so I had finished the now dog-eared volume. ⟨. . .⟩

At about the same time, I must have discovered Jules Verne; I still have my sixty-year-old copy of *A Journey to the Interior of the Earth*—a much more sensible title than the more usual *Journey to the Center* . . .! Oddly enough, I do not remember my first encounter with *From the Earth to the Moon* or *Twenty Thousand Leagues Under the Sea*, the two books which relate most closely to my own interests.

Rider Haggard (*When the World Shook*) and Conan Doyle (*The Lost World*—still my candidate for the perfect specimen of its genre) had also swum into my ken. And occasionally—perhaps once or twice a year!—I ran across other hardcover sf. ⟨. . .⟩

Soon after it was published in 1930, I discovered W. Olaf Stapledon's *Last and First Men;* I can still visualize the very shelf on which I found it in the Minehead Public Library. That such an imaginative work would be purchased by a provincial librarian was doubtless due to the reviews it had received. "As original as the solar system," said Hugh Walpole (how did he know?) while Arnold Bennett praised the author's "tremendous and beautiful imagination." Similar compliments came from a failed politician, then living by his wits—one Winston Churchill.

Though its opening chapters have been completely dated by events which make some of their political ideas seem naive, no book before or since has had such an impact on my imagination; the Stapledonian vistas of millions and *hundreds* of millions of years, the rise and fall of civilizations and entire races of Man, changed my whole outlook on the Universe and has influenced much of my writing ever since. Twenty years later, as Chairman of the British Interplanetary Society, I persuaded Stapledon to give us an address on the social and biological aspects of space exploration, which he entitled "Interplanetary Man?" His was one of the noblest and most civilized minds I have ever encountered: I am delighted to see a revival of interest in his life and work.

Arthur C. Clarke, *Astounding Days: A Science Fiction Autobiography* (1989; rpt. New York: Bantam Books, 1990), pp. 22–24

GREGORY FEELEY   In the decade following *The Foundations of Paradise*, announced as his last novel, readers saw poignant evidence that Clarke, however right he had been in sensing that he had no more to say, yet found himself (and this is hardly to his discredit) unsuited to a distinguished retirement. Clarke in fact published more in the 1980s than he had in the 1970s, although evidence of flagging inspiration was manifest. His novels for the decade amounted to this: one novel expanded from a 1958 story, two sequels to *2001* (whose germ of course dates from "The Sentinel" of 1951), and *Cradle*, a collaboration with NASA scientist Gentry Lee which was originally conceived as a movie project, and indeed bears a striking resemblance to the Disney feature *Cocoon* ⟨. . .⟩

It was the Lee collaboration, however, that most prompted foreboding, especially when trade papers announced in 1989 that Clarke agreed to write three more collaborations with Lee, the first of which would be that project Clarke had long resisted, a sequel to *Rendezvous with Rama.* ⟨. . .⟩

Rama II (out in time for Christmas 1989) was the opening salvo of this publisher's dream. At 420 pages, it was by far the longest novel Clarke had ever written—save for *Cradle*. Clarke had always been a spare writer, and his novels of the 1980s had not, like those of some of his peers, grown steadily longer to accommodate changing fashions. Readers may welcome Clarke's newfound prolificity, even with the proviso of collaboration with this very junior partner. They should be warned: there is good reason to hold the gravest doubts as to the extent of Clarke's contribution to this exploitative and amateurishly-written book. ⟨. . .⟩

Stylistic clumsiness aside, the sensibility of the book is simply not that of Arthur C. Clarke, nor is it one to which he might plausibly have made a major contribution. The handling of religious matters is simply the most obvious area: Clarke is a famously secular atheist, while *Rama II* was evidently written by a Roman Catholic. ⟨. . .⟩

I cannot imagine any lover of Clarke's fiction who would not feel cheated by this sub-contracting job (which Clarke presumably helped on the plotting and discussion stage). If I had paid for my copy, I would be in a rage.

Gregory Feeley, "Partners in Plunder; or, Rendezvous with Manna," *Foundation* No. 49 (Summer 1990): 59–60

TERENCE HOLT   In Arthur C. Clarke's *Childhood's End* (1953), children provide a ⟨. . .⟩ screen for a desire that becomes explicitly apocalyptic. Hiding behind its attempts to evade responsibility for this desire is an equally powerful wish to be the agent of apocalypse. In Clarke's novel, the structure of evasion involves a race of aliens that intervenes in human history to prevent atomic war. But this intervention simply relocates the familiar mislocation: under the aliens' tutelage, it is children—all of the children in the world—who obliterate Earth. The narrative tries to view this destruction as merely a side effect of an otherwise benign evolutionary process, but actually remains typically ambivalent about it. And here ⟨. . .⟩ ambivalence screens a single-minded wish for destruction. Although the narrative persistently points out that the aliens have saved the human race from itself, it also laments that in doing so they have also prevented us from reaching our potential. The novel figures this potential tellingly in terms of the space race, which both Clarke and history remind us was a competition to make total nuclear war technologically feasible. In both its approval of the alien intervention, and in its regret for the lost possibilities of human history, the novel expresses the same wish—to bring about the end of the world.

But although this ambivalence may be disingenuous, it does point to one of the most important features of apocalyptic fantasy. The dedication page of the book carries an odd warning that the author is "not responsible" for the opinions expressed within. This seems at first only a part of the novel's pervasive structure of mystification, which offers its narrative not as fiction but as a channel for some supernatural Truth, but this denial of responsibility is itself not the whole story. The narrative finds the aliens' version of the end of the world unsatisfactory because it takes that end out of human hands: it is important not merely that the end has come, but that *we* bring it about. Clarke's novel suggests this in its climactic scenes, which go to great lengths to provide one adult witness to Earth's destruction. As the world vanishes, this witness reports: "—oh, this is hard to describe, but just then I felt a great wave of emotion sweep over me. It wasn't joy or sorrow; it was a sense of fulfillment, achievement." ⟨. . .⟩ In its claim to offer something more than fiction, and in the desire that overwhelms the narrator of that revelation, *Childhood's End* reminds us that apocalyptic prophecy is always more than simple showing—as a narrative mode, prophecy seeks urgently not only to report but to fulfill its account. By adopting this prophetic stance, and by insisting on an individual narrator as the channel of its prophecy, the narrative seeks to gain control over these events, to be not merely their passive victim but their agent.

Terence Holt, "The Bomb and the Baby Boom," *TriQuarterly* No. 80 (Winter 1990–91): 212–13

NEIL McALEER   Clarke confesses he *wants* to believe that there is life elsewhere in the universe, "because it's very lonely if there's nobody else out there. But we haven't the slightest evidence for such existence. There's only statistical argument, and it's very tantalizing."

"The fact that we have not yet found the slightest evidence for life—much less intelligence—beyond this Earth does not surprise or disappoint me in the least," he said. "Our technology must still be laughably primitive; we may well be like jungle savages listening for the throbbing of tom-toms, while the ether around them carries more words per second than they could utter in a lifetime."

"One of the great lessons of modern science is that millennia are only moments," wrote Clarke, referring to the cosmic scale and the life cycles of stars and galaxies—and perhaps the universe itself. He admits to being skeptical about finding answers to the great questions and problems of existence that humans have debated for thousands of years. And the reason he is skeptical is that such questions will not likely be answered in such short time scales. He doubts that "we will really know much about the universe while we are still crawling around in the playpen of the solar system."

Make no mistake: Arthur C. Clarke has had a lot of fun playing. He has said more than once that he writes because it's fun—adding that he also likes to eat. Having "great fun" (one of his more common expressions) extends to all his explorations, cerebral and geographical—not just to his writing craft. He is somewhat coy about any deeper driving forces in his life.

"Actually, my motivation and aim in life is very simple," Clarke lightly confessed in 1990. "It's been expressed by a famous remark of a British prime minister (Stanley Baldwin, I think), who was talking about the newspaper world of Fleet Street in London and comparing its advantages with those of another profession: the privilege of the harlot through the ages, which is power without responsibility. I recently told the president of Sri Lanka that this was my goal and I'd now achieved it."

Neil McAleer, *Arthur C. Clarke: The Authorized Biography* (Chicago: Contemporary Books, 1992), p. 388

▣ Bibliography

Interplanetary Flight: An Introduction to Astronautics. 1950, 1960.
The Exploration of Space. 1951, 1959.

Prelude to Space: A Compelling Realistic Novel of Interplanetary Flight. 1951.

The Sands of Mars. 1951.

Islands in the Sky. 1952.

Expedition to Earth: Eleven Science-Fiction Stories. 1953.

Against the Fall of Night. 1953, 1956 (as *The City and the Stars*).

Childhood's End. 1953.

The Young Traveller in Space ⟨*Going into Space*⟩. 1954, 1971 (as *Into Space* [with Robert Silverberg]).

The Exploration of the Moon. 1954.

Earthlight. 1955.

Reach for Tomorrow. 1956.

The Coast of Coral. 1956.

The Making of a Moon: The Story of the Earth Satellite Program. 1957.

The Reefs of Tabrobane: Underwater Adventures around Ceylon. 1957.

Tales from the White Hart. 1957.

The Deep Range. 1957.

The Other Side of the Sky. 1958.

Voice across the Sea. 1958, 1974.

Boy beneath the Sea. 1958.

The Challenge of the Spaceship: Previews of Tomorrow's World. 1959.

Across the Sea of Stars ⟨*Childhood's End, Earthlight,* short stories⟩. 1959.

The First Five Fathoms: A Guide to Underwater Adventure. 1960.

The Challenge of the Sea. 1960.

Indian Ocean Adventure. 1961.

A Fall of Moondust. 1961.

From the Oceans, from the Stars ⟨*The Deep Range, The City and the Stars,* short stories⟩. 1962.

Tales of Ten Worlds. 1962.

Profiles of the Future: An Enquiry into the Limits of the Possible. 1962, 1973.

Dolphin Island: A Story of the People of the Sea. 1963.

Glide Path. 1963.

The Treasure of the Great Reef. 1964, 1974.

Indian Ocean Treasure (with Mike Wilson). 1964.

Man and Space (with the editors of *Life*). 1964.

Voices from the Sky: Previews of the Coming Space Age. 1965.

Prelude to Mars ⟨*Prelude to Space, The Sands of Mars,* short stories⟩. 1965.

An Arthur C. Clarke Omnibus ⟨*Childhood's End, Prelude to Space, Expedition to Earth*⟩. 1965.

Time Probe: The Sciences in Science Fiction (editor). 1966.

The Nine Billion Names of God: The Best Short Stories of Arthur C. Clarke.
    1967.

The Coming of the Space Age: Famous Accounts of Man's Probing of the Universe
    (editor). 1967.

2001: A Space Odyssey. 1968.

The Lion of Comarre and Against the Fall of Night. 1968.

An Arthur C. Clarke Second Omnibus ⟨*A Fall of Moondust, Earthlight, The
    Sands of Mars*⟩. 1968.

The Promise of Space. 1968.

Report on Planet Three and Other Speculations. 1972.

The Lost Worlds of 2001. 1972.

Beyond Jupiter: The Worlds of Tomorrow (with Chesley Bonestell). 1972.

The Wind from the Sun: Stories of the Space Age. 1972.

Of Time and the Stars: The Worlds of Arthur C. Clarke. 1972.

The Best of Arthur C. Clarke 1937–1971. Ed. Angus Wells. 1973.

Rendezvous with Rama. 1973.

Imperial Earth: A Fantasy of Love and Discord. 1975.

The View from Serendip. 1977.

Four Great SF Novels ⟨*The City and the Stars, The Deep Range, A Fall of
    Moondust, Rendezvous with Rama*⟩. 1978.

The Fountains of Paradise. 1979.

Vikram Sarabhai Memorial Lectures. c. 1980.

The Science Fiction Hall of Fame, Volume 3 (editor; with George Proctor).
    1982.

2010: Odyssey Two. 1982.

The Sentinel: Masterworks of Science Fiction and Fantasy. 1983.

1984, Spring: A Choice of Futures. 1984.

*Ascent to Orbit: A Scientific Autobiography: The Technical Writings of Arthur
    C. Clarke.* 1984.

The Odyssey File (with Peter Hyams). 1984.

Selected Works. 1985.

The Songs of Distant Earth. 1986.

Arthur C. Clarke's July 20, 2019: A Day in the Life of the 21st Century (editor).
    1986.

2061: Odyssey Three. 1987.

Tales from the Planet Earth. 1988.

A Meeting with Medusa ⟨with *Green Mars* by Kim Stanley Robinson⟩. 1988.

Cradle (with Gentry Lee). 1988.
Rama II (with Gentry Lee). 1989.
Astounding Days: A Science Fictional Autobiography. 1989.
The Ghost of the Grand Banks. 1990.
Opus 700. 1990.
Beyond the Fall of Night (with Gregory Benford). 1990.
The Garden of Rama (with Gentry Lee). 1991.
How the World Was One: Beyond the Global Village. 1992.
The Fantastic Muse. 1992.
The Hammer of God. 1993.
Rama Revealed (with Gentry Lee). 1993.
By Space Possessed. 1993.

Robert A. Heinlein
1907–1988

ROBERT ANSON HEINLEIN was born on July 7, 1907, in Butler, Missouri, and spent his childhood in Kansas City. In 1929 he graduated from the United States Naval Academy, and for the next five years he served as an officer on several ships including the aircraft carrier U.S.S. *Lexington*. In 1934 ill health forced him to retire from the Navy. He then sold real estate, involved himself in politics and silver-mining speculation, and studied physics at U.C.L.A.; in 1939 he wrote and sold his first story, "Life-Line," to John W. Campbell's *Astounding*.

Over the next three years Heinlein, with Campbell's guidance and support, moved from complete obscurity to a position of unrivaled dominance in SF, producing in that time four novels plus so many short stories that several were published pseudonymously in order to avoid having more than one story under Heinlein's name appear in any single magazine issue. All this fiction from Heinlein's first period, as well as most of his later work, has been reprinted in book form; much of it forms the nucleus to his "Future History" sequence, collected in the 1966 omnibus volume *The Past through Tomorrow*. Other work in these years ranged from SF-adventure potboilers such as *Sixth Column* (serialized 1941; book publication 1949) to sophisticated fantasies ("They," 1941; "The Devil Makes the Law," 1942). The core of Heinlein's SF, however, was and has remained matter-of-fact, provocative "hard SF" like *Beyond This Horizon* (serialized 1942; book publication 1948).

From 1942 to 1945 Heinlein worked as an aviation engineer at the Naval Air Experimental Station in Philadelphia. In 1947 he returned to SF, publishing a string of short stories in the *Saturday Evening Post* in addition to more novels and short works in the SF magazines. Throughout the 1950s he also wrote several SF novels for teenagers; later reissued without the juvenile-market packaging, some of them (notably *The Star Beast*, 1954; *Time for the Stars*, 1956; and *Citizen of the Galaxy*, 1957) have retained the interest of critics and adult readers as well. In 1956 he published one of his best-regarded novels, *Double Star*.

In 1959 Heinlein's career took a new direction with the explicitly militaristic *Starship Troopers*. This was followed in 1961 by *Stranger in a Strange Land*, which achieved tremendous popularity on college campuses for its apparent advocacy of sexual liberation; it was, however, later tainted by being one of the books that inspired Charles Manson and his followers. Heinlein's subsequent work, while reaching a much larger audience than most SF, was marked by greater and greater emphasis on complex political and religious polemics, generally of a conservative nature. Further novels include *Glory Road* (1963), *Farnham's Freehold* (1964), *The Moon Is a Harsh Mistress* (1966), and *I Will Fear No Evil* (1970). In 1973 Heinlein capped his long-neglected "Future History" series with *Time Enough for Love*, the "memoirs" of Lazarus Long, protagonist of *Methuselah's Children* (serialized 1941; book publication 1958).

Following an extended illness, Heinlein in 1980 published *The Number of the Beast*, a complex science-fantasy involving many characters from his own and other writers' previous works. His final four novels were *Friday* (1982), *Job: A Comedy of Justice* (1984), *The Cat Who Walks through Walls* (1985), and *To Sail Beyond the Sunset* (1987).

Heinlein was the recipient of the prestigious Hugo Award four times. He was married twice, first to Leslyn McDonald, then (from 1948) to Virginia Gerstenfeld. Robert A. Heinlein died on May 8, 1988. Since his death, several of his novels—including *Stranger in a Strange Land* and *The Puppet Masters*—have been issued in unabridged form.

⊠ *Critical Extracts*

ROBERT A. HEINLEIN   We here ⟨at the World Science Fiction Convention⟩, the science fiction fans, are the lunatic fringe! We are the crazy fools who read that kind of stuff—who read those magazines with the outlandish machines and animals on the cover. You leave one around loose in your home and a friend will pick it up. Those who are not fans ask you if you really read that stuff, and from then on they look at you with suspicion.

Why do we do it? I think I know. This is an opinion, but it is probably why we like science fiction. It is not just for the adventure of the story itself—you can find that in other types of stories. To my mind it is because science fiction has as its strongest factor the single thing that separates the human race from other animals—I refer to a quality which has been termed "time-binding." With a hyphen. It's a term that may not have come to your attention. It is a technical term invented by Alfred Korzybski, and it refers to the fact that the human animal lives not only in the present, but also in the past and the future.

The human animal differs from all other animals *only* in this respect. The definition includes both reading and writing. That is the primary technique whereby we are able to make records, to gather data and to look into the future. ⟨. . .⟩

Time-binding consists of making use of the multitudinous records of the past that we have. On the basis of those records, the data we have collected directly and the data that we get from others by means of time-binding techniques, including reading and writing, we are able to plan our future conduct. It means that we have lived mentally in the past and in the future, as well as in the present. That is certainly true of science fiction fans.

I like the term Future Fiction that Charlie Hornig gave it. It seems to me a little broader than Science Fiction because most of these stories are concerned with the future—what will happen.

In taking the future into account, trying to predict what it will be, and trying to make your plans accordingly, you are time-binding. The child-like person lives from day to day. The adult tries to plan for a year or two at least. Statesmen try to plan for perhaps twenty years or more. There are a few institutions which plan for longer than the lives of men, as for example, the Smithsonian Institution and the Catholic Church, that think not in terms of lifetimes, but in centuries. They make their plans that far ahead, and to some extent, make them work out.

Science fiction fans differ from most of the rest of the race by thinking in terms of racial magnitudes—not even centuries, but thousands of years. Stapledon thinks in terms of . . . how many years? How far does his time scale go? I don't know: the figures mean nothing to me.

That is what science fiction consists of—trying to figure out from the past and from the present what the future may be. In that we are behaving like human beings.

Robert A. Heinlein, "The Discovery of the Future" (1941), *Requiem: New Collected Works by Robert A. Heinlein and Tributes to the Grand Master*, ed. Yoji Kondo (New York: TOR, 1992), pp. 154–55

ORVILLE PRESCOTT   Sometime in the not too distant future, when the United States had become only one of many humble members of the World Federation of Free States and the moon had been profitably and thoroughly exploited, a human baby was born on Mars. His parents and the others on board the rocket ship died, but the child was raised by Martians. Some twenty-one years later a second rocket reached Mars and brought Valentine Michael Smith back to earth. In appearance he was human. In thought, habits, instincts and mysterious powers he was a Martian. His life on earth and how it affected the lives of numerous others is the story told in *Stranger in a Strange Land*.

So, just as eighteenth-century authors wrote the impressions of Europe drawn by imaginary Persians and Chinese, Mr. Heinlein writes of earthly and American matters from the supremely "unworldly" point of view of a Martian. But his satire of international politics, religion, various kinds of corruption and many ordinary customs is singularly ineffective, crude and tedious. Mr. Heinlein has little gift for characterization, a flippant and heavy-breathing style, a ponderous sense of humor and a sophomoric (high school, not college) enthusiasm for sex. ⟨. . .⟩

Strewn through *Stranger in a Strange Land* are numerous harangues by the doctor expressing an agnostic and skeptical philosophy about everything. They are very dull. But they are not so dull as the Martian's innumerable miraculous sleight-of-hand tricks or as the intricate ramifications of his Martian sex cult.

It is difficult to tell whether Mr. Heinlein thinks that his monotonous variations upon an erotic theme are funny, or whether beneath all the verbiage and leering lubricity there is supposed to be some serious plea for the "innocent" promiscuity of Smith's cult. In either case, much of *Stranger in a Strange Land* is puerile and ludicrous.

Orville Prescott, "Books of The Times," *New York Times*, 4 August 1961, p. 19

GEORGE EDGAR SLUSSER   The truly "classic" Heinlein is the allegorical writer who emerges from the numerous stories and novels I have examined. There is a basic pattern, shaped in the earliest tales, and carefully elaborated in his subsequent work. But there is also a distinct development of allegorical forms on a diachronic axis as well. The early stories and novellas are more obviously parables, and whatever action and adventure there is has an overtly symbolic or illustrative function. The middle novels are different: here, an allegorical purpose gradually informs and transforms conventional adventure. Rightfully, then, Heinlein's later "problem" novels are hybrids. In their didactic and "philosophical" emphasis, they mark a return to the more static patterns of the early stories. At the same time, however, their form has benefited from the development of Heinlein's art during the decade of juvenile writing. The curious subversion of the linear patterns of intrigue and initiation in these works has contributed as much to the form of *Stranger* ⟨*in a Strange Land*⟩ as the vertical configurations of a story like "Waldo."

In spite of this merger, these adventure forms have a certain life of their own in Heinlein. Running parallel to the revival of openly philosophical works on a grand scale in the 1960s is a current of shorter works in which the impetus of a decade of action and intrigue is sustained. Though the subtitle of *Podkayne of Mars: Her Life and Times* (1963) shows that it has been touched by some new interest in exemplary fiction, the novel remains basically a juvenile adventure. *Farnham's Freehold* is essentially a tale of adventure; this time, the motive force is time instead of space travel—a "tunnel in the sky" of a different sort. *The Moon Is a Harsh Mistress* (1965) is a story of political intrigue and revolution in the manner of *Double Star*. True, these novels eventually blend with the philosophical stream, if only through the fact that their heroes get progressively older. We go in the span of a decade from youth to middle age, and finally to senescence. In Heinlein's latest work, *Time Enough for Love*, adventure of all sorts (intrigue as well as the drama of coming of age) is absorbed into a new narrative center—the exemplary life of ancient and deathless Lazarus Long. ⟨. . .⟩

Overwhelmingly, the heroes of Heinlein's early stories are adults. His latest novels mark a complete return to this adult world and beyond. To a critic like Brian Aldiss, no maturity of understanding seems to result from this process. On the contrary these "adult" works provide a classic case of arrested development—the mature world continually cast in terms of a retentive childhood. Perhaps Heinlein is at his best when things are turned around. In *Glory Road* (as in *Space Suit*), the juvenile hero grapples with adult problems, but in some other distant world. When he returns to his own world, the growing up still waits to be done. It seems, moreover, that Scar Gordon (like Kip before him) accomplished what he did only because he remained a child. Indeed, the essence of Heinlein's philosophy in these two novels, with its refusal of limits of any kind, tyrannical or utopian, is merely the refusal of perpetual child-man to face the light of common day. There are differences, however, between *Glory Road* and its predecessor. Kip displays this buoyancy of youth in a well-defined dramatic situation— the climactic trial scene. Scar Gordon, on the other hand, proclaims it throughout. Heinlein later tried to repeat this tour-de-force of the first-person narrator in *The Moon Is a Harsh Mistress*. But once this opinionated discourse is taken from the mouth of the forever youth, it sours. The hero's voice in this later novel of revolution and adult intrigue bogs down in its own "seriousness" (not to mention the "new-Russian" newspeak it uses for conversing). With the passing of Scar Gordon, youth fades forever from Heinlein's universe.

George Edgar Slusser, *The Classic Years of Robert A. Heinlein* (San Bernadino, CA: Borgo Press, 1977), pp. 57–59

DAVID N. SAMUELSON   In *Stranger in a Strange Land*, solipsism is implicit in the manipulations of Mike and Jubal, especially in Mike's mental power over inanimate and animate matter. On the Martian plane, it is suggested or paralleled by the adult Martians' control of plants, by their cannibalistic rituals (like the snake devouring its own tail) and by their continuity with the Old Ones. More explicitly, Patty Paiwonski and "Alice" Douglas are both identified in heaven as "holy temporals" assigned to earthside duty, limited to individual human consciousnesses. And the Archangel Michael is identified as "one of the most eager Solipsism players in this sector." Even Jubal in a wry moment claims, once every leap year, to regard Creation as a matter of "sheer solipsist debauchery"; the rest of the time, if he thinks of it at all, he alternates between a "created" and a "noncreated" universe.

The true solipsist of the piece, however, is Heinlein himself, like any author willing his creations into existence. For all his claims, in various places, to want people to live by "the scientific method," his imagined societies work—on paper, despite the carpings of critics—because he wills them to. According to the dust jacket of *Stranger*, his admittedly unreachable "purpose in writing this novel was to examine every major axiom of Western culture, to question every axiom, throw doubt on it—and, if possible—to make the antithesis of each axiom appear a possible and perhaps a desirable thing—rather than unthinkable." This grandiose scheme seems conceivable only to an author who takes it for granted that he can create the real and unreal alike, and make his audience sit still for it. Like Jubal, he may be "fooling around," but for serious purposes. ⟨. . .⟩

The book's confusion, then, stems in part from the contradiction between an exemplary tale of men like gods and a solipsistic sense that it's all make-believe. The sophisticated reader may see this as confusion, rejecting both fantasies as adolescent wish-fulfillment. But the more naive audience might more easily accept what it wants to, from the satirical denigration of common knowledge and established tradition to the assumption of godlike powers. The audience in the Sixties, I suspect, has the latter reaction. Aside from the traditional science fiction subculture, Heinlein's readers were young, relatively untutored in literary analysis, certainly not schooled in literary readings of science fiction. College students, and other members of the "counterculture" that grew in the wake of the loss of John Kennedy's dream of Camelot, and in shared opposition to a technocratic society that had no use for them except as cannon fodder, devoured *Stranger in a Strange Land* and handed it on. Its reputation grew by word of mouth, as a "book of wisdom" for our time, an "underground classic." ⟨. . .⟩

Criticism of the book for bad taste in style or contents would hardly have been welcome, except as evidence of the critic's defense of the Establishment. Besides, old-fashioned ideas of taste were part of what the book attacked. In addition, it offered, with impenetrably confusing irony, a new program to establish utopia on Earth in which everyone who believed would love and share. It even seemed to be preaching revolution, at the cost of martyrdom if necessary. And the decade bore these supposed teachings out, in abortive form, from the Flower Children to the Weathermen. Even the most "shocking" aspects of *Stranger* seem pale against the background of the last seventeen years, and its solipsism fits right in to today's "laid-back" hedonism, in which everyone is trying to find—or create—the "real me."

David N. Samuelson, "*Stranger* in the Sixties: Model or Mirror?," *Critical Encounters: Writers and Themes in Science Fiction*, ed. Dick Riley (New York: Frederick Ungar Publishing Co., 1978), pp. 171–74

PHILIP E. SMITH II   The underlying fantasy-wish of *Beyond This Horizon* involves a justification of life and politics based on libertarian and competitive principles which are derived from a social Darwinistic interpretation of evolution. Heinlein's fictional utopia exhibits the author's vision of such a society—but it also includes his fantasy of transcending the biological limitations of evolutionary development as we know it by endowing the best specimens of the human race with telepathic powers and the certainty of reincarnation. The soul of Carvala, an aged female member of the Board of Policy, does not die with her body, but turns up in Felix's newborn daughter, Justina. This double fantasy, survival of the fittest humans coupled with the award to that elite group of telepathy and immortality, is a common one in Heinlein's fiction. Even in fictions where such transcendence is not provided, the happy endings usually affirm that the hero and the elite will be able to cope successfully with their problems.

In other early fictions Heinlein also portrays optimistically political systems which reconcile the need for social order with what he sees as the optimum condition for evolutionary advancement: maximum personal freedom and competition for the individual. In some cases, such as *The Day After Tomorrow* and " 'If This Goes On—' " elite revolutionary groups are depicted successfully overturning oppressive authoritarian regimes in order to reestablish the original political freedoms of the vanquished United States.

In *The Day After Tomorrow* (serialized 1941, published as a book 1949, originally titled *Sixth Column*) the United States has been conquered by the PanAsian hordes. A small band, or "sixth column," of patriots routs the yellow peril with racial rayguns which are able to " 'knock over all the Asiatics in a group and not touch the white men.' " People of other colors do not figure in this novel—America is made safe for the return of the white man's government. Heinlein's hero, Whitey Ardmore, plans that after the defeat of the invaders he will " 'locate all the old officials left alive and get them back on the job to arrange for a national election.' " Except for stopping the plot of a crazed American scientist who wants to establish a dictatorship, Ardmore shows no further concern for postwar politics. But he does make clear that the United States' original error consisted in not heeding a biological/political law: " 'We got into this jam by thinking we could settle things once and for always. . . . Life is a dynamic process and can't be made static.' "

Philip E. Smith II, "The Evolution of Politics and the Politics of Evolution: Social Darwinism in Heinlein's Fiction," *Robert A. Heinlein*, ed. Joseph D. Olander and Martin Harry Greenberg (New York: Taplinger, 1978), pp. 141–42

H. BRUCE FRANKLIN   The immediate ancestors of *Starship Troopers* are those World War II movies idealizing the military lives of our typical American combat men. In the novel, we see the familiar naïve, sloppy civilian being enlisted by the wounded, much-decorated, tough old recruiting sergeant, the brutal basic training that looks like "calculated sadism" administered by grizzled drill sergeants whose rhinoceros hides conceal their love for the recruits, and the thrilling, fearsome combat which demonstrates that every last bit of that training was vital. Half the pages are devoted to the details of our young hero's military training, first as a raw recruit going through basic training, later as a combat veteran making his arduous way through Officer Candidates School. Instead of the cross section of American youth featured in the World War II movies—the Iowa farm boy, the Texan or Virginian sharpshooter, the Jew from Brooklyn, and the Italian from the Bronx—we have a cross section of the youth of Earth's galactic empire—the martial-arts expert from Japan, the two Germans replete with dueling scars, the drawling, brawling southerner, miscellaneous "colonials" from Earth's galactic outposts, and our hero, Juan (Johnnie) Rico, son of a wealthy Philippine businessman.

But the resemblances between the World War II movies and *Starship Troopers* are somewhat superficial, for this is not about a mass conscript army called up in a war to defend democracy—that disappeared back in the twentieth century. *Starship Troopers* displays the superelite force designed to fight the permanent wars necessary to fulfill Earth's manifest destiny in the galaxy. And the Terran Federation, the society employing this force, is ruled entirely by veterans of this elite military machinery and its noncombatant auxiliaries.

Recently there has been some debate about whether *Starship Troopers* is as militaristic as it seems, and Heinlein himself disclaims any militaristic intentions. But to argue about whether or not *Starship Troopers* glorifies militarism would be as silly as arguing about whether or not "My Country 'Tis of Thee" glorifies America. Militarism shapes the speech and sets the tone of all the characters, including the narrator-hero; militarism animates every page; militarism—together with imperialism—is the novel's explicit message. What we must probe is not the quantity of militarism in *Starship Troopers* but its special quality. For *Starship Troopers* expresses its own time, and gives a striking vision of times to come. The difference between the World War II army movies and *Starship Troopers* measures the distance from the conscript army that fought against the Fascist-Nazi-New Order drive to conquer the world and the growing "military-industrial complex" (to use those words of President Eisenhower) that was attempting to hold and expand a worldwide empire against a rising tide of global revolution.

> H. Bruce Franklin, *Robert A. Heinlein: America as Science Fiction* (New York: Oxford University Press, 1980), pp. 111–12

BRIAN W. ALDISS and DAVID WINGROVE   Heinlein, as so many critics have commented, is a right-wing libertarian of the frontiersman breed. He is a champion of the freedom to *do* things: which is to say that he is champion of the strong and the competent. In his universe the weak and inefficient deserve to go to the wall. This stance has made several critics label him, incorrectly, a fascist. Like Campbell, Heinlein has a genuine hatred of bureaucracy, whatever its political colouring. His faults are sins of omission rather than commission. His characters are never evil and rarely callous. But they are unsympathetic.

If there are no free lunches, there is, at least, love, loyalty to one's cadre and longevity. In recent novels Heinlein has tried to combine all three: Gwen/Hazel in *The Cat Who Walks through Walls* (1985) is lover, commandant and grandmother to our protagonist. So it goes. To each his or her own fantasy. This is Heinlein's, it seems.

In *The Number of the Beast* (1980) Heinlein returned to territory he had explored in *Glory Road* (1963), presenting us with a whole series of alternate worlds of varying degrees of reality. For the first time in Heinlein's fiction a veil was torn aside. The fiction had become a game—a Godgame, as John Fowles has termed it—with Heinlein as God the Author. Talk had replaced the Burroughsian sword and sorcery adventure of *Glory Road*—an unending conversation inside the skull of Robert A. Heinlein.

The Number of the Beast, with its use of old Heinlein fictions and its eventual arrival at a science fiction convention, is self-indulgence of the worst kind. A game for the fans. Even so, many of the fans were concerned by what had been lost. The old Heinlein magic was absent from the novel.

Heinlein's next novel, *Friday* (1982), was a pleasant surprise. It deals with a future Earth not so different from our own, and works the seam so tirelessly mined by John Brunner in novels like *Stand on Zanzibar* (1968), *The Sheep Look Up* (1972) and *The Shockwave Rider* (1975). Earth's civilization is going to hell in a bucket: "You should leave this planet; for you there is nothing here." *Friday* is the nadir of Heinlein's feelings for Western civiliza-tion. We are beyond hope, he says in *Friday*. We have cocked it all up irredeemably, and not even special organizations can reverse what is hap-pening.

Friday, heroine of the novel, is a competent woman, an "AP" or Artificial Person, who gets gang-raped at the beginning of the novel and spends most of the rest fighting her way out of one hole or another. Eventually she comes across the capable "Boss" figure who dominates most Heinlein novels. Things go uphill from there. She ends up pregnant and happy and off-planet, finally belonging to a family group. Which is the be-all-and-end-all of Heinlein's message to us in this novel. Choose your friends well, and find a safe haven during a storm. As such it's preferable to the solipsistic escapism of *The Number of the Beast* and the selfish attitudes of *Time Enough for Love*.

Friday is also the most visual of Heinlein's modern novels and suffers least from his tendency to converse. It is a fast-paced, all-action adventure story in the old mould, a fact which won it favourable comparison from the critics with *The Moon Is a Harsh Mistress* (1966). Even so, the world we see in *Friday* is a false world. It does not encompass enough. Once again it is a world of the competent and the also-rans. And the also-rans aren't given a moment's consideration.

This over-simplified viewpoint is a kind of cartoon. Heinlein's world is rough-cast and unfinished. And so the world is, but it is also far subtler and more complex than Heinlein seems able to imagine. He treats his cartoon as the reality and makes his deductions accordingly.

Brian W. Aldiss and David Wingrove, *Trillion Year Spree: The History of Science Fiction* (New York: Atheneum, 1986), pp. 386–87

LEON STOVER   When *Farnham's Freehold* appeared, at the height of the Black Power movement, it met with a storm of critical indignation. The title hero is flung into a future in which the rule of North America has passed to the Black Muslims. ⟨. . .⟩ As in "If This Goes On—," yet another fundamentalist sect has come to power, and with the same disagree-able results. At the same time Heinlein dramatizes Mark Twain's prophecy of 1885 that within a hundred years the formerly enslaved blacks of America would turn things around and "put whites under foot." Or at least they might be disposed to do so, if emancipation were not completed with the elimination of racial prejudice. The unlovely victory of black culture in Heinlein's novel is nothing if not a testimony to Twain's enlightened plea for racial and cultural pluralism; yet for all that, a pluralism harmonized with the majority values of the nation's founders.

This patriotic note was another sore point with the critics. They jabbed at the novel's hero, Hugh Farnham, for the single-minded attention he gave to rescuing his family from black enslavement, and then for defending the family freehold upon the return of the Farnhams to the postwar anarchy of the "present" time. As it happens, the whole family had been thrown into the future by the mysterious effects of an atomic bomb blast, while hiding in their fallout shelter during World War III. Somehow getting back to their own time, in the midst of wartorn chaos, they establish their own freehold and fly the American flag over it. The critics found this offensive, for what appeared to them to be no more than pure selfishness united with racism, the whole miserable scene falsely wrapped in bunting.

But Hugh Farnham, in restoring his family to the best security he can manage, does nothing out of keeping with sound Christian doctrine. St. Paul says: "But if any does not take care of his own, and especially of his household, he has denied the faith and is worse than an unbeliever" (Timothy I, 5:8). The faithful are of course obliged to be helpful to others, loving one's neighbor as oneself, etc. But as the Bishop of Hippo (St. Augustine) observed, while the Roman Empire fell into anarchy all about his diocese in Tunisia, the religious person's "first duty is to look out for his own home, for both by natural and human law he has easier and readier access to their requirements" (*City of God*, chap. 14).

Yet when Heinlein defends the traditional ethics of Christian civilization, it is not seen in him; it is "rugged individualism" all over again, and worse. Moreover, Hugh Farnham frees himself and his family on the same principles that guide black emancipation in *The Narrative of the Life of Frederick Douglass: An American Slave* (1845). Its famous words, "No slave is ever freed, *save he free himself*," are those quoted by Heinlein elsewhere, without attribution in "Logic of Empire." He clearly expects the reader to recognize the source, this great classic of Afro-American Literature.

Leon Stover, *Robert A. Heinlein* (Boston: Twayne, 1987), pp. 60–62

FRED ERISMAN   A consistent theme throughout Robert A. Heinlein's works is the importance of intellectual breadth. From the outset, his

protagonists are multi-talented individuals, and, as his work and thinking
mature, he becomes steadily more overt in his insistence that a responsible
person must have a sound base of diverse knowledge. The theme is implicit
in the eclectic curriculum laid out for young Matt Dodson of *Space Cadet*
(1948), predicated on the belief that the person "who can think correctly
[i.e., in broad terms] will automatically behave morally." It becomes explicit
in *Have Space Suit—Will Travel* (1958) when Professor Reisfeld grumbles
that he "[deplores] this modern overspecialization." Lazarus Long, fifteen
years later, concludes a list of abilities that every human being should have
by asserting, "Specialization is for insects." And Heinlein himself, speaking
in his own voice, remarks in *Expanded Universe* (1980) that history, languages, and mathematics hold up "the 3-legged stool of understanding."
The theme exists. Of that there is no doubt.

What gives Heinlein's theme of breadth its larger significance, though,
is that he develops it through the presentation of a series of imaginary
societies. The expansion, he notes, is part of the science-fiction writer's
obligation to "create the scene and the culture and make it come alive."
If the culture portrayed is alive, rounded, and plausible, no matter how alien
it may otherwise be, it leads the reader to new perspectives on existence.
These perspectives, in turn, constitute what Heinlein sees as a major virtue
of science fiction. The genre necessarily deals with change; and change, if
it is to become progress, requires a solid foundation of knowledge. Thus, by
teaching readers that the world will change, science fiction "leads in the
direction of . . . adaptability [and] . . . preaches the need for freedom of the
mind and the desirability of knowledge."

Heinlein's determination to preach this need to young people (he calls
it his "own propaganda purposes") permeates his twelve Scribner juveniles
and the Scribner-rejected *Starship Troopers*. Within these books, his determination gives substance to the fictional characters' imaginary world, relating
it to the real world of the readers' present and giving life to the culture
described; outside them, it unobtrusively sensitizes young American readers
to their own involvement in a distinctive national culture. The result is a
cluster of provocative science fiction novels that handily document the
validity of E. D. Hirsch's theories of "cultural literacy" even as they provide
their young readers with visions of a future in which versatile knowledge
will be at a premium. ⟨. . .⟩

Heinlein's books leave no doubt as to the society he seeks. In them, the
American past and the changing future work together, suggesting to his

young readers how wide-ranging knowledge and forthright principle can collaborate to the advantage of the individual and the culture. That knowledge generally is of the broadest sort; it comes from all times, all places, and all peoples, enhancing the multi-cultural, independent world that is to come. But, significantly, welding it into a living and functional entity is a unifying socio-intellectual principle, deriving from the continuing American tradition and reinforced by the characters' knowledge of the nation's history and heritage. As the characters combine their fundamental Americanism with the evolving society of the future, they demonstrate for all to see how inevitable change may be transformed into genuine and truly democratic progress. Broadly informed and at home with a range of world knowledge, culturally literate in the very best sense of the term, Heinlein's young protagonists are, indeed, the citizens who will shape the imaginary worlds that they inhabit. If they succeed in communicating the importance of a corresponding and equally vital cultural literacy to the young readers of the American present, they will have more than justified Heinlein's efforts.

Fred Erisman, "Robert Heinlein, the Scribner Juveniles, and Cultural Literacy," *Extrapolation* 32, No. 1 (Spring 1991): 45–45, 51–52

Bibliography

The Discovery of the Future. 1941.

Rocket Ship Galileo. 1947.

Space Cadet. 1948.

Beyond This Horizon. 1948.

Sixth Column: A Science Fiction Novel of a Strange Intrigue ⟨The Day After Tomorrow⟩. 1949.

Red Planet: A Colonial Boy on Mars. 1949, 1990.

The Man Who Sold the Moon: Harriman and the Escape from Earth to the Moon! 1950.

Farmer in the Sky. 1950.

Waldo and Magic Inc. 1950.

Universe. 1951, 1963 (as *Orphans of the Sky*).

The Green Hills of Earth: Rhysling and the Adventure of the Entire Solar System! 1951.

Tomorrow, the Stars: A Science Fiction Anthology (editor; with Frederik Pohl
    and Judith Merril). 1951.
The Puppet Masters. 1951, 1990.
Between Planets. 1951.
The Rolling Stones. 1952.
Revolt in 2100: The Prophets and the Triumph of Reason over Superstition! 1953.
Assignment in Eternity: Four Long Science Fiction Stories. 1953.
Starman Jones. 1953.
The Star Beast. 1954.
Tunnel in the Sky. 1955.
Time for the Stars. 1956.
Double Star. 1956.
The Door into Summer. 1957.
Citizen of the Galaxy. 1957.
Have Space Suit—Will Travel. 1958.
Methuselah's Children. 1958.
The Robert Heinlein Omnibus ⟨*The Man Who Sold the Moon, The Green Hills
    of Earth*⟩. 1958.
The Menace from Earth. 1959.
The Unpleasant Profession of Jonathan Hoag. 1959.
Starship Troopers. 1959.
Stranger in a Strange Land. 1961, 1990.
Podkayne of Mars: Her Life and Times. 1962.
Glory Road. 1963.
Farnham's Freehold. 1964.
Three by Heinlein ⟨*The Puppet Masters, Waldo, Magic Inc.*⟩. 1965.
The Moon Is a Harsh Mistress. 1966.
A Robert Heinlein Omnibus ⟨*Beyond This Horizon, The Man Who Sold the Moon,
    The Green Hills of Earth*⟩. 1966.
The Worlds of Robert A. Heinlein. 1966.
The Past through Tomorrow: Future History Stories. 1967.
I Will Fear No Evil. 1970.
Time Enough for Love: The Lives of Lazarus Long. 1973.
The Best of Robert Heinlein 1939–1959. Ed. Angus Wells. 1973.
The Notebooks of Lazarus Long. 1978.
Destination Moon. Ed. David G. Hartwell. 1979.
A Heinlein Trio ⟨*The Puppet Masters, Double Stars, The Door into Space*⟩. 1980.
The Number of the Beast. 1980.

Expanded Universe: The New Worlds of Robert A. Heinlein. 1980.

Friday. 1982.

Job: A Comedy of Justice. 1984.

The Cat Who Walks through Walls: A Comedy of Manners. 1985.

To Sail Beyond the Sunset: The Lives and Loves of Maureen Johnson (Being the Memoirs of a Somewhat Irregular Lady). 1987.

Grumbles from the Grave. Ed. Virginia Heinlein. 1989.

Take Back Your Government: A Practical Handbook for the Private Citizen Who Wants Democracy to Work. 1992.

Requiem: New Collected Works by Robert A. Heinlein and Tributes to the Grand Master. Ed. Yoji Kondo. 1992.

Tramp Royale. 1992.

Fritz Leiber
1910–1992

FRITZ REUTER LEIBER, JR., was born in Chicago on December 24, 1910, the son of distinguished Shakespearean actor and theatrical manager Fritz Leiber and Virginia Bronson Leiber. Exposure to members of his mother and father's acting troupe introduced the young Leiber to a variety of interests, including reading, chess, and the stage. Leiber spent most of his childhood in Chicago, eventually enrolling in the University of Chicago, from which he graduated with a B.A. in 1932.

Upon graduating, Leiber served as an Episcopal minister but a crisis of conscience over his lack of religious faith sent him back to graduate school. After a brief but unsuccessful stint on the stage, Leiber returned once again to school, where he met Jonquil Stephens. The two were married in 1936 and moved to Hollywood to live with Leiber's parents while Fritz embarked on an abortive career in film. Their only son, Justin, was born in 1938. Over the next few decades, Leiber held a succession of jobs in publishing.

While at college, Leiber was introduced to the work of weird fiction writer H. P. Lovecraft, whom he would later cite as one of the most important influences on his writing. He corresponded with Lovecraft a short time before the latter's death in 1937 and sent his early efforts at fiction writing for Lovecraft's criticism. Also while in college, Leiber met Harry Otto Fischer, who shared many of Leiber's interests. In their correspondence, the two playfully imagined themselves as heroic fantasy characters named Fafhrd (Leiber) and the Gray Mouser (Fischer), who became the subjects of several stories by Leiber.

Leiber submitted several stories for publication to *Weird Tales* in the late 1930s, eventually selling his horror story "The Automatic Pistol" in 1938 (not published until 1940). To John W. Campbell's fantasy magazine *Unknown*, he sent the tales of Fafhrd and the Mouser that had been rejected by *Weird Tales*. The Fafhrd and Mouser stories, with their squabbling anti-hero characters and sly humor, were immediately recognized as alternatives to the stereotypical blood-and-thunder type of heroic fantasy that hitherto had dominated the pulp fantasy magazines. Leiber also made a mark with his horror fiction, updating the tropes of Gothic horror for modern urban settings inhabited by psychologically complex characters in stories such as "Smoke Ghost" and his first novel, *Conjure Wife* (serialized 1941; revised for book publication 1953; filmed as *Weird Woman* in 1948 and *Burn, Witch, Burn* in 1963). The latter, a rational treatment of the persistence of witchcraft in the modern world, became one of the most influential horror novels of the twentieth century.

When *Unknown* folded in 1943, Leiber concentrated on writing science fiction, producing the novels *Gather, Darkness!*, a futuristic novel satirizing religion, and *Destiny Times Three* for *Astounding Science Fiction*. His first book, the collection *Night's Black Agents*, was published in 1947. "You're All Alone" (final revision as *The Sinful Ones*, 1986), a short fantasy novel about alienation in the modern world, as well as stories Leiber wrote for the burgeoning science fiction market of the 1950s, blurred the boundaries of science fiction, fantasy, and horror through their imaginative expression of America's postwar angst. *The Big Time* (1961) is the centerpiece of a series of tales entitled The Change War, all probing the notion of time travel. *The Wanderer* (1964), about a mysterious planet that approaches the Earth, and *A Specter Is Haunting Texas* (1969), a political satire about a futuristic society, are among Leiber's more significant works of "hard" science fiction.

Over the last twenty-five years of his life Leiber amassed numerous awards for his writing, including seven Hugos, four Nebulas, and the World Fantasy Award for his novel *Our Lady of Darkness* (1977), a tale of urban paranoia set in his adopted town of San Francisco. He became the only writer to win lifetime achievement awards in the fantasy, horror, and science fiction fields. Although hobbled by health problems throughout the 1980s, Leiber continued to write, producing the lengthy and insightful autobiographical essay "Not Much Disorder and Not So Early Sex" for his collection *The Ghost Light* (1984) and a final collection of Fafhrd and Mouser stories, *The Knight and Knave of Swords* (1988). He died from complications of a series of strokes on September 5, 1992.

◈ Critical Extracts

AUGUST DERLETH   This swift-moving novel ⟨*Gather, Darkness!*⟩ is a compound of science-fiction and the orthodox weird, with emphasis on the former; it moves so rapidly that, once begun, the book will be difficult to put aside until the last page has been read. The three-way conflict among the priests, the followers of Asmodeus, and Brother Jarles makes for a rapid shifting in point-of-view, so that the reader is led to follow three separate chains of action all leading to the climax of the destruction of the hierarchy's power.

The growing following which science-fiction has developed will particularly enjoy this adventurous novel, which, despite its rapid action, is not without humor and satire. *Gather, Darkness!* tho primarily an entertainment, nevertheless focuses sharp attention on a present contemporary problem— shall the world of the future be guided by the scientists or by the people. Mr. Leiber's answer, like yours or mine would be likely to be, is ambiguous. But there is nothing ambiguous about his novel and its excellent readability.

August Derleth, "Here We Go, Into Second Atomic Age," *Chicago Sunday Tribune Magazine of Books*, 9 April 1950, p. 7

MARSHALL McLUHAN   In a story called "The Girl with the Hungry Eyes," by Fritz Leiber, an ad photographer gives a job to a not too promising model. Soon, however, she is "plastered all over the country" because she has the hungriest eyes in the world. "Nothing vulgar, but just the same they're looking at you with a hunger that's all sex and something more than sex." Something similar may be said of the legs on a pedestal. Abstracted from the body that gives them their ordinary meaning, they become "something more than sex," a metaphysical enticement, a cerebral itch, an abstract torment. Mr. Leiber's girl hypnotizes the country with her hungry eyes and finally accepts the attentions of the photographer who barely escapes with his life. In this vampire, not of blood but of spirit, he finds "the horror behind the bright billboard . . . She's the eyes that lead you on and on and then show you death." She says to him: "I want you. I want your high spots. I want everything that's made you happy and everything that's hurt you bad. I want your first girl . . . I want that licking

... I want Betty's legs ... I want your mother's death ... I want your wanting me. I want your life. Feed me, baby, feed me."

> Marshall McLuhan, *The Mechanical Bride: Folklore of Industrial Man* (Boston: Beacon Press, 1951), p. 101

DAMON KNIGHT   *Conjure Wife*, by Fritz Leiber, is easily the most frightening and (necessarily) the most thoroughly convincing of all horror stories. Its premise is that witchcraft still flourishes, or at any rate survives, an open secret among women, a closed book to men. Under the rational overlay of 20th-century civilization this sickly growth, uncultivated, unsuspected, still manages to propagate itself:

> ". . . I don't do much. Like when my boyfriend was in the army, I did things to keep him from getting shot or hurt, and I've spelled him so that he'll keep away from other women. And I kin annernt with erl for sickness. Honest, I don't do much, ma'am. And it don't always work. And lots of things I can't get that way.
> ". . . Some I learned from Ma when I was a kid. And some from Mrs. Neidel—she gots spells against bullets from her grandmother who had a family in some European war way back. But most women won't tell you anything. And some spells I kind of figger out myself, and try different ways until they work."

Tansy Saylor, the wife of a promising young sociology professor at an ultra-conservative small American college, is, like most women, a witch. She is also an intelligent, modern young woman, and when her husband happens to discover the evidence of her witchcraft (not his own easy advancement, which he ascribes to luck, but certain small packets of dried leaves, earth, metal, filings, &c.) he's able to convince her that her faith in magic is compounded of superstition and neurosis. She burns her charms; Norman Saylor's "luck" immediately turns sour. But this is not all—the Balance has been upset.

> The witches' warfare . . . was much like trench warfare or a battle between fortified lines—a state of siege. Just as reinforced concrete or armor plating nullified the shells, so countercharms and protection procedures rendered relatively futile the most violent onslaughts. But once the armor and concrete were gone,

and the witch who had foresworn witchcraft was out in a kind of
no man's land—

For the realistic mind, there could be only one answer. Namely
that the enemy had discovered a weapon more potent than
battleships or aircraft, and was planning to ask for a peace that
would turn out to be a trap. The only thing would be to strike
instantly and hard, before the secret weapon could be brought
into play.

Leiber develops the theme with the utmost dexterity, piling up alternate
layers of the mundane and outré, until at the story's real climax, the shocker
at the end of Chapter 14, I am not ashamed to say that I jumped an inch
out of my seat. From that point onward the story is anticlimax, but anticlimax
so skillfully managed that I am not really certain I touched the slip-cover
again until after the last page. Leiber has never written anything better . . .
which, perhaps, is all that needed to be said.

Damon Knight, "Campbell and His Decade," *In Search of Wonder* (Chicago: Advent,
1956), pp. 31, 33

JUDITH MERRIL   One way or another, Leiber keeps sorting out
the elements of his many "lives," using Shakespeare, sex, chess, science
and the supernatural, politics and pacifism, alcohol, Hollywood, Academe,
Church, Stage, and the publishing world, to cultivate his cunningly fashioned
demons and daemons of the world of today, using them in new modes when
he can, in old ones when he must. And in both veins, the young as well
as the old continue to listen, with pleasure. ⟨. . .⟩

In 1940, Leiber's story, "The Automatic Pistol," began:
"Inky Kozacs never let anyone but himself handle his automatic pistol,
or even touch it. It was inky-black . . ." And the last spoken line in it is:
"Two aces, Inky's little gun didn't protect him, you know. He didn't have
a chance to use it. Clubs and spades. Black bullets. I win." After which the
black gun inside the black suitcase fires at Inky's murderer and kills him.

There has been much learned discussion recently (and especially in reference to Vietnam) about the American refusal to acknowledge death. Well,
death has come home to us now, and our young people, at least, understand
fully that we can only live with death by looking on its face and recognizing
it. We cannot turn from *this* black face any more than from the twenty-

odd million living black faces among us. Not any more. We can conquer our fear the same way we can conquer our guilt. Our young people know this, and Leiber learned it in 1942—when he went from *Conjure Wife* to *Gather, Darkness!*

Black is Beautiful—*too*.

The hero of *A Specter Is Haunting Texas* is an animated skeleton (literally) known as *El Muerte* to the people of Texas (a country extending from Alaska to Acapulco, and from the Pacific Black Republic to the Black Florida Whosit). He is in love with two women: the pale Lady Death, and an earthly vital brunette; in the end he refuses to leave either one behind. And the lining of his hooded black cloak is a brilliant scarlet.

Judith Merril, "Fritz Leiber," *Magazine of Fantasy and Science Fiction* 37, No. 1 (July 1969): 59–61

JEFF FRANE   Leiber's second novel to receive the Hugo award for best novel was *The Wanderer*, a disaster story that, in some ways, became a formula for other writers to follow. What makes this book so much more satisfying than such later efforts as Larry Niven and Jerry Pournelle's *Lucifer's Hammer* is the added breadth of imagination and insight that carries it beyond the simple formula.

In most disaster novels, a prevalent sub-genre within science fiction, a natural cataclysm destroys most of civilization. The author frequently begins the story with the approach of the disaster—whether it be impending comet, flood, plague, or wind—and skips back and forth among a number of characters. After the cataclysm, the characters are drawn together in the struggle for survival, and the human element of interaction is used as a plot device.

In *The Wanderer* another level is added through Leiber's fertile imagination. It is also Leiber's first lengthy piece of what is commonly called "hard" science fiction, the type of story that requires a great deal of scientific research and extrapolation. ⟨. . .⟩

The Wanderer appears suddenly in the night sky, immediately following an eclipse of the moon. When first seen, it is a purple and gold yin-yang disc in the sky. As it rotates on its axis and revolves around Earth, the shape continues to change, stimulating any number of interpretations in the minds of the people who see it. Few of them accept immediately that what has appeared is indeed another planet ("planet" derives from the

Greek verb "to wander"), for they have not had any real warning and the idea of a planet suddenly appearing next to Earth in the Moon's orbit is too enormous a concept for their minds to grasp quickly, if at all.

For the most part, those characters who quickly assimilate the real nature of the Wanderer and its effects on the planet are those who are science-fiction readers. Leiber seems to feel that exposure to the "wild" ideas of science fiction may enhance the reader's ability to accept change more easily. This is a view very much in line with that expressed by the astronomer Carl Sagan: "The greatest human significance of science fiction may be as experiments on the future, as explorations of alternative destinies, as attempts to minimize future shock."

The appearance of the planet is enough in itself to cause enormous human disruption, for it drastically violates everyone's views of the natural state of the cosmos. In addition, the physical effects are disastrous. Leiber spent a great deal of time researching and calculating the "astronomy of the thing and a great deal more in the tidal effects, making out tidal charts for each place mentioned in the book." The Wanderer destroys and "devours" the Moon, and the tidal disruption of the Earth causes widespread earthquakes, tsunamis, floods, and fires. Leiber's first-page parallel with the Earth and the human soul is very important, for the "deep fissures" are physical and emotional. ⟨. . .⟩

At the conclusion of the novel, a second planet arrives and a cosmic battle between the two visitors is briefly featured. The Wanderer departs with the police planet in pursuit. Leiber leave us, however, with a feeling of ambiguity. Tigerishka has made it clear that humans can expect to be visited, and engulfed, by the galactic civilization in the near future. Although this disaster has ended, there is nothing that humans can do to avert a later and more final one.

Jeff Frane, *Fritz Leiber* (Mercer Island, WA: Starmont House, 1980), pp. 33–34, 36

JUSTIN LEIBER   In *You're All Alone* (1950) one of the narrowest and most dramatic expressions of paranoia that I have ever known is explored. The protagonist discovers that almost everyone in his present-day world operates like a Leibnizian "windowless" monad. They all are following a prearranged, automatic pattern that makes them look like they are interacting while in fact they are not. If you are one of the very few who can break out of the pattern, no one will notice you. And indeed they all continue "interacting" with the empty space you are programmed to occupy exactly as if you were there. The "all" does not include a small number of evil breakouts who are exploiting the situation and hunting down everyone else who has broken out of the automatic interplay. Eerie effects come from manipulation of the automaton normals, from retreating into the automatic patterns.

It's a scary story, and should one stand back and think about it, it suggests something about the writer (about a grim Chicago downtown business-and-bar world). But everything is done to lead the reader away from that issue, and the author has no place in the story. The title is "You're All Alone," not "I'm All Alone" or "We're All Alone."

On the other hand, *The Big Time* employs the same notion of breakout for the few whom the Snakes and Spiders can recruit. They do not break out of themselves, however, and Illy eventually suggests that the recruiter is really the demon-daemon Art. Here we have not the simple paranoiac punch but the gay, giddy, multileveled fabric of high art, of the "everybody and nobody," in which the Place, dancing with drama and history, is also revealed as the mind of Fritz Leiber and his Art (like "I" and "Borges").

Gather, Darkness! is one of the first (perhaps *the*) classical novels of a future, post–World War Three world dominated by an authoritarian, medieval church hierarchy whose inner circle employs a secret scientific technology to keep a superstitious public and lower priesthood under control. The action is dramatic and colorful, the technology cunning and charming, the plot stunningly well constructed. One idea that gives the work its classical balance is the logic of a revolution against such a hierarchy of white magic. The revolutionaries will play satanists, a hierarchy of black magic which will dismay, frighten, or win over people who are accustomed to thinking in magical, not scientific ways. (The French historian, Jules Michelet, saw medieval satanism as the only available expression for the antifeudal revolution. If the church hierarchy says that God wants wealth and power to go to the temporal and religious lords, who is on the side of the poor peasants? Who is their spiritual resource?)

But ⟨. . .⟩ when we get to *A Specter Is Haunting Texas* (1968), we have a more multileveled, more comic and realistic story of a post–World War Three future. Scully, actor from Circumluna, is dragged into the Hispanic revolution against hormone-hiked, conquering Texans, who identify the LBJ and (no doubt) a certain war. And Scully knows that history is seldom a tale of technologically inventive elites, coldly manipulating the credulous masses. You don't reason its craziness out, you sing, it, chant it, farce it out.

Justin Leiber, "Fritz Leiber and Eyes," *Philosophers Look at Science Fiction*, ed. Nicholas D. Smith (Chicago: Nelson-Hall, 1982), pp. 183–85

TOM STAICAR   Until Leiber began his cycle of stories which came to be known as the Change War series, SF writers had not strayed from the traditional view of time as a fragile, easily-shattered entity. Leiber built an image of time as a strong and inertia-prone progression of events in which a single action would have little effect. All known history could not be wiped out by saving Julius Caesar or Abraham Lincoln, for example. In The Change War, large numbers of alterations are required to produce a significantly different outcome to a single war, let alone the course of civilization's progress. No individual Wellsian Time Traveler could right the wrongs he saw in the future in a Change War tale. Where other authors had written of intrepid inventors working alone, Leiber created armies of time soldiers, each of whom played only a minor role in a drama that required the universe as a stage.

The keystone of his series is *The Big Time* (1961). Using that novel as the centerpiece, he wrote Change War stories for leading SF magazines such as *Galaxy* between 1958 and 1967. These share an overall background and, in a few instances, the same characters.

In "Try and Change the Past" (first published in *Astounding Stories* in 1958), Leiber has a character attempt to alter his own past in order to save himself from being shot and killed, but to no avail. Even with the gun itself removed from the room at the time of the shooting, a small meteorite makes its way to earth and hits him exactly where the bullet would have and causes the same type and size of hole. As the narrator of the story says:

> Change one event in the past and you get a brand new future?
> Erase the conquests of Alexander by nudging a Neolithic pebble?
> Extirpate America by pulling up a shoot of Sumerian grain?
> Brother, that isn't the way it works at all! The space-time
> continuum's built of stubborn stuff and change is anything but a
> chain-reaction. Change the past and you start a wave of changes
> moving futurewards, but it damps out mighty fast. Haven't you
> ever heard of temporal reluctance, or of the Law of Conservation
> of Reality?

Stories in the Change War series feature agents who struggle to make enough major changes in history to gain ultimate victory. Unlike the Bradbury story, "A Sound of Thunder," one tiny change will not be sufficient, because it would be damped out or negated by the other time soldiers. Major wars have to be altered in their outcomes and important people have to be rerouted in their careers or lives. ⟨. . .⟩

The Change War sometimes results in losses that cannot be remedied, eras of Greek or Roman history wiped out, leaders kidnapped as infants, and schools of thought disappearing because their originators were never born. Nuclear war seems like a lesser tragedy compared to the possibility that the very existence of a group of people could be obliterated from the past, present, and future. Not even a memory or a single record of their existence would remain, making their deaths all the more terrible.

Tom Staicar, *Fritz Leiber* (New York: Frederick Ungar Publishing Co., 1983), pp. 49–51

FRITZ LEIBER   I wrote "Coming Attraction" in 1951 when the McCarthy Era was getting into full swing and when atomic war was a chief matter for speculation and warning. My story was one more such.

Four influences were pushing me in the direction of science fiction writing in those days and some of them also helping equip me for writing it. First there was my job at *Science Digest,* where I read all the popularized science that came along in search of articles and book sections we could purchase for our magazine. It kept me thinking in the direction of new inventions and technical advances. It scanted pure science and the philosophy of science, to be sure, but made it a bit easier for me to delve into those things on my own.

Second there were the new magazines that were being launched, *The Magazine of Fantasy and Science Fiction,* which did much to raise literary standards in the field, and *Galaxy,* which was strong on the sociological side and breathed the "in the know" spirit of New York City.

Third there was ⟨John W.⟩ Campbell, who was once more encouraging me, even providing ideas, as for "The Lion and the Lamb." He was, by all odds, the best editor I've ever known at getting a writer going, if he chose to do so.

And fourth, there were the other science fiction editors, writers, and enthusiasts, whom I got to know with a rush at the 1949 World Science Fiction Convention, the Seventh, the "Cinvention." ⟨. . .⟩

⟨. . .⟩ The convention was for me a revelation—I just hadn't guessed how many people there were in this thing called science fiction—and a dizzying mixture of lost weekend and getting-acquainted party. I met Fred ⟨Pohl⟩, of course, and his wife Judith Merril, Lester del Rey, Horace Gold, a very young Poul Anderson, an engineer-author who was a lush like me and told me how he banished hangovers with hot-cold showers, even a "Miss Science Fiction of 1949," and any number of editors and publishers, especially editors and publishers soon-to-be. Nor was I too drunk to engage in and appreciate enough conversations about the fascination and exciting possibilities of science that told me I was really with my sort of people. ⟨. . .⟩ I got a tremendous shot in the arm that weekend and met a not inconsiderable fraction of my lifelong friends-and-colleagues.

> Fritz Leiber, "Not So Much Disorder and Not So Early Sex: An Autobiographic Essay," *The Ghost Light: Masterworks of Fantasy and Science Fiction* (1984; rpt. New York: Ace, 1991), pp. 358–60

JOHN HUNTINGTON   "Coming Attraction" describes a grim futuristic New York in which a few elements of fifties technology (automobiles, for instance) have become slicker and more dangerous. In this world emotion appears in perverse forms: erotic attention has been displaced from genital areas to the face, and women wrestlers who defeat men appear as objects of fascination. Having women display their bodies and mask their faces is a way of satirizing current prudishness about the display of the body. And the wrestling matches challenge conventional ideas of male domination, though, since the main effect of such matches is a masochistic humiliation of the man, it might well be argued that this particular violation of convention finally serves only to reinforce it. The story's knowingness about prudery and masculinity leads to a profound ambivalence.

The story itself is aware of its complicated attitude toward the place of emotion in the American future it depicts. A policeman's confused response to "Girls going down the street bare from the neck up"—an act of almost pornographic self-display in the story—is exactly the reaction we would expect of one of the story's readers to have to a woman bare from the neck down: "It was not clear whether he viewed the prospect with relish or moral distaste. Likely both." Like the masks themselves, which the narrator observes may be "heightening loveliness or hiding ugliness," fear is double valued. The frightened woman is both attractive and offensive. The protagonist's British conservatism—he comes from a society that does not seem much different from England in the mid-twentieth century—is seen as both morally straight in a world of American perversions and perhaps as foolish, cowardly, and stodgy.

The insecurities behind this ambivalence are made clear in a gratuitous scene midway through the story:

> The street was almost empty, though I was accosted by a couple
> of beggars with faces tunneled by H-bomb scars, whether real or
> of makeup putty, I couldn't tell. A fat woman held out a baby
> with webbed fingers and toes. I told myself it would have been
> deformed anyway and that she was only capitalizing on our fear of
> bomb-induced mutations. Still, I gave her a seven-and-a-half cent
> piece. Her mask made me feel I was paying tribute to an African
> fetish.

Contradictory responses of sympathy, distrust, contempt, fear, and shame pose an interpretative dilemma here: How are we, the readers, to respond to a narrator who tries to evade the beggar's plea for her deformed child by asserting that "she was *only* capitalizing on our fear of bomb-induced mutations"? Are we to agree that in a world of extravagant symbolic fantasies, beggars alone are not to "capitalize" on our fears? And what does he mean by "it would have been deformed anyway"? The attitudes here are common enough; the question is are we to accept or to challenge them? Is the British narrator, the representative of the familiar world, to be understood as morally sound or as hypocritical? The whole story is riddled with this sort of dilemma. Is Theda, the enigmatic woman who engages the narrator, victim or "capitalizer"? If the latter, what is her profit? And by befriending her, is the narrator acting as a good samaritan or a conned sucker? And if the latter, is it his fault or hers?

The essential moral displacement that characterizes "Coming Attraction" would seem to allow these questions to remain open. ⟨...⟩ "Coming Attraction" ⟨...⟩ imagines new sexual relations and emotional values, thereby at least potentially disqualifying conventional judgments and responses. The intrepretative problem posed by the story is whether we are to read the kinky future as an emancipation from our own inhibitions or as a degeneration from the "wholesomeness" of our own, however limited, system of gender roles.

John Huntington, *Rationalizing Genius: Ideological Strategies in the Classic American Science Fiction Short Story* (New Brunswick, NJ: Rutgers University Press, 1989), pp. 104–6

BRUCE BYFIELD   What is significant in Leiber's five decades of development is the way in which his circumstances and his reading constantly combine to give him better understanding of his craft. Lovecraft's example helped Leiber to analyze himself during his crisis of confidence in the mid-1940s, and to identify the rudiments of his symbolism, then, when his ambivalence about his symbolism emerged, the timely publication of ⟨Robert⟩ Graves' *Seven Days in New Crete* focuses his misgivings and gives him something to react against. In much the same way, Leiber's discovery of Jung in the late 1950s justified his shift to personal concerns, and extended his understanding of his symbolism. When Leiber's recovery from grief in the mid-1970s interested him in individuation, ⟨Joseph⟩ Campbell, De Quincey, and Ibsen allowed him to present his symbolism by artful allusion, and to find still another new direction.

This cross-influence of life and reading is not unique to Leiber, but what does seem unusual is how aware Leiber has been of the process. Many writers absorb literary and environmental influences unconsciously, so much so that they are afraid to analyze them too closely lest self-consciousness prevent them from writing. By contrast, Leiber seems to have used his fiction as the main instrument in a fifty year process of individuation. Developing slowly and deliberately, sometimes too self-consciously to be successful, at other times hiding from the implications of his work through whimsy, irony, or ambiguity, Leiber appears to have thought through most of the major changes in his work. In this respect, he disproves the critical stance that writers cannot be the best judges of their own work. Although he can be vague or reticent about details, his nonfiction about his influences and his life indicates a writer with a clear idea of how he operates in his craft. If this awareness has sometimes given his fiction a contrived feel, it has more often allowed him greater control, enabling him to pinpoint his themes and to find ways of reinforcing them. In general, the more personal or painful his material has been, and the more he has struggled to control it, the greater his artistry has been. It is when he ignores or contradicts his attitudes, or responds to the market, that his fiction is usually at its weakest.

This consciousness of his craft explains the sudden advances that Judith Merril observes in his work. Leiber defines himself as a thorough rather than a quick thinker, yet, once he becomes aware of his own tendencies, he realizes them quickly, and in a rather small number of works. As a consequence, he has paced developments in science fiction as no other writer has done. Even if Leiber was not worth studying for his own sake, he would still be an important figure because his development is a microcosm of the field's. Leiber and his chosen field have matured and become more literary together, and science fiction would lack some of the respect it has today without Leiber's quiet influence on better-known writers.

> Bruce Byfield, *Witches of the Mind: A Critical Study of Fritz Leiber* (West Warwick, RI: Necronomicon Press, 1991), p. 68

▩ *Bibliography*

Night's Black Agents. 1947.

Gather, Darkness! 1950.

Conjure Wife. 1953.

The Green Millennium. 1953.

The Sinful Ones ⟨with *Bulls, Blood, and Passion* by David Williams⟩. 1953, 1972 (as *You're All Alone*), 1986 (as *The Sinful Ones*).

Destiny Times Three. 1957.

Two Sought Adventure: Exploits of Fafhrd and the Gray Mouser. 1957.

The Big Time ⟨with *The Mind Spider and Other Stories*⟩. 1961.

The Silver Eggheads. 1962.

Shadows with Eyes. 1962.

H. P. Lovecraft: A Symposium (with others). 1963.

The Wanderer. 1964.

A Pail of Air. 1964.

Ships to the Stars ⟨with *The Million Year Hunt* by Kenneth Bulmer⟩. 1964.

The Night of the Wolf. 1966.

Tarzan and the Valley of Gold. 1966.

The Secret Songs. 1968.

The Swords of Lankhmar. 1968.

Swords against Wizardry. 1968.

Swords in the Mist. 1968.

A Specter Is Haunting Texas. 1969.

The Demons of the Upper Air. 1969.

Night Monsters. 1969.

Swords and Deviltry. 1970.

Swords against Death. 1970.

The Best of Fritz Leiber. 1974.

The Book of Fritz Leiber. 1974.

The Second Book of Fritz Leiber. 1975.

The Worlds of Fritz Leiber. 1976.

Our Lady of Darkness. 1977.

Swords and Ice Magic. 1977.

Rime Isle. 1977.

The Change War. 1978.

Sonnets to Jonquil and All. 1978.

Bazaar of the Bizarre. 1978.

Heroes and Horrors. Ed. Stuart Schiff. 1978.

Ship of Shadows. 1979.

Ervool. 1980, 1982.

The World Fantasy Awards: Volume 2 (editor; with Stuart David Schiff). 1980.

The First World Fantasy Convention: Three Authors Remember (with Robert
        Bloch and T. E. D. Klein). 1980.

Riches and Power: A Story for Children. 1982.

The Mystery of the Japanese Clock. 1982.

Quicks around the Zodiac: A Farce. 1983.

The Ghost Light. 1984.

The Knight and Knave of Swords. 1988.

The Leiber Chronicles: Fifty Years of Fritz Leiber. Ed. Martin H. Greenberg.
        1990.

Gummitch and Friends. 1992.

C. L. Moore
1911–1987
Henry Kuttner
1915–1958

HENRY KUTTNER was born in Los Angeles on April 7, 1915, to Henry Kuttner, a dealer in rare books, and Annie Lewis Kuttner. Kuttner's father died when he was five and his mother and two older brothers moved from San Francisco, where the family had settled, back to Los Angeles. Upon graduating from high school he took a job at a Beverly Hills literary agency and the experience stimulated him to try writing himself. Kuttner had become enamored of fantasy through his reading of L. Frank Baum and Edgar Rice Burroughs, and his earliest efforts were fantasy and horror fiction. His first professional fiction sale, "The Graveyard Rats," appeared in the March 1936 issue of *Weird Tales* and strongly reflected the influence of his mentor and correspondent H. P. Lovecraft. From that point on, Kuttner attempted to make a living as a writer, trying his hand at many types of popular fiction including science fiction and earning an early reputation as a competent but derivative writer.

It was in the pages of *Weird Tales* that Kuttner first came upon the fiction of C. L. Moore. Catherine Lucille Moore had been born in Indianapolis, Indiana, on January 24, 1911, to Otto Newman Moore, a machinist, and Maude Estelle Jones Moore. Sickly as a child, Moore picked up an early love of reading from her mother, who taught her for many years at home. Moore pursued an interest in romance literature at Indiana University but her education was cut short by the depression. She was working as a secretary at a trust company when she sold her first story, "Shambleau," to *Weird Tales*. An uncommonly mature space opera with a discreetly erotic subtext, it immediately thrust Moore into the spotlight as a writer of significance.

At Lovecraft's behest, Kuttner wrote a fan letter to "Mr. C. L. Moore," unaware initially that the recipient was a woman. A correspondence ensued and the two met for the first time in 1938. Their first collaboration, "Quest of the Starstone," appeared in the November 1937 issue of *Weird Tales*. They were married in New York on June 7, 1940.

Kuttner and Moore proved compatible not only as husband and wife but as writing partners, and it is nearly impossible to determine what their respective contributions were to the torrent of fiction they produced from 1940 onward. When Kuttner was discharged from military service in 1943 for illness, he and Moore began writing prodigiously for the science fiction and fantasy magazines. So great was their output that they were compelled to use more than a score of pseudonyms, the best known being Lewis Padgett and Lawrence O'Donnell.

Under his own name, Kuttner wrote wacky stories about human beings frustrated in their efforts to understand technology, several of which were collected as *Robots Have No Tails* (1952). Under her name, Moore wrote brooding tales of galactic empires in conflict, the best example of which is *Judgment Night* (1952). Under pseudonyms, they wrote stories that emphasized the persistence of human nature, for better or for worse, in futuristic and technologically sophisticated worlds. Their work did much to dispel the belief that characters were fated to play second fiddle to the ideas in science fiction. Their most famous Padgett story, "Mimsy Were the Borogoves," inaugurated an entire branch of science fiction which proposed that children, unbiased by adult thought processes, could apprehend alternate forms of logic. As O'Donnell, they produced the time travel masterpiece "Vintage Season." Under dual bylines, they wrote psychologically complex fantasy novels that showed the influence of A. Merritt. So highly regarded and ubiquitous was their work in the 1940s that many readers assumed any story of merit by an unfamiliar name was a pseudonymous Kuttner-Moore collaboration.

By 1950 their science fiction output had slowed to a trickle and the couple enrolled at the University of Southern California, eventually obtaining their college degrees. They were embarked upon careers as script writers for Warner Brothers when Kuttner died of a heart attack on February 3, 1958. Moore continued writing for television and married businessman Thomas Reggie in 1963. She died after a long period of illness on April 4, 1987.

◙ Critical Extracts

H. P. LOVECRAFT   As to the work of C. L. Moore—I don't agree with your low estimate. These tales have a peculiar quality of cosmic weirdness, hard to define but easy to recognise, which marks them out as really unique. "Black God's Shadow" isn't up to the standard—but you can get the full effect of the distinctive quality in "Shambleau" & "Black Thirst". In these tales there is an indefinable atmosphere of vague *outsideness* & *cosmic dread* which marks weird work of the best sort. How notably they contrast with the average pulp product—whose bizarre subject-matter is wholly neutralised by the brisk, almost *cheerful* manner of narrative! Whether the Moore tales will keep their pristine quality or deteriorate as their author picks up the methods, formulae, & style of cheap magazine fiction, still remains to be seen. A. Merritt fell for the pulp formula, hence never realised his best potentialities. Miss Moore may do the same. But at present she certainly belongs in the upper tier of W⟨eird⟩ T⟨ales⟩ contributors along with ⟨Clark Ashton⟩ Smith, ⟨Robert E.⟩ Howard, &c.

     H. P. Lovecraft, Letter to William Frederick Anger (28 January 1935), *Selected Letters 1934–1937*, ed. August Derleth and James Turner (Sauk City, WI: Arkham House, 1976), pp. 92–93

LIN CARTER   I first read *Earth's Last Citadel* back in the old *Argosy*, and it was quite nice to re-live that fine story once again—my *Argosy* copies having long since gone the Way of All Old Pulps. That is the best fantasy novel you've printed for quite a while; you'll have to go some to find a better one than that.

Naturally, any collaboration of the talents of C. L. Moore and Henry Kuttner would be something special. But this one was actually superb. So rich with color and imagery, such lavish Merrittesque description—indeed that adjective might be used to classify the entire story. This is probably the finest imitation of Merritt's style since Hannes Bok's "Sorcerer's Ship." I can't seem to praise the novel enough. So seldom does a work of such heights of imagination appear in print, that it almost paralyzes one's powers of description.

     Lin Carter, Letter to the Editor, *Fantastic Novels* 4, No. 3 (November 1950): 127

FREDERIK POHL   Kuttner is about as agile a man with a typewriter as science-fiction possesses, and it is no secret that in these and practically all of his other stories of the last decade he has had the expert help of his wife, otherwise known as C. (for Catherine) L. Moore. When this impressive duo sets out to construct a story that is funny (as in the title yarn), you are going to find yourself laughing out loud; when they want to throw a scare into you (witness "The Twonky" and "Mimsy Were the Borogoves"), you will not escape the sensation of teetering at the edge of a dangerous height. The world the Kuttners create is a nightmare world—nightmare fear, and even nightmare humor—but it is a nightmare you'll want to explore, at a safe distance.

> Frederik Pohl, [Review of A Gnome There Was and Other Tales of Science Fiction and Fantasy], Super Science Stories 8, No. 1 (April 1951): 37–38

ANTHONY BOUCHER   Henry Kuttner and his wife, C. L. Moore, have written science-fantasy under nineteen names (of which the best known is Lewis Padgett); and although publishers have made vain attempts to distinguish their identities, they say "It is almost impossible now to tell which of us wrote what part of any particular story." As a collective entity, they are best described as the author who once began (and, da capo, closed) a science fiction novel with the line "The doorknob opened a blue eye and looked at him," and who memorably made strict science fiction out of Lewis Carroll's "Jabberwocky."

They bring to science fiction the surrealistic (but logical) vividness of the best fantasy. They are among the most imaginative, technically skilled and literarily adroit of all today's science-fantasy writers; and this volume of 60,000 of their better words is a top-ranking newsstand bargain. The ten stories appeared during the last eleven years under four of their assorted names; two have been previously anthologized, which makes their inclusion regrettable, when so much first-rate Kuttner-Moore remains unreprinted. But it's still a book to be bought, not only by the enthusiast, but by the short-story reader who thinks he doesn't like science fiction.

> Anthony Boucher (as "H. H. Holmes"), [Review of Ahead of Time], New York Herald Tribune Book Review, 19 July 1953, p. 12

J. FRANCIS McCOMAS   First published in the magazines of 1945, Lewis Padgett's famed series of "Baldy" stories rank today as the classic exploration of all the ramifications of that inevitable conflict between man and—not superman, but psi-man. Those tales of the hairless telepaths are now gathered together and published as a novel ⟨*Mutant*⟩; this novelistic unification does not seem at all strained, since each story was originally a single episode in a general history. In fact, when read in sequence they add up to such a brilliant total that the connecting device added in the present volume seems an awkward, distracting appendage. ⟨. . .⟩

So perfect, so complete is this study of people with extra talents that all writers who have tried the theme since Padgett's first story have been confined within his all-embracing framework. And, as always, Lewis Padgett propounds his ideas in a beguiling story rich in reading entertainment.

J. Francis McComas, "Spaceman's Realm," *New York Times Book Review*, 20 December 1953, p. 17

JAMES BLISH   The reappearance of Lewis Padgett in the September, 1953 *Astounding*—and with that Baldy story, at that—provides a fresh reminder for those of us who need it of how many worlds the Kuttners are away from the technical universe occupied by most of the new writers. "Humpty Dumpty" is not, to my eyes, the best Baldy story of the series, partly because it has its share of the symbols of resignation and defeat which have been creeping into the Kuttners' most recent writings, but it is an object lesson in how to construct a science-fiction novelette.

It manages to be so in spite of the fact that its basic construction follows a plan developed by the Kuttners a long time ago, and follows it rather mechanically at that. Padgett stories for years have begun in just this way: The narrative hook, almost always dealing with incipient violence, madness, or both; enough development of the hook to lead the story into a paradox; then a complete suspension of the story while the authors lecture the reader on the background for a short time, seldom more than 1,000 words. The lecture technique is generally taboo for fiction, especially in the hands of new writers, and only two science-fiction writers have managed to get away with it and make the reader like it, Heinlein being the other. "Humpty Dumpty" is no exception; it follows the pattern so predictably as to suggest that the Kuttners do not have their entire attention on their work.

And yet, automatic though some of the writing seems to be, the story is beautifully rounded as a structure, and, as is usual with the Kuttners, does not contain an unnecessary word. As a writing team the Kuttners evidently subscribe to Chekhov's principle of plot economy (the Russian writer once remarked that if in a story he mentioned that an ornamental gun hung on the wall of a room, that gun must go off before the story is over). For a single example, note the mention in "Humpty Dumpty" of the way Cody perceives the minds of the goldfish. Any other writer would have been so pleased with this as a bit of coloring matter—for, while it's logical enough that a telepath should be able to read the minds of animals, few other writers in the field would have conveyed the point in so bizarre a way— that he would have let it stand just as it was. Not so the Kuttners; that bit of color has to be for something, not just color for its own sake, and so toward the end of the story the goldfish are used as a springboard into understanding the mind of the child. This, gentlemen, is story-telling; and if more than half of ⟨John W.⟩ Campbell's current stable could be forced to drink from the Kuttners' goldfish pond, *Astounding* would be a hell of a lot more readable than it is these days.

> James Blish (as "William Atheling, Jr."), "Negative Judgments" (1953–54), *The Issue at Hand: Studies in Contemporary Magazine Science Fiction* (Chicago: Advent, 1964), pp. 89–91

DAMON KNIGHT   When Kuttner married Catherine Moore in 1940, two seemingly discordant talents merged. Kuttner's previous stories had been superficial and clever, well constructed but without much content or conviction; Moore had written moody fantasies, meaningful but a little thin. In the forties, working together, they began to turn out stories in which the practical solidity of Kuttner's plots seemed to provide a vessel for Moore's poetic imagination. Probably the truth is a good deal more complex; the Kuttners themselves say they do not know any more which of them wrote what (and I've always been uncertain whether to review them as a single or double author); at any rate, the two elements still seem to be present, and separable, in their work.

The Ballantine collection, *No Boundaries*, gives only a taste of this blend-ing: of the five stories, I take one, "Vintage Season," to be almost entirely

C. L. Moore's, and two, "The Devil We Know" and "Exit the Professor," to be equally pure Kuttner.

To dispose of these first: "Vintage Season" is the hauntingly memorable story, from *Astounding*, about the brief visit of a group of cruel pleasure-seekers from the future, which fairly drips with a blend of love, luxury and fear—a specific emotional color, so intense that you can almost taste it. The story is a rounded whole, complete and perfect in itself, except for a rather awkwardly prolonged ending. In an unfolding puzzle story like this one, the argument and the physical action ought to come to a point at once, like the intersection of a fist and a chin.

"The Devil We Know" is a deplorable potboiler from *Unknown*, with one paragraph of good writing in it—the description of the demon on page 55—; the rest is bromides and desperation. "Exit the Professor" is one of the funniest of the unfailingly funny Hogben stories; these, I have said before, belong in a book of their own.

The two remaining stories, "Home There's No Returning" and "Two-Handed Engine" are recent ones; the latter was published in *Fantasy and Science Fiction* for August, 1955; the former appears for the first time in this book. Both are about robots, a subject which has intrigued the Kuttners separately before.

Here it's no longer possible even to guess what part is Kuttner's and what Moore's: the hypnotically deft treatment of Deirdre's robot body in "No Woman Born" is clearly echoed in these stories, but so is the ingenious improvisation of ENIAC in "The Ego Machine." The result is a series of brilliant and penetrating images, in which the robot, that clanking servitor of hack writers, becomes a vehicle for allegory and symbol. The blunt weapon suddenly has a point so sharp and fine that it tickles you at the heart before you know you have been touched.

"Home There's No Returning" deals with the robot as savior, and has a stiff little moral at the end: "Two-Handed Engine" deals with the robot as destroyer—the Fury of Greek myth, who pursues a malefactor to his doom. Which of the two stories you like better probably depends partly on the meaning these symbols have for you, and partly on how far the emotional experience succeeds in distracting you from the details of the plotting. Stripped of their elaborations, both plots are banal; the sociological backgrounds are no better than they should be, and the other sciences are worse; in one, the physical action of the story is so arbitrarily arranged as to be flatly incredible. Yet these are stories you won't soon forget: probably because science fiction is so full of stories in which the technical data are correct and soundly handled, but the people are so many zero-eyed integers—as blank-faced, but not a hundredth part as meaningful, as the Kuttners' shining robots.

Damon Knight, "Genius to Order: Kuttner and Moore," *In Search of Wonder: Essays on Modern Science Fiction* (1956; rev. ed. Chicago: Advent, 1967), pp. 144–45

JAMES GUNN   What the Kuttners brought to science fiction, which broadened it and helped it evolve, was a concern for literary skill and culture. The Kuttners expanded the techniques of science fiction to include techniques prevalent in the mainstream; they expanded its scope to include the vast cultural tradition available outside science fiction ⟨. . .⟩ The significance of the Kuttners' work rests in the fact that much of the development in science fiction over the past twenty years has come along the lines they pioneered.

This is not to say that everything the Kuttners wrote (not even the stories they wrote for *Astounding*) was without precedent; certainly man's cultural heritage and a concern for style were a part of science fiction in its beginnings, in the work, for instance, of Mary Shelley and Edgar Allan Poe, both of whom, directly or indirectly, benefited from a classical English education. And there was H. G. Wells. But those classical and literary traditions were lost in the science fiction ghetto created by Hugo Gernsback in 1926; they were replaced by newer pulp traditions of action and adventure, and eventually of scientific accuracy and informed speculation about one science after another, beginning with geography and mesmerism and progressing through chemistry, electricity, physics, and mathematics to computers, psychology, sociology, and biology.

Many areas of human experience, as contrasted with human knowledge, were considered unimportant or inappropriate to science fiction, either consciously—as in the case of sexual relationships and such other basic functions as eating and excreting—or unconsciously in areas in which writers were unaware or uneasy, such as cultural traditions and stylistic methods.

In the latter areas the Kuttners moved with growing skill and familiarity. Insofar as one can disentangle the gestalts they created, Moore seems to have contributed most of the unusual romantic involvements and perhaps all the classical references to myth, legend, and literature which served to expand and enrich the Kuttners' best work. Kuttner provided insights into the minds of children—he seemed to have a particular fondness for what has become known as the generation gap—and his literary references, perhaps appropriately, were almost entirely restricted to *Alice in Wonderland* and *Through the Looking Glass.*

James Gunn, "Henry Kuttner, C. L. Moore, Lewis Padgett *et al.*," *Voices for the Future: Essays on Major Science Fiction Writers,* ed. Thomas D. Clareson (Bowling Green, OH: Bowling Green University Popular Press, 1976), Vol. 1, pp. 194–95

SUSAN GUBAR   〈"Shambleau"〉 perfectly epitomizes the nature of Moore's contribution to the history of SF: what is striking is first the lack of technological hardware; secondly, the revisionary myth-making, specifically of a myth central to women's identity; and finally, the concomitant portrait of the woman as alien, specifically the obsession with the ways in which her body is experienced as foreign and dangerous. This last motif finds expression not only in the monstrous Shambleau, but in the exceptionally beautiful heroines of Moore's stories too; in the Minga girls on Venus in "Black Thirst" (1933), for example, who have been bred to such exquisite grace that their loveliness is almost "soul-destroying" to Northwest Smith when he attempts to help one member of the harem escape the prison guarded by their keeper-creator. Both the ugly and the beautiful heroines—perhaps especially the latter—use their looks as a tactic for survival and retribution in a fallen world where female assertion and autonomy are defined as impossible or unnatural. The beauty of many of Moore's heroines is especially potent through the alluring adornments of costuming, cosmetology, and cosmetics, as they are exotically practiced in extraterrestrial worlds. In a story she published in *Astounding* (March 1944), "The Children's Hour," Moore describes the fated infatuation of a soldier for a lovely alien girl who is closely identified with Danae, divine in a shower of gold.

Moore's sensitivity to the ethical issues surrounding the mystique of female beauty is probably best illustrated by "Vintage Season" (1946), her most frequently anthologized story, in which she creates a race of aesthetes whose physical perfection and sensitivity lead to a narcissistic quest for sensation: time-travelling to spectacular disasters in history, this race of beautiful people has lost all sense of responsibility or sympathy. The human hero of this story is destroyed when the aliens—most conspicuously the girl he falls in love with—come to watch voyeuristically the destruction of his city and his own demise. As in "The Bright Illusion" (1934), where the Great God's priestess and the Great Goddess's priest can only realize their love in death because they are of different species, the planetary worlds of SF repeatedly allow Moore to dramatize the gulf between men and women. Her image for the two sexes is that they come from different worlds, with different cultures and languages and different physical forms. The two main characters in this story—priest and priestess—cannot realize their love until they leave their physical form because each finds the other's appearance repulsive. If, as Eric Rabkin, Robert Scholes, and a number of other theoreticians of the genre argue, SF provides a "narrative world . . . at least somewhat different from our own," for female SF writers at least up to Moore's time the world that is "our own" is inexorably patriarchal, and the "different" term is the female, seen now in all her alienation. But this means that "our own" is really theirs, and that "they" are really "us." It is in its play with such categories that SF by women distinguishes itself.

Susan Gubar, "C. L. Moore and the Conventions of Women's Science Fiction," *Science-Fiction Studies* 7, No. 1 (March 1980): 20–21

FREDERICK SHROYER   Reading Kuttner's fiction, one is first struck by the extent and precision of his vocabulary. It was with him as with Mark Twain, who said that the difference between the right word and the almost right word was the difference between lightning and a lightning bug. Kuttner was also a master of plotting, dialogue, and, not infrequently, three-dimensional characterization. Although he was imitative in his early years, he soon achieved his own style.

All in all, it is probably the humor that sets Kuttner's work apart from earlier science fiction. The genre was, in the main, deadly serious and didactic. Kuttner galvanized it with an often zany humor that is truly memorable. One need but read his Galloway Gallegher stories (collected in book form in 1952 as *Robots Have No Tails*), which featured an entirely "human" robot named Joe, to realize that robots could never be the same again after Joe, petulant and opinionated, emerged fully assembled from the author's mind. Beyond this humor was an inventive, imaginative bent that often resulted in stories that throw new light on the human predicament.

One memorable story has a great deal to say about the differences between children and adults. Entitled "Mimsy Were the Borogoves" (1943), it tells of a scientist of the far future who uses a box of his children's old toys as ballast for a time-transportation experiment. The box lands in the present, and two children, finding it, begin to play with the toys therein. They are instructional toys. The flexible, unquestioning minds of the two children accept the new ideas the future toys generate without difficulty. The more they learn from their play, the farther they are drawn toward a new, far-future world where their parents can't follow. The assumption is that when Lewis Carroll wrote *Alice in Wonderland*, he knew of this transitional path along which only young children can walk. Adults are puzzled by Carroll's interpolated verse—lines such as "All mimsy were the borogoves, and the mome raths outgrabe"—and they are too inflexible in their thinking to follow this path; but children, with the right guidance, can walk the maze unerringly into a new world, leaving the old one and its adults behind them. With this story, Kuttner rubs shoulders, and as an equal, with H. G. Wells and his tale "The Magic Shop."

> Frederick Shroyer, "C. L. Moore and Henry Kuttner," *Science Fiction Writers*, ed. E. F. Bleiler (New York: Charles Scribner's Sons, 1982), p. 166

PATRICIA MATHEWS   Whether science fiction or fantasy, ⟨the⟩ works by C. L. Moore all share a set of definable and complex values reflected in their plots. First among these values is her basic belief that people's actions matter. All the battles Jirel of Joiry fights are won by her own actions, directly, as when she fights her way out of a trap ("Hellsgarde") or, indirectly, when she enlists an ally, whose actions help her in victory ("The Dark Land"). In "Vintage Season," what the tourists do, or deliberately refrain from doing, have the harshest of consequences. In "No Woman Born," the entire issue is what Harris will do, what Malzer will do, and most of all, what Deirdre will do. Even in *Judgment Night*, the most fatalistic of all Moore's works, in which every plan comes to disaster, the defeats are based on the failure of human beings to make the right decisions and to do the right thing, not on whim or chance or a malignant or playful universe.

Not only do people's actions matter, but in Moore's universe, victory is possible, given will, intelligence, and strength. Jirel of Joiry triumphs, always, by her own efforts. Deirdre, in "No Woman Born," succeeds in making a metal body her own, and she succeeds against all odds, in her chosen profession after her return as a cyborg. Victory is not inevitable—this is not Hollywood—but even in defeat, we feel that it is still possible. Oliver, in "Vintage Season," has desperately tried to warn his contemporaries of the disasters the tourists know of but are bound by oath not to speak of. He is too sick to succeed. Here, realistically, is a portrait of someone who has done his best according to his or anybody's standards but was defeated by forces too strong for him. Yet, in another, less overpowering disaster, Oliver might well have succeeded; the story is tragic, but not defeatist. Likewise, Juille in *Judgment Night* fails because, while she tried her best, her best was informed by tragically wrongheaded values. Had she made other choices, she could have saved civilization, if not her empire. Victory is possible, if not inevitable.

To C. L. Moore, abilities, intelligence, and strength are unqualified good; evil only comes with the misuse of these abilities.

Patricia Mathews, "C. L. Moore's Classic Science Fiction," *The Feminine Eye: Science Fiction and the Women Who Write It*, ed. Tom Staicar (New York: Frederick Ungar Publishing Co., 1982), pp. 21–22

ROBERT SILVERBERG   Kuttner was prolific, versatile, clever, and technically adept. His stories were tightly constructed, but most of them prior to his marriage to Moore tended to be little more than facile pulp-magazine stuff. Moore's early work depended more on emotional intensity and evocative coloration than on intricacy of plot or swiftness of action; her stories were long and moody and slow, and often culminated in a swirl of powerful but impenetrable strangeness that defied rational analysis. Each writer thus complemented the other; and when they worked as collaborators they were triumphantly able to merge their strongest talents and produce fiction superior to anything either had done alone. That their work is largely out of print today is both saddening and perplexing to me. There were no science-fiction writers I studied more closely, in that enormously formative period of my teens, than C. L. Moore and Henry Kuttner. In everything they wrote—even the stories that Kuttner seemed to have tossed off in an hour or two before lunch to pay the rent—they seemed supremely in command of their craft. I still feel that way about them; and I still go back often to read with pleasure, and to ponder, the myriad stories they produced singly and in collaboration.

It is difficult and dangerous to try to figure out who wrote what in the Kuttner-Moore canon. Apparently, virtually everything that either one published from the time of their marriage until Kuttner's early death in 1958 was to some extent a joint work. The byline is no clue. Most of their work was published under pseudonyms—Lawrence O'Donnell, Lewis Padgett, Keith Hammond, and a dozen more. It is easy enough to say that the richer, warmer stories are Moore's and the quick clever ones are Kuttner's, but it seems more probable that scarcely any story left their household without having been jointly planned, written, and revised. Trying to identify distinctive Kuttner or Moore traits is almost hopeless. *Fury,* a novel that bore the O'Donnell pseudonym when it was serialized in a magazine, is thought by students of this remarkable team to be largely Kuttner's work, and was published under Kuttner's name alone when it appeared in book form. It is a sequel to the O'Donnell story "Clash by Night," which is thought to have been written mainly by Moore. Yet *Fury* has more of a Moore tone to it than the earlier story. Had he so fully absorbed her style by then that he could speak in her voice or did she have a hand in the story? We'll probably never know.

Robert Silverberg, "The Silverberg Papers," *Science Fiction Chronicle* 9, No. 2 (November 1987): 46

SARAH GAMBLE   As well as exploring the difficulties of communication between the sexes, within her stories Moore symbolically hints at the possible discovery of a kind of *écriture féminine.* This is mainly expressed through the recurring motif of some type of random configuration—most commonly a pattern or design, although sometimes music or (as in the case of Julhi) colour. Whatever form it takes, it is a system of non-linguistic representation which holds no meaning at all for (Northwest) Smith, but which is understood well enough by the alien women he encounters. The pattern is often linked to Smith's descent to the other world in which all his patriarchal values are reversed. In 'The Tree of Life', when Thag's priestess runs into the shadow of the grille, Smith sees a hidden significance revealed in the pattern that

ran over her like a garment, curving to the curve of her body in
the way all shadows do. But as she stood there striped and laced
with the darkness of it, there came a queer shifting in the lines of
black tracery, a subtle, inexplicable movement to one side. And
with that motion, she vanished.

The mysterious tracery of the pattern thus functions in a metaphorical sense,
opening the way into the female creative space, in the same way that, in
the words of Hélène Cixous, *écriture féminine*, 'the language of 1,000 tongues
which knows neither enclosure nor death' enables the female artist 'to pass
. . . into infinity'. The parallel between the pattern and female creativity is
even more obvious in Moore's story 'Scarlet Dream' (1934). As in 'The
Tree of Life' a pattern is the means by which Smith enters a world clearly
aligned with the female principle—this time a pattern woven into a piece
of cloth, which, when he studies it, gives him the impression of hidden
power, opening the normal world to 'undreamed-of vastnesses where living
scarlet in wild, unruly patterns shivered through the void'. The piece of
cloth is in fact a shawl, and its bright scarlet colour, as well as its association
with an item of exclusively female apparel, is reminiscent of the dangerous
female sexuality of Shambleau and Julhi. The power of the pattern is such
that it becomes, in Smith's dreams, 'one mighty Word in a nameless writing,
whose meaning he shuddered on the verge of understanding, and woke in
icy terror just before the significance of it broke upon his brain'.

Eventually, of course, the twisting design leads him to the other world
that is awaiting him below the surface of the text. And again it is clearly
associated with the female space. In this realm of literal representation, a
symbolic colour (scarlet) actually becomes that which it symbolises in all
of Moore's stories—blood, described by the critic Susan Gubar as 'one of
the primary and most resonant metaphors provided by the female body'.
Blood has always been closely associated with women through the biological
processes of menstruation and childbirth, and it is also commonly associated
in feminist criticism with female art, symbolising 'woman's use of her own
body in forms of artistic expression', and echoing the plight of 'the woman
artist who experiences herself as killed into art . . . bleeding into print'
⟨Susan Gubar⟩. In 'Scarlet Dream' the metaphor is surrounded by a strange,
yet meaningful, ambiguity—the inhabitants of this world drink blood for
their food, yet they also shed it as random victims of a nameless 'Thing'.
Blood is thus simultaneously associated with life and death, in the same
way as it can create both the space and the means for female creativity,

while at the same time marking out women as circumscribed 'others' in a male society.

Sarah Gamble, " 'Shambleau . . . and Others': The Role of the Female in the Fiction of C. L. Moore," *Where No Man Has Gone Before: Women and Science Fiction*, ed. Lucie Namitt (London: Routledge, 1991), pp. 40–41

◈ *Bibliography*

Works by C. L. Moore and Henry Kuttner:
The Brass Ring. 1946.
The Day He Died. 1947.
Fury ⟨*Destination Infinity*⟩. 1950.
A Gnome There Was and Other Tales of Science Fiction and Fantasy. 1950.
Tomorrow and Tomorrow, and The Fairy Chessmen. 1951.
Clash by Night. 1952.
Well of the Worlds. 1953.
Mutant. 1953.
Beyond Earth's Gates. 1954.
Line to Tomorrow and Other Tales of Fantasy and Science-Fiction. 1954.
Remember Tomorrow. 1954.
Way of the Gods. 1954.
There Shall Be Darkness. 1954.
No Boundaries. 1955.
Bypass to Otherness. 1961.
Return to Otherness. 1962.
Earth's Last Citadel. 1964.
Valley of the Flame. 1964.
The Time Axis. 1965.
The Dark World. 1965.
The Mask of Circe. 1971.
Clash by Night and Other Stories. Ed. Peter Pinto. 1980.
Chessboard Planet and Other Stories. 1983.
The Startling Worlds of Henry Kuttner ⟨*The Portal of the Picture, Valley of the Flame, The Dark World*⟩. 1987.

Works by C. L. Moore:
Judgment Night: A Selection of Science Fiction. 1952.
Shambleau and Others. 1953.

Northwest of Earth. 1954.

The Challenge from Beyond (with A. Merritt, H. P. Lovecraft, Robert E. Howard, and Frank Belknap Long). 1954.

Doomsday Morning. 1957.   .

Jirel of Joiry ⟨*Black God's Shadow*⟩. 1969.

The Best of C. L. Moore. Ed. Lester del Rey. 1975.

Scarlet Dream. 1981.

Works by Henry Kuttner:

Dr. Cyclops. 1940.

Man Drowning. 1952.

Robots Have No Tails. 1952, 1983 (as *The Proud Robot: The Complete Galloway Gallegher Stories*).

Ahead of Time: Ten Stories of Science Fiction and Fantasy. 1953.

As You Were. 1955.

Sword of Tomorrow. 1955.

The Murder of Ann Avery. 1956.

The Murder of Eleanor Pope. 1956.

Murder of a Mistress. 1957.

Murder of a Wife. 1958.

The Best of Kuttner. 1965–66. 2 vols.

The Creature from Beyond Infinity. 1968.

The Best of Henry Kuttner. 1975.

Elak of Atlantis. 1985.

Kuttner Times Three. 1988.

Frederik Pohl
b. 1919

FREDERIK POHL was born in Manhattan on November 26, 1919. His father was a machinist whose work took him to the Panama Canal shortly after his son's birth, and the family lived a peripatetic life in Texas, New Mexico, and California before settling down in Brooklyn several years later. Pohl was sickly as a child and did not enter grade school until the age of eight. In 1930 he came across a copy of the pulp magazine *Science Wonder Quarterly* at a newsstand and became hooked for life on science fiction.

A high school dropout at seventeen, Pohl became an active member of the Brooklyn Science Fiction League and later the Futurians, an influential club of New York science fiction fans that would number among its ranks Damon Knight, James Blish, Isaac Asimov, Cyril M. Kornbluth, Robert A. W. Lowndes, and other writers and critics who shaped the course of science fiction in the postwar years. The Futurians looked upon their interest in science fiction not only as a hobby but as an outgrowth of their social and political philosophies, and it was during his affiliation with them that Pohl refined his belief in science fiction as a tool for reflecting on culture. When he became editor of the low-budget magazines *Astonishing Stories* and *Super Science Stories* in 1940, Pohl enlisted his colleagues' help to fill issues with fiction and artwork.

Although Pohl wrote fiction under a variety of pseudonyms used by the Futurians, it was not until the 1950s, when he had given up working as a literary agent for science fiction writers, that he began writing under his own name. Much of his early fiction was written in collaboration with Cyril M. Kornbluth, including his first novel *The Space Merchants* (1953), a dystopia about a near-future America governed by advertising companies that displayed his bent for social satire and is renowned as one of the most prescient, if cynical, novels of modern science fiction. Other collaborators during these years included Lester del Rey, Isaac Asimov, Jack Williamson, and his third wife, Judith Merril.

Pohl spent most of the 1950s and '60s fulfilling dual careers as an editor of Ballantine Books' *Star Science Fiction* series and the magazine *Galaxy*, while at the same time writing his own tales of near future Earths learning to cope with the ramifications of technological advancement. With the publication of the Hugo– and Nebula Award–winning *Gateway* in 1977, Pohl clarified an idea introduced in a 1971 story regarding the human race's advancement through its use of artifacts of the extraterrestrial "Heechee" civilization, not always for the best ends. The saga, which extends over four books written over thirteen years, shows Pohl to be an astute observer of human nature who does not flinch at the suggestion that mankind's future may not be as rosy as the image put forth through more traditional science fiction.

Pohl has spent much of the 1980s and '90s as a promoter and spokesman for science fiction. His strong interest in the impact of science upon civilization led him to write *Terror* (1986), *Chernobyl* (1987), and other nongenre novels that examine the point where science fiction gives way to science fact. He currently lives with his fifth wife, Elizabeth Anne Hull, in Chicago.

▨ *Critical Extracts*

ROBERT A. W. LOWNDES   When this ⟨*The Space Merchants*⟩ came out in *Galaxy* as "Gravy Planet", it seemed to be merely an entertaining hunt-and-chase thriller, with the background of advertising horrors for laughs, a satire on the way things are now. Since then I've taken a closer look at the gruesomeness of the advertising we have grown numb to and it begins to look more like a trend than a joke.

If advertising is used to sell cigarettes, chewing gum, labor unions, opinions of the NAM, candidates for election, and movies, why shouldn't it make the smart deadly move of selling itself? Self-preservation is the business law that works every time.

Could the American public be sold on the idea that advertising men are the aristocracy of the Earth? Could they believe that advertising is the foundation of American business? Could they be convinced that the first duty of a patriot and a man of principle is to buy things the advertisements tell him to buy, whether he wants them or not? ⟨. . .⟩

In its revised form, *The Space Merchants*, this novel is even smoother and more entertaining in plot, but I have not been able to read more than a few pages at a time before the background gives me the whillies.

Will the Senator from Nutra-Cola please take the floor?

Robert A. W. Lowndes, [Review of *The Space Merchants*], *Dynamic Science Fiction* 1, No. 6 (January 1954): 26, 36

ANTHONY BOUCHER   In one of the oddest and most individual of recent imaginative novels ⟨*Search the Sky*⟩, the authors of last year's admirable *The Space Merchants* combine an ingenious scientific theme (the effect of known genetic laws on small planetary colonies) with a lively picaresque adventure novel, in which our hero zooms along a transgalactic Yellow Brick Road, escaping perils and adding strange companions to his entourage. But the primary emphasis is on neither science nor adventure, but on a series of satires in the grand tradition of the eighteenth century's Imaginary Voyages. For each planet encountered represents a *reductio ad absurdum* of some trend in contemporary civilization—one ruled by women, one by "senior citizens," one that has achieved absolute conformity, and so on. You may, like me, refuse to believe that all of these civilizations can have diverged so, over the course of centuries, with no linguistic changes at all; but suspension of disbelief is easily attained in a tale so animated, adroit, witty and, in short, sheerly entertaining as this.

Anthony Boucher (as "H. H. Holmes"), [Review of *Search the Sky*], *New York Herald Tribune Books*, 21 February 1954, p. 13

S. E. COTTS   Perhaps the most outstanding feature ⟨of *Tomorrow Times Seven*⟩ is Pohl's own brand of humor which provides the main tone of the volume. He does not try to force it on the reader by blunt or obvious satire. It is humor of a far more elusive kind. As nearly as it can be pinned down, it seems to rely on taking some of Earth's seedier characters and putting them in contact with some of the most original outworlders this reviewer has ever seen. Thus, in "Survival Kit," we follow the fortunes of a petty crook as he tries to make a dishonest dollar out of a time traveler. In "The Gentle Venusian," an alcoholic survey man from Earth has a run-in with the law on Venus, where the creatures spend their entire lives playing games. In "The Day of the Boomer Dukes," a New York gang collides with another time traveler.

The spice and originality of these ideas are further enhanced by the author's invention of certain delicious words for names of men and objects, and by the contrasting dialogue between the Earth people and the Spacers. And if in the ends of most of the stories, the aliens seem to get the best of us or have the last word, no one can really object because it is all such good fun.

S. E. Cotts, [Review of *Tomorrow Times Seven*], *Amazing Stories* 33, No. 2 (November 1959): 139–40

KINGSLEY AMIS   ⟨Pohl's⟩ field of interest is contemporary urban society and its chain of production and consumption. He is thus in some sort a novelist of economic man, or, rather, of two overlapping personages within that concept, the well-to-do customer and the high-level executive who keeps the consumer consuming. An occasional space-ship flashes across his page, but no BEM ⟨bug-eyed monster⟩ ever raises its heads there and aliens do not appeal to him; the adventure-story component of his work is incidental. His mode is typically the satirical utopia, with comic-inferno elements rarely absent; his method is selective exaggeration of observable features of our society, plus the concrete elaboration noted in ⟨Robert⟩ Sheckley.

Kingsley Amis, *New Maps of Hell: A Survey of Science Fiction* (New York: Harcourt, Brace & World, 1960), pp. 118–19

DAMON KNIGHT   Like one of John Campbell's psionics machines, the heads of Frederik Pohl's characters are empty except for little cards labeled "career soldier," or "con man," or whatever. In the stories collected as *Tomorrow Times Seven*, they gabble brightly at each other, pose and pirouette through the motions of frantic plots. Pohl's ideas are ingenious, his backgrounds carefully detailed, his pace swift. Over and over again, his greedy people are scheming, conniving, sweating to get their hands on something of value—in "The Haunted Corpse," a mind-transferring gadget; in "The Gentle Venusian," diamond-studded boomerangs; in "The Day of the Boomer Dukes" and "Survival Kit," two bags of tricks from the future; and in "The Knights of Arthur," a brain in a prosthetic tank. The eerie and disturbing thing about all these stories (and about the dismally ill-formed "The Middle of Nowhere") is that in spite of all the emphasis on wealth and cupidity, it quickly becomes plain that not one of these characters really gives a damn. ⟨. . .⟩

The subject of "My Lady Green Sleeves" ⟨in *The Case against Tomorrow*⟩ is race prejudice, and the story attacks it in a typical display of *Galaxy*'s agonized irony, by substituting "wipes" (common laborers) for Jews, "figgers" (clerks) for Negroes, "greasers" (mechanics) for Mexicans, and, variously, "civil service people" and "G.I.'s" for white Anglo-Saxons. The point of all this, when we eventually get to it, seems to be that fostering class distinctions based on occupations has canceled out others based on race or religion—so that the heroine can ask, in honest ignorance, "What's a Jew?"

In its own corkscrew fashion, I suppose this is intended as a contribution toward racial egalitarianism. But it seems to me that rubbing the reader's nose repeatedly into racial hate-words in this way is the worst possible way to go about it. The story is such a mishmash of viewpoints that it's impossible to tell where (if anywhere) the author's sympathies lie; reading it as straight satire, it seems to me, you could easily construe it as an expression of bigotry. And on top of everything else, a pure racial stereotype turns up in the story itself, in the description of a man named Hiroko: "Beads of sweat were glistening on his furrowed yellow forehead." (For God's sake, Fred, "yellow man" is an epithet—Japanese have brown skins.)

Damon Knight, "New Stars," In Search of Wonder: Essays on Modern Science Fiction (1956; rev. ed. Chicago: Advent, 1967), pp. 193–94, 196

RICHARD D. ERLICH   In *The Space Merchants* and *Gladiator-at-Law* the pattern of the heroic quest is essentially the one familiar to us from romance and romantic comedy: the hero is going to overcome his adversaries, get the girl, and bring fertility. This pattern is worked out, however, in worlds far removed from those of Romance or Comedy. Not quite the horrors we find in Orwell's *1984* or Kafka's *Penal Colony*, still, the worlds presented in these books do approach what Northrop Frye has called the "demonic," and they have portions of their geography which are explicitly likened to Hell. These works are more optimistic than many satires only insofar as they assume that the world might be saveable (*Gladiator-at-Law*) or at least leaveable (*The Space Merchants*).

In both novels we start with worlds controlled by greedy capitalists, typified in *Space Merchants* by a pair of older men running fantastically powerful ad agencies, and, in *Gladiator*, by some old "Titans of Industry," and by Green, Charlesworth: two downright ancient incarnations of money-power and pride. In *Space Merchants* the world is an ecological disaster area, with the population divided politically into (1) the very rich, (2) the executive and "staff" class, and (3) the wretched consumers. In *Gladiator* the world of the novel is a United States where contract workers serve their corporations for pay and for the privilege of living in magnificent GML "bubble houses"—and where those who lack contract status live in horrible suburban slums, represented mostly by Belly Rave (once Belle Reve). In these brave new worlds the people in general are confined, spied upon, oppressed: most are slaves or only a little better than slaves. Both worlds are dystopian and sterile, in need of saviors. And it comes to pass (in the fulness of time, undoubtedly) that our heroes appear in the midst of these wastelands.

Now heroes, of course, are often the highly unlikely sort: seventh sons of seventh sons, talented (if unsightly) frogs, babes found abandoned or in mangers; but Pohl and Kornbluth go quite far in the direction of the Anti-hero. In *Space Merchants*, Mitch Courtenay is "an ill-tempered, contriving, Machiavellian, selfish pig of a man," so resistant to education that he flunks his first initiation and has to go through the entire Heroic cycle—including the Return and the Reconciliation with the Father—before he is ready to begin doing what can be done to save humanity. In *Gladiator*, Charles Mundin is a criminal lawyer who lusts after the remunerative glories of corporation law: he begins the novel as part of the problem more than part of the solution. Moreover, he shares the Hero's journey with Norvell (usually called "Norvie") Bligh: a lost soul who starts the story as a writer of "scripts" for gladiatorial spectacles; a man dominated and manipulated by his wife, daughter, boss, associates, and "friend"; a man who shuts out the world with psychosomatic deafness.

Odd men, indeed, for the archetypal tasks of rejuvenating a wasteland or saving humankind! Saviors they are, though, and we would do well to examine the highly displaced methods their creators use to initiate them into their heroic roles.

Richard D. Erlich, "Odysseus in Gray Flannel: The Heroic Journey in Two Dystopias by Pohl and Kornbluth," *Par Rapport* No. 1 (Summer 1978): 127

DAVID N. SAMUELSON   Throughout the 1960s, Pohl was also experimenting with "sketches" in which the story proper hardly interferes at all with the satire or speculation. Displaying a verbal economy surpassing his previous efforts, they are essentially static, crammed with information rather than action. Four of them feature aliens, but not as the melodramatic menaces of hoary tradition. The first of these, "The Martian Stargazers" (1962), comments obliquely on our history and conceit, explaining through speculative Martian lore why they killed themselves long before men landed there. "Earth 18" (1964) is a fictional guidebook to the paucity of attractions Earth offers, despite continuing "development" by conquering aliens. "The Day After the Martians Came" (1967) uses the Martians as the butt of racist jokes, irrelevant to a Florida hotel-keeper, but worth their weight in gold to his black bellman. And "Speed Trap" (1967) implies alien involvement in a suspected conspiracy to use travel, conferences, and administration to keep real research from being done.

The best of these, "Day Million" (1966), is a self-proclaimed love-story imagining really altered people and conditions in the future (the millionth day, A.D.). Genetic engineering and social change have modified the meaning of gender, the forms human bodies can take, and the immediacy and exclusiveness of a love relationship. Without actually telling us a "story," the narrator presents us with the two "genetic males" who "marry" by obtaining electronic replicas of each other to use for that era's version of a "full" love relationship. The jolting shift of perspective common to many Pohl stories occurs not once but several times in this story, as contemporary terminology proves inadequate, even misleading, for describing the future. The richness of this verbal experience may be marred for some readers by the narrator's direct address, even browbeating them into taking historical change into account when they look past tomorrow. The overall effect, however, is contemplation of, not recoil from, the supposedly outrageous circumstances, and vindication of the claim that this is indeed a "love story."

"Day Million" and *The Age of the Pussyfoot* suggest the maturing of Pohl and his greater control of fictional techniques during the 1960s. Editing as many as four magazines at once, he was living through a change in social conditions which, along with more important things, made all kinds of SF seem vaguely respectable, and both allowed and expected it to be all things to all people. Changes were also happening in SF, if not most overtly displayed in his magazines, as the "New Wave" writers in England and their American counterparts rebelled against the old editorial formulas.

Long considered an apostle of doom, Pohl reversed his field slightly late in the decade, calling in an editorial for more hopeful and constructive stories in SF. Backing this call with at least limited action, he printed in *Galaxy* and *IF*, as other SF magazines did also, paid advertisements for and against the American presence in Vietnam, signed by other SF professionals, and announced a contest to seek feasible solutions to this problem then ripping apart the fabric of American society. But the magazines soon were sold, and he resigned as editor, entering a stage of depression in which he claims even living lost its appeal.

> David N. Samuelson, "Critical Mass: The Science Fiction of Frederik Pohl," *Science-Fiction Studies* 7, No. 1 (March 1980): 87–88

MARTHA A. BARTTER   Newton's third law of motion, that for every action there is an equal and opposite reaction, holds true in *Gateway* in the psychological as well as the physical sense. Broadhead's reaction to emotional trauma is to lose his memory, to avoid the pain involved in trying to remember, and by quite literally ceasing to live on any but the most basic physical level. We have already noted that he refused to make the normal passage to maturity expected of a man of twenty-six and that he hoped, from Gateway, to derive eternal youth. Invariably, though subconsciously, he equates maturity with death; it is significant that these statements are recorded by Sigfrid but not recalled by Broadhead. Consciously, he equates positive feelings with youth: "I don't know if I can make you feel it, how the universe looked to me from Gateway: like being young with Full Medical." He is, moreover, a physical year younger than his actual age, whatever that may be, as the book opens, for he literally lost a year in the black hole. And there is no question that he has not been truly living in the sixteen years since he left Gateway; his life has been a mere holding pattern of activity, misery, and surgery: "I hesitated, rubbing my belly. I have almost half a meter of new intestine in there now. They cost fearfully, those things, and sometimes you get the feeling that the previous owner wants them back."

Physically and psychologically, Broadhead has lost both his sense of the passage of time and his sense of self. And his experience in the black hole fuses the three scientific principles of reaction, relativity, and entropy into one event. A black hole is a region in space where mass has become so concentrated that its gravity will allow nothing, not even light, to escape. In a black hole, time literally stops; space itself collapses; entropy, apparently, is reversed. It is a relativistic anomaly; it also seems to represent everything Broadhead has been seeking in his life.

After studying the data obtained from the trip in which Broadhead "killed" his ship, scientists decide to send two heavily armored ships to a single dangerous destination. The bonus offered is gigantic. Broadhead, financially and emotionally destitute, volunteers, as do almost all the people with whom he is emotionally involved. The two ships emerge from tau space within the event horizon of a black hole. They have insufficient power to escape; their only chance is to add an extra kick to the drive. Putting all the people into one ship, they load the other with their gear and fire both drives simultaneously, hoping that the ship with the people will break free with the help of the sacrificial boost from the other one. In the haste and confusion, Broadhead is trapped in the abandoned ship; the ships are launched (did he launch them?), and once again his luck is with him. Although there is no way to predict which, if either, of the ships will escape, it happens that Broadhead's ship breaks free and returns.

His life has been saved. By an equal and opposite psychological reaction, it has been destroyed. He loses his love and his past in pain and guilt, and with them his very identity.

Martha A. Bartter, "Times and Spaces: Exploring *Gateway,*" *Extrapolation* 23, No. 2 (Summer 1982): 194–95

ERIC S. RABKIN   In Frederik Pohl's *Man Plus* (1976), we find yet another treatment of Martians. This time the Martians do not contrast with the humans either to warn us about where we are heading or to urge us to return to what once we should have been. This time the Martians don't contrast with us at all. Pohl's main character is an astronaut named Roger Torraway who is told he must migrate to another planet if Earth is to be saved. In order to put Roger on Mars, the scientists must change his physiology, for they do not intend to provide Roger with a space suit.

. . . what if one reshapes a human being?

> Suppose one takes the standard human frame and alters some
> of the optional equipment. There's nothing to breathe on Mars.
> So take the lungs out of the human frame, replace them with
> micro-miniaturized oxygen regeneration cat-cracking systems. One
> needs power for that, but power flows down from the distant sun.
>   . . . The solar panels [attached to his shoulder blades] . . . did
> resemble bat wings.
>   . . . by the time he was on Mars, he would really need to eat
> only about one square meal a month . . . of the diagnostic signs of
> manhood . . . what was left was nothing at all. [Roger Torraway
> became] a strange devil-like creature.

But he is not a devil in the mold of Clarke's *Childhood's End*, for he is
emphatically *not* alien. Throughout the novel we sympathetically follow
Roger's plight, feel his struggle to fulfill his human mission against the
incredible assault of his image of himself. When he finally succeeds in
surviving on the surface of Mars, a pioneer who makes possible the following
of other humans, we understand Roger as human. He is not a Wellsian
monster nor even one of Bradbury's gentle throwbacks: he is an image of
man freed from the chauvinism of any particular bodily form. ⟨. . .⟩

Pohl's novel has a rather interesting twist at the end. The last chapter
begins with this sentence: "We had gone to a lot of trouble at every point
along the line, and we were well pleased." "We" turns out to be the worldwide, autonomous and linked consciousness of "machine intelligence," a
voice that speaks for "every brother in the net." In an instant, the reader
realizes that the computer output that had urged Roger's reconstruction
had been a conclusion not of men using computers but of the computers
themselves. If Roger was a prisoner of the "brother" on his back, then we
are all in danger! And yet, within half a page, we come to discard that
homocentric attitude. After all, the world was in danger of catastrophic war
and the Mars Project did save it. So we have to agree when the computer
voice says, "We had saved our race. And in the process we had significantly
added to the safety of human beings, as well." And, by the way, a perfectly
fit and desirable human woman elects to stay on Mars as Roger's lover.

Eric S. Rabkin, "Science and the Human Image in Recent Science Fiction," *Michigan
Quarterly Review* 24, No. 2 (Spring 1985): 261, 263

THOMAS CLARESON   In *Black Star Rising* (1985), Pohl has produced a delightfully caustic satire deserving a high place in the tradition

going back through Orwell, Huxley, and Swift. It surpasses anything that such of his contemporaries as Ray Bradbury and Kurt Vonnegut have attempted. ⟨. . .⟩

To reveal the mindset of the Yankee Americans as quickly and vividly as possible, Pohl shifts the narrative focus to the youthful Jupe (Jupiter), a "blazing patriot" preparing to venture forth to Space City to celebrate the long-awaited arrival of the yacht of that most mythical of all beings, the President of the Real Americans. Handsome in his uniform (every American wears a tailored uniform from the age of ten) and practicing "fierce military expressions before a glass," Jupe represents that "tiny minority of males" on World who are "not merely combat ready" but are "combat-*prone*" because "they are warriors." A product of "his age and life . . . and gender," he longs to fight for his lost Homeland: "Recapture! Recover! Revenge! Those were the key words in the litanies he had learned with his first lisped baby words." Cloaked in military paraphernalia, Jupe is Pohl's caricature of that macho image which shapes so many American males and goes back, in part at least, to the popularized myths of the cowboy and the frontiersman.

Incarnate in the Yankees on World is that hawkish, combative self-righteousness which characterizes so much of contemporary America. In addition, male sexual fantasies have been structured into their society. During the thirty-one-year space voyage, the astronauts aboard the *Intrepid* "enjoyed" themselves as they chose, but they carefully preserved the monthly ova of the twenty-eight women aboard as well as selected sperm from the males so that, when they arrived at Van Maanen's star, they had twelve thousand eight-day embryos and "twenty-five robust young adults"—the result of the single occasion when the twenty-eight women received embryo implants. On World, into the third generation, this "lost colony of human beings" has been "breeding like maggots"; they number eighty-five hundred. As in the manipulation aboard the *Intrepid*, the number of males is kept minimal, one male to each "nest" of one-hundred-seventy "sisters." Necessarily the women run the society, including the government (Governor, Senators, and "Congressones"). Ironically, because they are kept pregnant, "once a year at most, usually," Jupe explains to Miranda—they represent the sexually submissive woman who eagerly desires to serve any male available. Yet trained to fight if necessary, they avidly share the vision given the Yanks by the Original Landers: ". . . arming themselves . . . readying themselves to invade the Earth at whatever cost in life and destruction."

Aided and abetted by the erks, "America was alive and well on World, and growing."

Thomas Clareson, *Frederik Pohl* (Mercer Island, WA: Starmont House, 1987), pp. 143, 147–48

FREDERIK POHL   If we suppose—as I think most of us do—that science fiction is something more than mere escapist entertainment, it is because we believe that at its best science fiction gives its readers some new and otherwise unobtainable insights into our world—in fact, into all our possible worlds. I do believe that. I think that through science fiction we can see, for instance, how many of the customs and "truths" we live by are logically inevitable, and thus "right," and how many are mere accidents of decisions taken, or even of our mammalian biology and the physical constraints of the particular planet on which we happened to evolve. Science fiction is the only literature we have that can give us this objective perspective on our human affairs—what Harlow Shapley once, in a considerably different context, called "The View from a Distant Star."

When science fiction writers explore the implications of what that God's-eye view of our world reveals, they enter many touchy areas. That can't be avoided. Most writers don't even try to avoid it, and this is true not only of those writers who set out to explore large questions but even of the authors of the space operas and the pulpy adventure stories of the 1920s and 1930s. ⟨. . .⟩

It is fair to ask if the political aspects of all this political science fiction are deliberately inserted by the author. Fair to ask, but hard to answer, for attempting to untangle an author's purposes is one of the high-risk activities of literary criticism.

However, there is one author whose intentions I do know something about—much of the time, anyway—and that is myself. Many of my own works, including some of the ones I like best, are overtly political, even propagandistic in their central themes. *The Years of the City* is an explicit attempt to describe the stages of political evolution in America over the next century or two; the starting assumptions of *Jem* deal with what I imagined to be the future of international politics after the Cold War had run its course.

If it is chancy for a critic to try to discern an author's purposes, it is even more adventurous for a writer to assume that what is true of himself must be common among all other writers. Still, I do not doubt that every writer does necessarily put something of himself into everything he writes; that personally unique and idiosyncratic view of the world is really all that any writer has to sell. Indeed, as some perceptive person—identity unfortunately not known to me—once pointed out, the true and proper title of any book should be *How to Be More Like Me*. And, of course, in this political age (with frequent political change institutionalized in countries like the United States, irregular and sometimes extraordinarily violent in others), our politics is one of the ways by which we define ourselves.

So it is inevitable that politics should be a part of science fiction. And fortunately, I think, for how much better it is to attempt to work out the consequences of political change in a science fiction story than to play them out in the bloodier, harsher, and less-forgiving real world we live in.

Frederik Pohl, "The Politics of Prophecy," *Extrapolation* 34, No. 3 (Fall 1993): 205–7

Bibliography

Beyond the End of Time (editor). 1952.

The Space Merchants (with C. M. Kornbluth). 1953, 1985.

Shadow of Tomorrow: 17 Great Science Fiction Stories (editor). 1953.

Danger Moon. 1953.

Star Science Fiction Stories. 1953–59. 6 vols.

Search the Sky (with C. M. Kornbluth). 1954, 1985.

Assignment in Tomorrow (editor). 1954.

Undersea Quest (with Jack Williamson). 1954.

Star Short Novels (editor). 1954.

Preferred Risk (with Lester del Rey). 1955.

A Town Is Drowning (with C. M. Kornbluth). 1955.

Gladiator-at-Law (with C. M. Kornbluth). 1955, 1986.

Undersea Fleet (with Jack Williamson). 1956.

Presidential Year (with C. M. Kornbluth). 1956.

Alternating Currents. 1956.

Sorority House (with C. M. Kornbluth). 1956.

The God of Channel 1. 1956.

Turn the Tigers Loose (with Walter Lasly). 1956.

Slave Ship. 1957.

The Case against Tomorrow: Science-Fiction Stories. 1957.

Edge of the City. 1957.

Undersea City (with Jack Williamson). 1958.

Wolfbane (with C. M. Kornbluth). 1959, 1986.

Tomorrow Times Seven: Seven Science Fiction Stories. 1959.

Drunkard's Walk. 1960.

The Man Who Ate the World. 1960.

Star of Stars (editor). 1960.

Turn Left at Thursday: 3 Novelettes and 3 Stories. 1961.

The Wonder Effect (with C. M. Kornbluth). 1962, 1977 (as *Critical Mass*).

The Expert Dreamers (editor). 1962.

Time Waits for Winthrop and Four Other Short Novels from Galaxy (editor). 1962.

The Abominable Earthman. 1963.

The Reefs of Space (with Jack Williamson). 1964.

The Best Science Fiction from Worlds of If Magazine (editor). 1964.

The Best Science Fiction from Worlds of Tomorrow (editor). 1964.

The Seventh Galaxy Reader (editor). 1964.

Starchild (with Jack Williamson). 1965.

A Plague of Pythons. 1965, 1984 (as *Demon in the Skull*).

The Eighth Galaxy Reader (editor). 1965.

The Frederik Pohl Omnibus. 1966.

The If Reader of Science Fiction (editor). 1966.

Digits and Dastards. 1966.

The Ninth Galaxy Reader (editor). 1966.

The Tenth Galaxy Reader (editor). 1967.

The Second If Reader of Science Fiction (editor). 1968.

The Eleventh Galaxy Reader (editor). 1969.

Rogue Star (with Jack Williamson). 1969.

The Age of the Pussyfoot. 1969.

Day Million. 1970.

Nightmare Age (editor). 1970.

Practical Politics 1972. 1971.

The Gold at the Starbow's End. 1972.

The Best Science Fiction for 1972 (editor). 1972.

Science Fiction: The Great Years (editor; with Carol Pohl). 1973–76. 2 vols.

Jupiter (editor; with Carol Pohl). 1973.

The Best of Frederik Pohl. Ed. Lester del Rey. 1975.

The Science Fiction Roll of Honor (editor). 1975.

Farthest Star: The Saga of Cuckoo (with Jack Williamson). 1975.

Man Plus. 1976.

In the Problem Pit. 1976.

Science Fiction Discoveries (editor; with Carol Pohl). 1976.

The Best of C. M. Kornbluth (editor). 1976.

The Early Pohl. 1976.

Gateway. 1977.

The Starchild Trilogy ⟨*The Reefs of Space, Starchild, Rogue Star*⟩ (with Jack
      Williamson). 1977.

The Way the Future Was: A Memoir. 1978.

Science Fiction of the Forties (editor; with Martin Harry Greenberg and Joseph
      D. Olander). 1978.

Jem: The Making of a Utopia. 1979.

Beyond the Blue Event Horizon. 1980.

Nebula Winners 14 (editor). 1980.

Before the Universe and Other Stories (with C. M. Kornbluth). 1980.

The Great Science Fiction Stories (editor; with Martin H. Greenberg and Joseph
      D. Olander). 1980.

Galaxy: Thirty Years of Innovative Science Fiction (editor; with Martin H.
      Greenberg and Joseph D. Olander). 1980–81. 2 vols.

Science Fiction: Studies in Film (with Frederik Pohl IV). 1981.

Not This August (with C. M. Kornbluth). 1981.

The Cool War. 1981.

Starburst. 1982.

Planets Three. 1982.

BiPohl ⟨*The Age of the Pussyfoot, Drunkard's Walk*⟩. 1982.

The Syndic (with C. M. Kornbluth). 1982.

*Yesterday's Tomorrows: Favorite Stories from Forty Years as a Science Fiction
      Editor* (editor). 1982.

Syzygy. 1982.

Wall around a Star: The Saga of Cuckoo (with Jack Williamson). 1983.

Midas World. 1983.

The Saga of Cuckoo ⟨*Farthest Star, Wall around a Star*⟩ (with Jack Williamson).
      1983.

Heechee Rendezvous. 1984.

Pohlstars. 1984.

The Years of the City. 1984.

The Merchants' War. 1984.

Black Star Rising. 1985.

Venus Inc. (with C. M. Kornbluth). 1985.

The Coming of the Quantum Cats. 1985.

Terror. 1986.

Tales from the Planet Earth (with Elizabeth Anne Hall). 1986.

Worlds of If (editor). 1986.

Annals of the Heechee. 1987.

Our Best: The Best of Frederik Pohl and C. M. Kornbluth. 1987.

Chernobyl. 1987.

Land's End (with Jack Williamson). 1988.

The Day the Martians Came. 1988.

Narabedla Ltd. 1988.

Homegoing. 1989.

The Gateway Trip: Tales and Vignettes of the Heechee. 1990.

Outnumbering the Dead. 1990.

The World at the End of Time. 1990.

Stopping and Slowyear. 1991.

Our Angry Earth (with Isaac Asimov). 1991.

The Singers of Time (with Jack Williamson). 1991.

Mining the Oort. 1992.

The Voices of Heaven. 1994.

Mars Plus (with Thomas T. Thomas). 1994.

Theodore Sturgeon
1918–1985

THEODORE STURGEON was born Edward Hamilton Waldo on February 26, 1918, to Edward and Christine Hamilton Waldo on Staten Island, New York. Sturgeon's parents were divorced in 1927. His mother remarried two years later, whereupon he was adopted by his stepfather and legally changed his name to Theodore Hamilton Sturgeon. He attended Overbrook High School in Philadelphia, where an early enthusiasm for gymnastics was cut short by a bout of rheumatic fever at the age of fifteen.

After spending three years on various jobs at sea, Sturgeon sold the first of more than forty stories to *McClure's* in 1937. He was persuaded by friends to try his hand at writing science fiction in 1939. During the next two years Sturgeon sold more than a dozen short stories to the field's most influential editor, John W. Campbell, and quickly established himself as one of science fiction's most accomplished writers. His first collection, *Without Sorcery*, was published in 1948 to critical acclaim. Sturgeon's short stories continued to receive praise throughout his career; he published more than twenty collections (among the more significant are *E Pluribus Unicorn*, 1953; *Caviar*, 1955; and *A Touch of Strange*, 1958) and won the Hugo and Nebula Awards for his short story "Slow Sculpture" (1970).

Sturgeon's first novel, *The Dreaming Jewels*, was published in 1950 to mixed reviews. Its reputation has grown with time, however, because of its stylistic richness and its concern with themes that would become Sturgeon trademarks, particularly the creative imagination of children and the stifling of the individual by a stagnant and thoughtless society.

More Than Human (1953) was Sturgeon's breakthrough novel, and remains to the present day one of science fiction's most respected works. Its three connected novellas relate the growth to maturity of *homo gestalt*, humanity evolved to the state of integrated group consciousness. It was universally praised in the field and was one of the first science fiction novels to receive significant critical notice outside the genre. Although none of Sturgeon's subsequent novels had the immediate impact of *More Than*

Human, they all received more praise than criticism and remain touchstones for the science fiction field. The most significant are *The Cosmic Rape* (1958) and *Venus Plus X* (1960).

Sturgeon also wrote a significant body of work in other fields. Among his celebrated works of horror are the novelette "It" (1940; issued separately in 1948) and the nonsupernatural vampire novel *Some of Your Blood* (1961). He also wrote Westerns (*The King and Four Queens*, 1956) and detective stories (*The Player on the Other Side* [1963], written under the name Ellery Queen).

During the 1960s Sturgeon wrote little fiction, although he reviewed science fiction voluminously for the *National Review* between 1961 and 1973; in 1971, however, a collection of short stories, *Sturgeon Is Alive and Well*, appeared. Several more retrospective collections followed, culminating in *Alien Cargo* (1984). In his last decade he wrote little except for the Star Trek novel *Amok Time* (1978) and book reviews for *Twilight Zone* magazine.

As one of the first writers of science fiction to place more emphasis on character development and stylistic concerns than on plot, and as one of the earliest to deal with controversial sexual themes, Sturgeon's permanent place in the field is assured. He was married four times and had eight children. After a long illness Sturgeon died on May 8, 1985, in Eugene, Oregon. A short novel, *Godbody*, appeared posthumously in 1986, the same year he was posthumously awarded the life achievement award by the World Fantasy Convention. Two collections of stories appeared subsequently, *To Marry Medusa* (1987) and *A Touch of Sturgeon* (1988).

▨ *Critical Extracts*

THEODORE STURGEON   I think what I have been trying to do all these years is to investigate this matter of love, sexual and asexual. I investigate it by writing about it because ⟨. . .⟩ I don't know what the hell I think until I tell somebody about it. And I work so assiduously at it because of a conviction that if one could understand it completely, one would have the key to cooperation itself: to creative inspiration: to self-sacrifice and that rare but real anomaly, altruism: in short, to the marvelous orchestration which enables us to keep ahead of our own destructiveness.

In order to do this I've had to look at the individual components. In "The Deadly Radio" (the "definitive" syzygy story; its original title was "It Wasn't Syzygy") I had two lovers, only one of whom was real. In "Bianca's Hands" only one of them was human. In "Rule of Three" and "Synthesis" I had (in reverse order) a quasi-sexual relationship among three people, and one among six so it could break down into three couples and be normal. In "The Stars Are the Styx" I set up several (four, as I remember) different kinds of love motivations for mutual comparisons. In "Two Percent Inspiration" it was hero worship, a kid and a great scientist. In "Until Death Do Us Join" it was the murderous jealousy between two personalities in a schizophrenic, both in love with the same girl. In "Cactus Dance" (upcoming in *Zane Grey's Western*) it is non-physical, perhaps even non-substitute physical love, as represented in several symbiotic relationships between humans and yucca plants. In "Killdozer" it was a choked-up worship for the majesty of a machine. By this time you get the idea.

"Bianca's Hands" and "The World Well Lost" cause the violently extreme reactions they do because of the simple fact that the protagonist was happy with the situation. No one was churned up (in these areas) by "Until Death Do Us Join" because the crazy mixed-up little guy was killed in the end. "Killdozer" didn't bother anyone, because love for a machine (as expressed) is too remote for most readers' ability to identify. But write a story well enough to force identification, and have the protagonist indulging in something weird, and let the guy be happy about it, and people explode all over the place. It is fashionable to overlook the fact that the old-shoe lover *loves* loving old shoes. Write that, and all the old-shoe lovers will love the story; all the deviates who equate their specialty with old-shoe loving will love the story; all the aberrates who so specialize or so equate but feel guilty about it will hate the story and you too.

Theodore Sturgeon, "Why So Much Syzygy?" (1953), *Turning Points: Essays on the Art of Science Fiction*, ed. Damon Knight (New York: Harper & Row, 1977), pp. 271–72

ANTHONY BOUCHER   Theodore Sturgeon, as distinctively talented a writer as any in the science-fantasy field today, has long been preoccupied with the theme of human symbiosis—not merely the no-man-is-an-island concept of the need of human beings for each other, but the thesis that, with intelligent sentient beings, the sum of one and one is (both richly and disturbingly) a great deal more than two.

His finest expression of this theme to date was in last year's long *Galaxy* novelette, "Baby Is Three"—an extraordinary study of a group of children,—ranging from a Mongolian idiot savant to a clever girl with para-psychological skills, who together constituted one unified being—possibly the precursor of a new symbiotic race, *Homo Gestalt*. In *More Than Human* we have the full novel of which that story is the mid-section; there are equally long portions before and after describing how the children came together, and how later they learned to fulfill their highest potential. These sections are on the same high level of writing and thinking—and, as is fitting to the theme, the novel as a whole adds up to much more than the sum of its three parts.

This is—surprisingly for so generally prolific a writer—only Sturgeon's second novel. One fears to toss about words like "profundity" and "greatness" in connection with the literature of entertainment; but it's hard to avoid them here. And one hastens to add that purely as entertainment, the book is a masterpiece of provocative storytelling.

> Anthony Boucher (as "H. H. Holmes"), [Review of *More Than Human* and *E Pluribus Unicorn*], *New York Herald Tribune Book Review*, 22 November 1953, p. 19

JAMES BLISH   All of Sturgeon's major work is about love, sexual love emphatically included. He has so testified, but had he kept mum about the matter it would have been discovered anyhow; it is right there on the page. This, for Sturgeon, is far from a limited subject, for he has stretched the word to include nearly every imaginable form of human relationship. Here again I think he is probably always in danger of embarrassing a large part—the juveniles—of his audience; the rest of us are fortunate that, if he is aware of this danger, he evidently doesn't give a damn. ⟨. . .⟩

Directly under this heading belongs Sturgeon's love affair with the English language, which has been as complicated, stormy and rewarding as any affair he has ever written about. He is a born experimenter, capable of the most outrageous excesses in search of precision and poetry; people who do not like puns, for example, are likely to find much Sturgeon text almost as offensive as late Joyce (and I am sorry for them). Nobody else in our microcosm could possibly have produced such a stylistic explosion as "To

Here and the Easel," a novella based in language as well as in theme on Ariosto's 16th-Century epic *Orlando Furioso*, because in fact nobody else would have seen that the subject couldn't have been handled any other way. ⟨. . .⟩ And even Sturgeon's verbal excesses are his own; he does not call upon exotic or obsolete words for their own sakes, or otherwise the multitudinous seas incarnadine; he never says anything is ineffable or unspeakable, the very ideas embodied in those words being foreign to his artistic credo; he does not splash color on with a mop, or use the same colors for everything; and he does not say "partly rugose and partly squamose" when he means "partly rough and partly scaly."

This quality of freshness of language even when it is out of control—which is not often—is due primarily to the fact that Sturgeon is an intensely visual writer. His images come almost exclusively from what he sees, as Joyce's came almost exclusively from what he heard. ⟨. . .⟩ Readers who do not think in terms of visual images—a very large group, as the electroencephalographers have shown us; perhaps as many as half of us—are likely to be baffled by this, or at least put off. They will get along much better with a writer like Poul Anderson, who follows a deliberate policy of appealing to at least three senses in every scene. Sturgeon's extremes of visualization probably lie at the root of the rather common complaint that he is a "mannered" writer.

James Blish (as "William Atheling, Jr."), "Caviar and Kisses: The Many Loves of Theodore Sturgeon" (1961), *More Issues at Hand* (Chicago: Advent, 1970), pp. 70–72

DAVID N. SAMUELSON   Not sharing the preference of many writers and fans for "pure" science fiction, Sturgeon is conscious nevertheless of the need to overcome the reader's disbelief of the improbable. He does so, however, primarily by literary, rather than by "scientific" (science fictional) means. Sturgeon by no means assumes a lawless universe—psi powers in *More Than Human* are subject to rules and limitations—but he does not feel it incumbent upon him to give a detailed explanation of the laws of nature which apply to his fictional world. Little or no explicit rationalization is offered for his characters' ability to defy natural laws apparently operable in the real world; he merely demonstrates their abilities in action, as they appear both from outside and from within the characters' minds.

Sturgeon does not attempt to anchor his fantasy in the basic assumptions of science; empiricism, determinism, and relativism are all somewhat subverted in this novel. Psi powers may be an objectively observable reality in the fictional world, but they are not subjected to or described in terms of quantitative measurement, and their objective reality is subordinated to their subjective reality, with which empiricism is not qualified to deal. Naturalistic determinism is invoked, in a way: the children's loneliness and rejection, resulting from some kind of maltreatment, is implied as a causal factor—necessary but not sufficient—in their parapsychological development. But loneliness and rejection are at least partly subjective, Sturgeon indicates, relieved by positive social interaction (love, affection, belonging). And the real determinism of the book is teleological: the goal of maturity, explicit in the characters and implicit in the structure of events, requires the success of the gestalt. Scientific relativism is operable in that each individual gestalt is regarded as an experiment of nature; the race (*homo gestalt*) welcomes each success, but it destroys each failure which does not dissolve or destroy itself. Moral relativism is more heavily stressed, especially in the character of Gerry, for whom the gestalt is largely a means to his playing the role of superman. Having no respect for merely human beings, laws, or institutions, he feels no obligation to use his power for good, nor does he even recognize a distinction between "good" and "evil" until his final confrontation with Hip.

The basic *goals* of science, prediction and control, are clearly present in *More Than Human*, but they are also basic desires of every man, which fantasy can achieve in literature where science cannot in the real world. The lesson of science, that we can achieve what we want only if we accept and take advantage of how the world is really constructed (i.e. not in accordance with our wishes alone) seems not to matter here. The ease with which certain "elect" persons achieve goals unreachable in the world outside the fiction is reminiscent of the ease with which seduction is managed in works of pornography. Sturgeon avoids intellectual pornography to some extent, however, by making his characters suffer and struggle in other ways, and by leading them toward a sense of ethical values. By treating psi powers as other writers treat mechanical technology, Sturgeon even avoids drifting completely beyond the borders of science fiction. By showing psi powers at work, as a matter of "fact," not of mystery, and by showing the skepticism of other characters overcome in the novel, he undermines our disbelief somewhat, even though we know he is using the literary equivalent of a conjuror's tricks. Since he does not refute the basic assumptions of science, and since the world he displays is still an orderly one, we are not so much led to a belief in "disguised spiritism" ⟨. . .⟩ as we are reminded that there may be wonders in the world which are still unexplained.

David N. Samuelson, "Theodore Sturgeon: *More Than Human*," *Visions of Tomorrow: Six Journeys from Outer to Inner Space* (New York: Arno Press, 1974), pp. 177–80

THOMAS M. DISCH   Theodore Sturgeon's *More Than Human* ⟨. . .⟩ is a book that even today I cannot praise highly enough. Among its many excellences is the fact that it uses its considerable power *as a daydream* to inculcate ethical values and spiritual insights usually entirely absent from genre writing. For instance, the book's insistence on mutual interdependency (and, by implication, on psychic integration) is in sharp contrast to the legion of stories in which the hero discovers the fate of the world to rest in his sole power. Another theme of the book—the need to bide one's time—is of obvious utility to any fourteen year old. But the largest subliminal lesson is latent in the fantasy of possessing secret powers. What this represents, I believe, is an assurance that there *is* a world of thought and inner experience of immense importance and within everybody's grasp. But it is only there for those who cultivate it.

Thomas M. Disch, "The Embarrassments of Science Fiction," *Science Fiction at Large: A Collection of Essays, by Various Hands, about the Interface between Science Fiction and Reality*, ed. Peter Nicholls (London: Victor Gollancz, 1976), p. 146

DONALD M. HASSLER   Sturgeon's protean sense of play, that is his style, can perhaps be more fully understood now after seeing that playfulness can be a very serious idea indeed—an idea that allows some balance between the longing for anthropocentrism and perhaps even the cessation of change on the one hand and the realizations of an open universe on the other. Sturgeon's style, in short, allows him the flexibility not to have to dwell for long at either pole of that opposition. He writes about people and love and loneliness (only humans can be lonely for other humans and even our pets, particularly our pets, we anthropomorphize as fellow humans); but he lets us know that there are many more things in heaven and earth as well. And his style is the way both to convey and to endure this complexity. Finally, then, the style of proliferation and the content of love and concern are blended in Sturgeon's work. It is a truism in literary studies that style and content are related, but with Sturgeon the relationship goes beyond the truism and becomes intriguingly almost incestuous. His changes and his virtuosity are both his way of loving and his way of avoiding loneliness.

Obviously, Sturgeon the stylist and literary form-changer is the same Sturgeon who is the lover. Form and content in the overall effects of his work are one, and his continual interest in the nature of change and newness is closely related to his interest in style. ⟨. . .⟩ a high ideal for Sturgeon as a writer is that he works "assiduously," not at ideas, but at writing images. The result is, as in some theories of Renaissance art, a richly proliferating aping of nature that conveys finally the most valuable idea *from* nature: its complexity and continually changing newness. As James Blish comments in *The Seedling Stars* about various species changes of a lively nature: "But why should any of them think of form-changing as something extraordinary, and to be striven for? It's one of the commonplaces of their lives, after all." The commonplace of at least a major portion of Sturgeon's literary life is that style and loving concern are counterparts of one another because it is the comprehension of all the complexity, done through style, that allows the most genuine love. Perhaps in a simpler, more anthropocentric universe love could be more single minded; and we might prefer that. But the comic tension of our complex universe arms us to love things as they are, and Sturgeon's complex literary fabrications contribute to the expression of this comic tension.

Donald M. Hassler, "Images for an Ethos, Images for Change and Style," Extrapolation 20, No. 2 (Summer 1979): 186–87

LAHNA DISKIN   Sturgeon, like ⟨D. H.⟩ Lawrence, believes in the sanctity of desire, in the life-giving, rippling act of loving, in transmitting the palpable and potent stream of desire which exists in everybody to flow preternaturally from person to person, creature to creature, growing thing to growing thing, ever outward, ever ongoing.

Sturgeon's style changes with each story. The idea and characters determine and generate his whole mode from diction and imagery to syntax. Thus each work has its own attributes as prose, based on what he once called "harmony and/or contrast." This versatility has led some critics to call him a "mannered" writer. James Blish, however, praised Sturgeon's skill at changing manners, at adopting or casting off a style according to the demands of the story.

Sturgeon's sensuous imagery may be the only constant element in his prose. Its tactile quality comes from his effect of *touching* the object of his description with his discerning eyes and ears as well as with his sensitive fingers—with his most cultivated sensibilities. His details are always alive with the *feel* of a facial expression, the sound of a person's voice, the movement of people and things, the fiber, the pulse and coloring of a setting. His consummate sense of texture controls all his best imagery. Whether he is shaping sounds, places, or actions, he perceives the unexpected, the unnoticed, the unobvious, the unlooked-for. ⟨. . .⟩

Occasionally, even a few of Sturgeon's staunchest admirers among the critics blanch at his audacity. They feel uneasy when he sets out to slay latter-day dragons, the perpetuators of benighted social attitudes. They become especially upset when he strikes his blows combating rigid sexual taboos. If their nervousness, this dis-ease, blurs their view of Sturgeon's art as a bold fabulator and social critic, it may be because his subject is distasteful and disturbing to them. And if they do suffer a temporary occlusion, their incapacity stops them from seeing beyond the issue of sex per se to recognize that Sturgeon deals with the whole spectrum of human intercourse (in its broadest sense) in which the physical and spiritual aspects are inseparable, interdependent. Sometimes, therefore, the critics have failed Sturgeon in direct proportion to the breadth (or more properly, the limitations) of their own attitudes and sensibilities, to the extent that they have viewed sex as an end unto itself rather than, like Sturgeon, as an element—a vital element—in a complex compound in the chemistry or composition of human relationships.

Lahna Diskin, *Theodore Sturgeon* (Mercer Island, WA: Starmont House, 1981), pp. 15, 17

LUCY MENGER   In *The Cosmic Rape*, Sturgeon shows man through his own innate capacities outdoing the "network of force-beams" described in "The Stars Are the Styx." Where the force-beam network was only similar to "the synaptic paths of a giant brain," the Human-Medusa hive *is* a giant brain. The hive, moreover, does something the force-beams could not: it links all its members together through telepathic understanding.

More Than Human, The Cosmic Rape, and others of Sturgeon's works involving telepathic union may have had their genesis in a wish to answer a question evoked by "Bianca's Hands," written in the earliest days of Sturgeon's career. That story had told of a young man, Ran, who was destroyed by the very union he desired. The question the story evoked was: Can total union (such as Ran desired) have any end other than dissolution?

In pursuing an answer to this question, Sturgeon postulated and then examined many different types of union. These ranged from loose, subliminal associations to unbreakable bonds. ⟨. . .⟩

The union portrayed in *The Cosmic Rape* combines the most desirable elements of the other telepathic fusions considered in his fiction. Within the Human-Medusa hive, individuals are free to follow their own bents. They have the use of the knowledge of others in the hive, and are protected by the hive. More, they are aware of the hive and are aware of, and in mental communication with, every other individual in the hive. There is no threat of dissolution to hive members. Instead, individuality is supported and nurtured.

The all-embracing concept of the Human-Medusa hive seems to be Sturgeon's definitive statement on the subject of union. His final answer to the question evoked by "Bianca's Hands" is unequivocal: yes—union can be both total *and* safe.

With this answer, the subject of unions, telepathic or otherwise, vanished from Sturgeon's fiction for decades.

Sturgeon was, nevertheless, far from finished with his examination of the potentials and problems of mankind. In subsequent works, however, he would refocus from the cosmic panorama to more earthly and earthy subjects.

Lucy Menger, *Theodore Sturgeon* (New York: Frederick Ungar Publishing Co., 1981), pp. 84–85

STEPHEN KING   Sturgeon's emphasis on psychology instead of blasters prepared the way for such modern masters of the genre as Robert Silverberg, Gregory Benford, John Varley, Kate Wilhelm. When science fiction made its crucial shift from pulp action to a careful consideration of what the future might hold for the emotions and the psyche as well as for the techno-toybox, Sturgeon was in the van.

Only a science fiction writer, but in "Baby Is Three" (part of *More Than Human*) and *The Dreaming Jewels* he brought Joycean stream-of-consciousness techniques to a field which until 1954 or so had considered the prose styles of such stalwarts as E. E. "Doc" Smith and Ray Cummings perfectly adequate. ⟨. . .⟩

Only a science fiction writer was all Theodore Sturgeon was. Check the obits and see if I'm not right. But he also entertained, provoked thought, terrified, and occasionally ennobled. He fulfilled, in short, all the qualifications we use to measure artistry in prose.

Stephen King, "Theodore Sturgeon (1918–1985)," *Washington Post Book World*, 26 May 1985, p. 11

BEN BOVA   If Ted Sturgeon were to paraphrase Harlan Ellison's famous line, it would come out, "Sex ain't nothing but love misspelled."

Godbody is Theodore Sturgeon's last testament to his readers. As in all his other works, the theme of this short novel is human love. ⟨. . .⟩

Godbody is nothing less than an attempt to retell the fundamental myth of Christ: God in a human body, showing the way to benighted people, being killed, and rising from the dead. It is no more science fiction than the Gospel according to St. Luke. That will not deter Sturgeon's legions of science-fiction followers: they have come to expect Sturgeon's stories to be uniquely Sturgeon, not standard science fiction.

Would a reader who is not interested in science fiction, who does not know of Sturgeon's place in the field, enjoy *Godbody?* Certainly. This story contains the kind of tale we all want to believe in, written in a relaxed naturalistic style that makes the miraculous seem quite plausible.

Will *Godbody* take its place as the capstone to Sturgeon's long career? Probably not. When the sentiment engendered by his death fades away, this slim novel will be seen as a good first draft, perhaps a very good first draft, of what could have been a truly beautiful novel if only the author had lived to finish the task.

Ben Bova, [Review of *Godbody*], *Los Angeles Times Book Review*, 13 April 1986, p. 1

JOHN   HUNTINGTON   Theodore   Sturgeon's   "Macrocosmic God" (1941) finds itself sucked into the social contradictions that Gernsback avoided in his depiction of the innocent genius. Sturgeon tells about a genius, James Kidder, who, after some brilliant inventions of his own, increases his output by developing a race of tiny, intelligent creatures, "Neoterics." He keeps the Neoterics in a large, complex laboratory and makes them evolve rapidly. By making them solve catastrophic crises that he, the "god" of their tiny world, originates, he forces them to invent materials and techniques that he then offers to the human world. Kidder's banker, Conant, who begins as an ally, later tries to use Kidder's invention, a power transmitter, to take over the United States government. When Kidder tries to stop him, Conant attacks Kidder's island with an armed force. Kidder and his Neoterics finally defeat Conant and, with an engineer named Johansen, retreat from the world beneath an impenetrable dome. The story ends with an anxiety, familiar from horror tales, about what may happen when the Neoterics decide to leave their dome. ⟨. . .⟩

At one level we are observing a confusion arising from the overlap of two aspects of capitalism. The entrepreneurial banker and the inventor, both essential to the mythography of technological development, represent different phases of it. The story evades the contradiction involved in admiring both of them by seeing Kidder as a social hero and Conant as a selfish villain. The good-evil dichotomy solves at the narrative level what is a moral puzzle: as Fredric Jameson puts it, how can my enemy "be thought of as being *evil* (that is, as other than myself and marked by some absolute difference), when what is responsible for his being so characterized is quite simply the *identity* of his own conduct with mine." This sort of split, as Jameson argues, is characteristic of romance. The romance narrative, which SF is often considered, with its absolute oppositions based on identity, serves an important ideological function by validating on moral grounds an antipathy whose real origin is political. After all, though Sturgeon's story seems to subscribe to the idea that Conant is a social leech while Kidder is a producer, at another level, hidden from all the world, the genius, secretly manipulating and robbing his Neoterics, is just as parasitical as the banker. ⟨. . .⟩

The deep ambiguity in Sturgeon's story, whether conscious or not, enacts a crucial dilemma. While it cannot give up the idea of genius—after all, Kidder, with his little world, is much like a young SF author—the story also acknowledges the socially destructive aspect of the genius. By using the psychological device of "splitting" the character into Kidder and Conant, the author manages to give the destructive aspect play without destroying the idealization. In the fantasy of the Neoterics, the story invents a form of social progress that escapes the dilemma of the genius, but the story also abstains from pursuing the social implications of this idea. In the fantasy of the Neoterics we can see hints of an idea that neither American SF enthusiasts nor scientists themselves have much encouraged: that progress is a cultural (rather than individual) product. Recently one can find this idea argued explicitly by Paul Feyerabend in "Creativity—A Dangerous Myth" and, in a slightly different form, by Robert Weisberg in *Creativity: Genius and Other Myths*. I do not mean to suggest that Sturgeon's story makes such an argument, but that at some level it is aware of it. In such a story one observes a process of cultural (rather than individual) thought.

John Huntington, *Rationalizing Genius: Ideological Strategies in the Classic American Science Fiction Story* (New Brunswick, NJ: Rutgers University Press, 1989), pp. 53–54, 57, 59

THOMAS D. CLARESON   One gains a sense of the reception given *Venus Plus X* by the reaction of Alfred Bester, the book reviewer for *F&SF*, who asserted that Sturgeon "has permitted himself to blunder into the trap that undoes many lesser American authors, . . . a deadly and stultifying seriousness about sex." Sturgeon structured the novel as a classic utopia; Charlie Johns, seemingly an American aviator who has survived a crash, is guided through the kingdom of Ledom by the historian Philos, who asks Johns to judge the society. From the outset the only mystery remains the sexual identity of its inhabitants until Johns sees two of them pregnant; Philos and others allow him to infer that he has somehow revived in a future time when humanity has mutated so that it is hermaphroditic. Although this makes him uncomfortable, he accepts it and learns that an all-encompassing love, particularly for their children, governs the lives of the Ledom.

Against this unfolding but essentially static background Sturgeon inserts a series of sharply satirical vignettes focusing primarily on Herb and Jeannette Raile and their two preschool children in order to attack the hypocrisy and inconsistencies in the prescribed sex roles characteristic of mid-century, suburban American society. In addition to referring to a wide variety of sources including Ruth Benedict, Margaret Mead, Erich Fromm, and

G. Rattray Taylor (*Sex in History*, 1954), Sturgeon drew heavily on Philip Wylie's *The Disappearance* (1951), which separates the sexes for four years in parallel worlds so that Wylie can condemn masculine domination and misjudgment. Sturgeon follows Wylie in denouncing humanity's virtual loss of the ability to love and man's breeding women to be submissive. He concludes that throughout history the father-dominated religious orders have been a key element in the Western refusal to adopt "a charitic religion and a culture to harmonize with it." Although *Venus Plus X* retains historical importance because it precedes the women's movement, it remains effective primarily when Sturgeon allowed the vignettes to speak for themselves. His most telling point is the episode in which Jeanette Raile thinks herself "rotten clear through" because she feels sexual desire.

> Thomas D. Clareson, *Understanding Contemporary American Science Fiction: The Formative Period (1926–1970)* (Columbia: University of South Carolina Press, 1990), pp. 144–45

◈ *Bibliography*

It. 1948.

Without Sorcery. 1948, 1961 (abridged; as *Not Without Sorcery*).

The Dreaming Jewels ⟨*The Synthetic Man*⟩. 1950.

More Than Human. 1953.

E Pluribus Unicorn: A Collection of Short Stories. 1953.

Caviar. 1955.

A Way Home: Stories of Science Fiction and Fantasy. Ed. Groff Conklin. 1955.

I, Libertine. 1956.

The King and Four Queens. 1956.

Thunder and Roses: Stories of Science-Fiction and Fantasy. Ed. Groff Conklin. 1957.

The Cosmic Rape. 1958.

A Touch of Strange. 1958.

Aliens 4. 1959.

Beyond. 1960.

Venus Plus X. 1960.

Some of Your Blood. 1961.

Voyage to the Bottom of the Sea. 1961.

The Player on the Other Side. 1963.

Sturgeon in Orbit. 1964.

Two Complete Novels 〈. . . *And My Fear Is Great, Baby Is Three*〉. 1965.

The Joyous Invasions. 1965.

Starshine. 1966.

The Rare Breed. 1966.

Sturgeon Is Alive and Well: A Collection of Short Stories. 1971.

The Worlds of Theodore Sturgeon. 1972.

To Here and the Easel. 1973.

Sturgeon's West (with Don Ward). 1973.

Case and the Dreamer. 1974.

Visions and Venturers. 1978.

Amok Time. 1978.

Maturity: Three Stories. 1979.

The Golden Helix. 1979.

The Stars Are the Styx. 1979.

Slow Sculpture. 1982.

Alien Cargo. 1984.

Godbody. 1986.

To Marry Medusa. 1987.

A Touch of Sturgeon. Ed. David Pringle. 1988.

A. E. van Vogt
b. 1912

ALFRED ELTON VAN VOGT was born near Winnipeg in Manitoba, Canada, on April 26, 1912, to parents of Dutch descent. He was raised in rural Neville, Sasketchewan, where his father was an attorney and co-owner of a grocery store with his brothers. Van Vogt was a self-conscious child, and his family's move to the larger city of Winnipeg when he was fourteen intensified his introspectiveness and contributed to his poor performance at school. He began reading voraciously to compensate, and in 1926 discovered the science fiction magazine *Amazing Stories*, which he read faithfully for several years.

While working as a census taker in Ottawa in 1931, van Vogt took a writing course at the Palmer Institute of Authorship. Over the next few years he embarked upon a professional writing career, contributing to high-paying "true confession" magazines and writing radio plays. In 1938 he came upon a copy of *Astounding Science-Fiction* and was struck by Don A. Stuart's story "Who Goes There?" Unaware that Stuart was a pseudonym for the magazine's editor, John W. Campbell, van Vogt submitted his first science fiction story, "The Vault of the Beast," to *Astounding*. Campbell, impressed by the story's energy and audacious ideas, bought it, although it did not see print until 1940. The appearance of van Vogt's first published science fiction story, "Black Destroyer," side by side with Isaac Asimov's first sale to *Astounding* in the July 1939 issue, is considered the beginning of science fiction's Golden Age.

Readers responded enthusiastically to van Vogt's dazzling and complex reworkings of familiar themes into the stuff of mind-boggling science fiction. Van Vogt explained his formula for success in 1946 by admitting that he tried never to write scenes longer than 800 words, a technique that allowed him to accommodate any idea that came to mind and to maintain a furious pace through narrative cross-cutting. Although many critics derided his confusing style of writing and imperfect grasp of science, readers hailed his stories as instant classics, particularly the novel *Slan* (serialized 1940; published as a book 1946), which is told from the point of view of a mutant superman, and *The World of A* (1948) and its sequel *The Pawns of Null-A* (1956), which promulgated Alfred Korzybski's general semantics movement and induced other writers to explore the ramifications of Korzybski's interest in non-Aristotelian logic in their own science fiction.

Van Vogt's ingenious and sometimes infuriatingly opaque epics of characters who realize their destiny as supermen in time to overthrow futuristic despotic monarchies dominated the pages of *Astounding* in the 1940s, where he contributed stories under his own name and in collaboration with E. Mayne Hull, whom he had married in 1939. He moved to the United States in 1944. His preoccupation with L. Ron Hubbard's self-help science Dianetics led to his withdrawal from writing science fiction in the 1950s, although several "fix-ups"—novels assembled from loosely interconnected stories that had been published previously—appeared during these years, most notably *The Voyage of the Space Beagle* (1950), *The Weapon Shops of Isher* (1951), *Empire of the Atom* (1956), and *The War against the Rull* (1959).

Van Vogt returned to writing science fiction in the late 1960s but few of his recent novels have fared well critically. Since the publication of his autobiographical *Reflections of A. E. van Vogt* and the death of E. Mayne Hull in 1975, he has led a quiet life in California, publishing only sporadically. He married Lydia I. Byerman in 1979. In 1985 a third Null-A novel, *Null-A Three*, was issued.

◈ *Critical Extracts*

DAMON KNIGHT   I have been progressively annoyed by van Vogt ever since *Slan*. The first part of this article has vented much of that annoyance, but there is a remainder: there are trends in van Vogt's work as a whole which either do not appear strongly in *The World of A*, or could not be treated in a discussion of that story without loss of objectivity.

There is the regiphile trend, for example. It strikes me as singular that in van Vogt's stories, nearly all of which deal with the future, the form of government which occurs most often is the absolute monarchy; and further, that the monarchs in these stories are almost always depicted sympathetically. This is true of the "Weapon Shops" series and the "Mixed Men" and of such single stories as "Heir Apparent"—the hero of the latter being a "benevolent dictator," if you please.

I am attacking van Vogt on literary, not political grounds, so I shall not say what I think of a man who loves monarchies. Neither do I think it relevant that these stories were written and published during a time when both van Vogt's country (Canada) and ours were at war with dictatorships, except insofar as it serves to accentuate this point: Obviously van Vogt is no better acquainted with current events than he is with ancient or modern history.

The absolute monarchy was a form of government which evolved to meet feudal economic conditions everywhere, and which has died everywhere with feudalism. Modern attempts to impose a similar system on higher cultures have just been proven, very decisively, to be failures. Monarchy is dead, and it can never revive until the economic conditions which produced it recur. It is no crime for van Vogt as a private citizen to wish it were not so; but ignorance, for an author, is a crime.

Another trend which appears in van Vogt's work is an apparently purposeless refusal to call things by their right names. "A" and "lie detector" are two examples; another is the term "robot" which was employed throught the "Mixed Men" series. Etymologically the usage was correct; the word, as first used by Capek, meant an artificially created protoplasmic man. But it has since been altered through wide use to mean a mechanical device which performs some or all of a human being's functions. "Android"—first used, as far as I know, by Jack Williamson—has assumed the original meaning of "robot" in science fiction.

"Robot," in the aforementioned series, was a key word; to garble its meaning was to render the entire story meaningless. Van Vogt certainly is aware of the changed meaning of the word, as shown by his use of the term "roboplane"; yet he did not hesitate on that account to call his androids "robots." I do not pretend to know why.

Still another trend is the plot wherein two opposing parties turn out to be identical (*Slan*, "The Weapon Shop"). This trend, however, appears not only in van Vogt's work but in that of several other *Astounding* writers; and I suspect that final responsibility for it rests with ⟨John W.⟩ Campbell.

The plot device was used by G. K. Chesterton to beautiful effect in *The Man Who Was Thursday*, and it was effective precisely because the impression the author wanted to give was of utter and imbecilic pointlessness. In van Vogt's hands it gives the same impression, but without Chesterton's charm.

In general, van Vogt seems to me to fail consistently as a writer in these elementary ways:

1. His plots do not bear examination.

2. His choice of words and his sentence-structure are fumbling and insensitive.

3. He is unable either to visualize a scene or to make a character seem real.

Damon Knight, "Cosmic Jerrybuilder: A. E. van Vogt" (1945), *In Search of Wonder: Essays on Modern Science Fiction* (1956; rev. ed. Chicago: Advent, 1967), pp. 58–60

A. E. VAN VOGT   Very well, then, let us suppose you have conceived an excellent idea for a science fiction story. Now, you are sitting down to write. What next?

Think of it in scenes of about 800 words. This is not original with me, but I have followed that rule religiously ever since I started to write. Every scene has a purpose which is stated near the beginning, usually by the third paragraph, and that purpose is either accomplished or not accomplished by the end of the scene ⟨. . .⟩

By adopting this "secret" of the 800 word scene (it can be 600 words or a 1000 words), I wrote and sold my first story and it has formed a solid base for all the stories I have sold since then.

Readers have a habit of being right about an author. Some years ago, in a "little" magazine—they call them fanzines in the science fiction and fantasy field—I was described as an "idea" man. Meaning that my science fiction stories abounded in ideas, twists and odd angles.

This description startled me for I had never thought about it in that way. But, almost immediately, I recognized the accuracy of the description. Ever since I started writing for the science fiction field, it has been my habit to put every current thought into the story I happened to be working on. Frequently, an idea would seem to have no relevance, but by mulling over it a little, I would usually find an approach that would make it usable.

There are writers who would warn you against putting all your ideas into one story. Hold them back, they say, for soon there will be another story coming along where they may be more useful. This has a certain logic to it, but let me issue a counter warning: The brain does not develop on negative expectations. If a person attaches too much importance to one idea, then the brain will concentrate around that idea, and will stop manufacturing new ones.

My own experience has been that the brain thrives on positivity. Take it for granted that ideas will come as you need them—and they do. Don't hoard, but start a flow. Once such a flow is under way the problem will be to turn it off, not to keep it going.

> A. E. van Vogt, "Complication in the Science Fiction Story," *Of Worlds Beyond,* ed. Lloyd Arthur Eshbach (Reading, PA: Fantasy Press, 1946), pp. 54, 56

P. SCHUYLER MILLER   "Black Destroyer" was and is one of the finest science fiction stories of the last fifteen years. It now serves as curtain-raiser for a series of episodes in which the crew of the *Space Beagle,* outward bound through the fringes of our own galaxy to the Andromeda universe, meet, are threatened by, and defeat the monstrous representatives of rival races. The second longest of these adventures appeared here as "Discord in Scarlet," and a short connecting link has been published elsewhere as "War of Nerves."

The complete rewriting of these stories to give them some of the unity needed in a novel has created the character of Elliott Grosvenor, Nexialist of the expedition, a diffident exponent of the new science of things as a whole. Nexialism in this book might be considered the parallel of the Null A philosophy in van Vogt's previous volume in this series, but it has not been so well developed, either through explanation or example, as the world of A. Grosvenor is retiring to the point of being exasperating, and neither his own struggle for recognition nor the built-up feud between Morton and Kent for directorship of the expedition gives the book the unity a novel needs. The catlike Couerl, the birdlike Riim, the red devil Ixtl, the gaseous, whispering Anabis of the final episode are interesting enough concepts, but this is one case where the whole is less than the sum of the original parts.

> P. Schuyler Miller, [Review of *Voyage of the Space Beagle*], *Astounding Science-Fiction* 47, No. 3 (May 1951): 152

ANTHONY BOUCHER   Van Vogt has been known to the hard-cover reading public chiefly as the author of vast, intricate and ponderous novels; now at last this collection ⟨*Destination: Universe!*⟩ (curiously labeled by the publishers as "an anthology") displays what the magazine-reader has long known: his mastery of the economical short story adventurously developing a startling imaginative idea. As usual, his prose is graceless, even cumbrous; and the introductory analysis of science fiction in general and his own work in particular is faintly embarrassing. But here are some of the most striking concepts in the last ten years of imaginitive fiction, with a fine sense of vigorous storytelling and a small-scale, convincing impact lacking in more pretentious works.

Anthony Boucher (as "H. H. Holmes"), [Review of *Destination: Universe!*], *New York Herald Tribune Books*, 1 June 1952, p. 12

COLIN WILSON   As a typical example of the best type of popular science fiction, consider A. E. van Vogt's volume of stories *Destination Universe*. Its opening story, "Far Centaurus," deals with the problem of reaching the stars. A scientist discovers a drug capable of keeping men in a state of suspended animation. This partly answers the problem of how men could keep alive through the enormous periods of time that it would take to reach the nearest stars—even for a space ship that could travel at the speed of light. Several drugged men are shot towards Alpha Centauri. They wake up after fifty years or so, take more of the drug, and sleep for another fifty years. In this way they are still young men when they reach the star. But when they arrive, a surprise awaits them. Since their space ship set out, human science has made immense advances, and has constructed space ships that can cover the journey in a fraction of the time. When they arrive, the star is already colonised by men from earth. Unfortunately, the author has no idea how to finish his story, but the first part is impressive because it makes the reader aware of the immensity of space. The men who leave earth on a two-hundred-year-voyage are severing themselves from all their human connections, and from the human race. By the time they arrive on the star, all their relatives on earth will be dead. The story jars the reader's imagination to a new viewpoint. Our imaginations are anthropocentric, earthbound; they prefer to deal with the emotions with which they are familiar—human love and hate. In this sense, a story like van Vogt's can be considered as a new departure for the human imagination, which since Homer has dealt with warmer and more familiar emotions. For its first half, the story is an excellent example of the almost theological note sounded by the best science fiction. It recalls Pascal's phrase about the 'eternal silences of these infinite spaces', and it also has the merit of bringing these home to the imagination more forcibly than Pascal does.

Colin Wilson, *The Strength to Dream: Literature and the Imagination* (London: Gollancz, 1962), p. 111

AVRAM DAVIDSON   Nothing kept me at *The Beast* except that it was straight SF, of which the column's been short—*and* the fact that it's by the great A. E. van Vogt. Surely (I kept telling myself), surely any minute now things will start getting good. Surely paper characters, cliché situations, poor writing, flapdoodle and flumadiddle about Mysterious Super Engines, Secret Mysterious Organizations, Super Mysterious Powers, Mysterious Secret Caves in the Moon, Secret Super Communist Nazis, Super Secret Mysterious Neanderthal—surely all this must momentarily give way to the Great van Vogt Stimulating Concepts for which *Slan, The World of Null-A, The Weapon-Shops of Isher*, were famous . . . surely? Well, give way it did—for a while—but only to make room for Super Mysterious Equalized Man-Like Women, Mysterious Super Intelligent Arc-lights Living in a Pit, Secret Super Kidnapping Colonies on Venus—

But why go on. Apparently this collection of rubbish has been confected out of three stories originally published in *Astounding*, the dates of which are meretriciously not given, but I'd guess not long after the War, with perhaps the dates re-set later to bring it (ha ha) up to date; which, if I'm correct, failed miserably in its intention: and, if I'm wrong, merely convicts van Vogt of here being a poor prophet as well as (here) a poor writer. The only redeeming features of the book are good paper, clear typography, an arresting jacket design by Howard Burns. In short, I feel quite savage about having wasted on it an entire evening which I might have better spent bubbling my lips for the amusement of my little boy.

Avram Davidson, [Review of *The Beast*], *Magazine of Fantasy and Science Fiction* 25, No. 5 (November 1963): 68–69

DONALD A. WOLLHEIM   Van Vogt swings back and forth, like his victim of Isher, making all time and space his field, and showing in innumerable ways that man is equal to the greatest potential and is godlike in himself. Man may vary—he may advance himself by conquest of his own mind or by evolutionary development of the next race, or he may deliberately remake himself into a scientifically constructed superior form, as in the recent Van Vogt novel *The Silkie*, whose hero is a being of that classification, able to change shape at will, able to be a space ship and a submarine, able to think with computerlike capacity and speed, able to play God as far as the old-style humans are concerned.

To the uninitiated layman all this may smell of megalomania and perhaps paranoia, but Van Vogt remains atop the lists of the most favored and best-selling science-fiction writers. There must be a reason and that reason is as I have outlined before: he has an instinctual belief in humanity, he believes in the invincibility of humanity, he refuses to accept the boundaries of time and space.

The fact is that science fiction readers agree with him. They, too, cannot believe that humanity has limitations.

> Donald A. Wollheim, "Of Men Like Gods," *The Universe Makers: Science Fiction Today* (New York: Harper & Row, 1971), pp. 47–48

PAUL A. CARTER   Part of the continuing effectiveness of Mary Shelley's *Frankenstein* lies in its being told in substantial part from the monster's point of view. A. E. Van Vogt made his initial mark in science fiction with three stories (all in *Astounding Science-Fiction*) about humans in conflict with extraterrestrial creatures—"Black Destroyer" (vol. 23, July 1939), "Discord in Scarlet" (vol. 24, December 1939), and "Vault of the Beast" (vol. 25, August 1940)—in which the viewpoint of the alien is presented at the beginning of the story, before the reader is introduced to its human opponents. When the time came to undertake his first book-length novel, *Slan* (ASF: 26, September, October, November, December 1940; first hard-cover book version 1946), Van Vogt in effect translated the theme of those earlier stories into a conflict between man and superman—but this time he told the story *entirely* from the alien's point of view. As the author remarked to a circle of fans at the Fourth World Science Fiction Convention (the "Pacificon," Los Angeles, 1946), "I imagined one of my alien beings, but put him in a human body. The result was Jommy Cross," the superboy hero of *Slan*.

Actually, Jommy Cross is no more "alien" than Edmond Hall ⟨in Stanley G. Weinbaum's *The New Adam*⟩, and he is considerably less so than ⟨Olaf Stapledon's⟩ Odd John. He has two hearts, convenient enough should one of them conk out, and he has tendrils on his head, a feature genetically linked with a faculty of telepathy, but otherwise he is a human—and, at the beginning of the story, badly frightened—little boy. And that, as editor John Campbell was the first to point out, was the way Van Vogt solved the superman problem, using one of the oldest dodges in the book—simple reader identification.

The opening of *Slan* is a fast-paced chase scene, in which Jommy's mother is shot down by mutant-hunting policemen, and her nine-year-old son makes his escape on the rear of a bumper car in which sits the human police chief who is directing the hunt. The suspense is maintained with very little let up until the final instalment, which closes with a double surprise ending. It is a pulp plot, if you will, but in its day it was very good pulp; *Slan* was one of the earliest novel-length magazine stories to be reprinted in hard covers by a major commercial publisher, and a post-pulp generation in science fiction has continued to find it readable.

The basic literary and philosophical problem—how an ape is to tell a man's story, or a man a superman's—remains unsolved. However, as Van Vogt had shown, telepathy offered an easement of this dilemma. J. B. Rhine's ESP (extra-sensory perception) experiments at Duke University were quite well known to readers and writers of science fiction, and in the stories ESP could plausibly be described by analogy with sight, touch, and hearing. Thus the coming superman could be described as a conventional specimen of *Homo sapiens*, except for the ability to use ESP to read others' minds. Indeed, telepathy and ESP (or "psi," as it came to be called) need not be a foretaste of human evolution at all; they might be traits that humans unknowingly have always possessed.

Paul A. Carter, *The Creation of Tomorrow: Fifty Years of Magazine Science Fiction* (New York: Columbia University Press, 1977), pp. 152–53

BRIAN STABLEFORD   One has to admire van Vogt. He doesn't write very well, but whereas common mortals with this affliction try to cope with it in the ordinary, tedious way (i.e. by trying to write better) van Vogt goes to extraordinary lengths to turn his incompetence into an advantage.

He has difficulty in saying what he means—well then, obscurity will become the hallmark of his prose, and he will cultivate it assiduously. He cannot characterise properly—well then, let the motivations of his characters be relentlessly absurd, let their illogicality at least be blessed with the compulsion of obsession. He loves to throw into his plots any and every idea that occurs to him during the time of writing, whether it fits or not and despite the fact that it prohibits him ever making a sensible resolution to the plot and its contents—well then, forget fitting things together and to hell with sensible resolutions; make disorder the rule and go in for magical formulae whose mere recitation will be said (no proof need be given) to have made everything satisfactory. Tell the reader *that* while staring them straight in the eye, and tell them that your climactic miracle, as well as resolving your irresolvable plot, has also resolved all the problems of mankind, and maybe a few of God's as well, and even though they will *know* that you are telling the most blatant lies imaginable, they will have to respect you for it. Who else has ever told them such breathtakingly appalling lies?

It isn't Literature, but in its own sweet way, it's magnificent.

Brian Stableford, [Review of *Cosmic Encounter*], *Foundation* No. 20 (October 1980): 82

LESLIE A. FIEDLER   ⟨Brian⟩ Aldiss fails to do justice to the three great father figures of the American Golden Age, Heinlein, Asimov, and especially A. E. Van Vogt, whose "creative insanity" he is willing to acknowledge, but whose most influential and central book he completely ignores. Given his prejudices, one does not expect Aldiss to speak of *Slan* as hyperbolically as does ⟨Sam⟩ Moskowitz, who calls it Van Vogt's "most famous and perhaps best work"; but one expects at least a mention of it in so compendious and inclusive a history of the genre as *Billion Year Spree.*

Van Vogt is a test case, not just for Aldiss; since an apology for or analysis of science fiction which fails to come to terms with his appeal and major importance, defends or defines the genre by falsifying it. If a writer as widely sympathetic to sf in all its varieties as Aldiss flunks that test, what can we expect of later, more academic, elitist, and rigorous critics like Rabkin and Scholes but total disaster. Indeed, they tell us in their ambitious and otherwise useful study, *Science Fiction: History, Science, Vision* (1977), that Van Vogt has not worn well, and that *Slan*, whose centrality to his work they do not deny, proves him "precisely the sort of writer that has given science fiction a bad name among serious readers." My heart sinks at the phrase "serious readers," and when Rabkin and Scholes go on to say of the same novel that "this is not fiction for adults," I lose all hope. It is, after all, the availability to children and the childlike in us all, along with the challenge to the defunct notion of the serious reader which characterizes not just Van Vogt but all sf at its most authentic.

Any bright high school sophomore can identify all the things that are *wrong* about Van Vogt, whose clumsiness is equaled only by his stupidity. But the challenge to criticism which pretends to do justice to science fiction is to say what is *right* about him: to identify his mythopoeic power, his ability to evoke primordial images, his gift for redeeming the marvelous in a world in which technology has preempted the province of magic and God is dead. To do this, structuralism and its spin-offs, those strange French (or naturalized Slavic) gods after whom recent scholars of fantasy and popular literature have gone a-whoring, are of little help—as, indeed, they are of little help with any good-bad literature, whose virtues are independent of the text and therefore immune to semiotic analysis.

> Leslie A. Fiedler, "The Criticism of Science Fiction," *Coordinates: Placing Science Fiction and Fantasy*, ed. George E. Slusser, Eric S. Rabkin, and Robert Scholes (Carbondale: Southern Illinois University Press, 1983), pp. 10–11

DAVID G. HARTWELL   No one has taken Van Vogt seriously as a writer for a long time now. Yet he has been read and *still is*.

What no one seems to have noticed is that Van Vogt, more than any other single SF writer, is the conduit through which the energy of Gernsbackian, primitive wonder stories has been transmitted through the Campbellian age, when earlier styles of SF were otherwise rejected, and on into the SF of the present. James E. Gunn comes closest to understanding the importance of Van Vogt when he says, "Van Vogt was creating the mythology of science, writing stories of science as magic or magic as science" (*Alternate Worlds*, New Jersey: Prentice-Hall, 1975, p. 163). The style hardly matters. And as Knight proved, Van Vogt's awkwardness is certainly easy to ridicule—but to do so without an appreciation of Van Vogt's virtues misses the point.

While literary criticism has never admitted complication as a virtue in fiction, complication has always been central to the mainstream of science fiction. This is derived from the focus on plot and story (above character, theme, structure, stylistic polish) and of course setting. The novels of Jules Verne were complicated by the insertion of immense amounts of scientific and technological detail. There is substantial evidence that Verne's Victorian audience saw detail as edifying and pleasurable. That dense and almost preliterate classic of modern SF, Hugo Gernsback's *Ralph 124C41+* (1911), has almost nothing to it but its complications. Les del Rey described it in *Science Fiction: 1926–1976* (New York: Garland Publishers, 1979, p. 33):

> As fiction, it is simply dreadful. . . . The plot is mostly a series of events that help to move from one marvelous device to another.
>
>   But never mind that. It is one of the most important stories ever written in the science fiction vein. It is a constant parade of scientific wonders—but they are logically constructed wonders, with a lot of keen thought behind them. The novel forecasts more things that really came true than a hundred other pieces of science fiction could hope to achieve. There is television (which was named by Hugo Gernsback), microfilm, tape recording, fluorescent lighting, radar—in fact most of the things that did eventually make up our future.

Obviously, Gernsback's book depends entirely on its extraliterary virtues. And Van Vogt most of all sums up and transmutes this part of the science fiction tradition and transmits it forward to a large and influential body of better stylists who come after him.

David G. Hartwell, *Age of Wonders: Exploring the Worlds of Science Fiction* (New York: Walker, 1984), pp. 131–32

JOHN HUNTINGTON   The important figure for ⟨Philip K.⟩ Dick, as has long been recognized, is A. E. van Vogt, known for his confusingly intricate plots. But it is not the model of the plots themselves that we need to be aware of so much as the rule by which he generated them. Van Vogt advised young writers that in order to keep their readers' interest they should introduce a new idea every 800 words. For van Vogt this is not a "philosophical" rule, but simply a practical technique to make the story interesting, on the level with the rule which requires that the first paragraph of a story make mention of each of the five senses. In van Vogt's own work one is aware of a disorienting series of changes which may be exhilarating

as long as one is able to hold on. Often the change at 800 words involves
a blatant reversing of the values some character or thing has represented:
a friend turns out to be an enemy, an enemy a friend, what we thought was
useful is useless, an escape is a trap, etc. Often the reversals are given some
coherence by the continuity offered by the hero (as in *Slan*) or by a fixed
deep structure (such as the truth in "The Weapon Shop" that the armed
strangers are liberators, while the familiar authorities are oppressors). What
is remarkable about these fairly mechanical and hasty exercises is how
profound they can seem. The van Vogt rule of a new idea every 800 words
is a way of generating complexity and of enforcing at least the illusion of
a relentless dialectic.

What I am calling the 800-word rule is an explicitly acknowledged device
for van Vogt. I do not know of any such explicit acknowledgement on
Dick's part. Yet the central importance of van Vogt's practice for Dick's
sense of SF is easily documented. In his interview with Charles Platt, Dick
twice points to *The World of Null-A* as a central text which "absolutely
fascinated" him. "A lot of what I wrote, which looks like taking acid, is
really the result of taking van Vogt very seriously."

> John Huntington, "Philip K. Dick: Authenticity and Insincerity," *Science-Fiction
> Studies* 15, No. 2 (July 1989): 153–54

ALEXEI and CORY PANSHIN   In something of the same way
in which Jommy Cross was a relatively superior human being, able to do
what the ordinary person could not do, so we may see van Vogt as a relatively
superior SF writer, able to imagine what the ordinary science fiction writer
of 1940 could not imagine.

Throughout the modern scientific era, as we have taken some pains to
notice, existence has been divided into two parts—an area of securely known
things and another area of unknownness. But van Vogt no longer observed
this distinction between *here* and *out there*, between the Village and the
World Beyond the Hill. To his way of thinking, knowledge and mystery
were inextricably intertwined in all times and places.

As van Vogt saw it, so great was the imperfection of our perception and
thought that even the here-and-now was all but a total mystery to us. At
the same time, however, the farthest star and the most remote moment

were part of the same ultimate Unity as we, and consequently in some sense might be knowable by us.

This new construction of things allowed van Vogt to operate freely and easily in mental and physical territory that was too far out for his more conventional colleagues. And it also allowed him to imagine utter strangeness close at hand where ordinary perception would never expect to find it.

To an audience that was still struggling to come to terms with materialism and the apparently accidental and meaningless nature of existence, van Vogt's new perspective seemed mysterious and elusive. It permitted him to come at his readers from impossible directions and to show them marvels completely beyond their ability to anticipate.

Even John Campbell was captivated, charmed and awed by the sheer inexplicability of A. E. van Vogt. Shaking his head in wonder, Campbell would say, "That son of a gun is about one-half mystic, and like many another mystic, hits on ideas that are sound, without having any rational method of arriving at them or defending them."

However, nearly fifty years after the original serialization of *Slan*, with the advantages lent to us by hindsight, by the changes that have taken place in thinking patterns during the intervening time, and by van Vogt's own self-explanations, we don't need to be quite as baffled or as hypnotized by the story as readers were in 1940. We can see that what was present in *Slan* to be taken away by a reader—whether consciously or not—was precisely those elements that van Vogt had labored so long and so hard to put into his story in the first place: Names of significance. A sense of the mutability of things. Sudden emotional and intellectual recognitions. Patterns and relationships. Awareness of the whole.

Alexei and Cory Panshin, *The World beyond the Hill: Science Fiction and the Quest for Transcendence* (Rigelsville, PA: Elephant Books, 1989), pp. 484–85

◈ *Bibliography*

Slan. 1946.
The Weapon Makers ⟨*One against Eternity*⟩. 1947, 1952.
The Book of Ptath ⟨*Two Hundred Million A.D.*⟩. 1947.
The World of A ⟨*The World of Null-A*⟩. 1948, 1970.

Out of the Unknown (with E. Mayne Hull). 1948, 1969.

The Voyage of the Space Beagle ⟨*Mission: Interplanetary*⟩. 1950.

Masters of Time ⟨*Earth's Last Fortress*⟩. 1950.

The House That Stood Still. 1950, 1960 (as *The Mating Cry*).

The Weapon Shops of Isher. 1951.

The Mixed Men ⟨*Mission to the Stars*⟩. 1952.

Away and Beyond. 1952.

Destination: Universe! 1952.

The Universe Maker. 1953.

Planets for Sale (with E. Mayne Hull). 1954.

The Pawns of Null-A. 1956.

The Hypnotism Handbook (with Charles Edward Cooke). 1956.

Empire of the Atom. 1956.

The Mind Cage. 1957.

Triad ⟨*The World of A, The Voyage of the Space Beagle, Slan*⟩. 1959.

The War against the Rull. 1959.

Siege of the Unseen ⟨with *The World Swappers* by John Brunner⟩. 1959.

The Wizard of Linn. 1962.

The Violent Man. 1962.

The Beast. 1963.

The Twisted Men ⟨with *One of Our Asteroids Is Missing* by Calvin M. Knox⟩.
    1964.

Rogue Ship. 1965.

Monsters ⟨*The Blal*⟩. Ed. Forrest J. Ackerman. 1965.

The Winged Man (with E. Mayne Hull). 1966.

A van Vogt Omnibus, Volume 1 ⟨*Planets for Sale, The Beast, The Book of Ptath*⟩.
    1967.

The Far-Out Worlds of A. E. van Vogt. 1968.

The Silkie. 1969.

Quest for the Future. 1970.

Children of Tomorrow. 1970.

The Battle of Forever. 1971.

More Than Superhuman. 1971.

A van Vogt Omnibus, Volume 2 ⟨*The Mind Cage, The Winged Man, Slan*⟩.
    1971.

The Proxy Intelligence and Other Mind Benders. 1971.

M33 in Andromeda. 1971.

The Darkness on Diamondia. 1972.

The Money Personality. 1972.

The Book of van Vogt ⟨*Lost: Fifty Suns*⟩. 1972.

Two Science Fiction Novels ⟨*The Three Eyes of Evil, Earth's Last Fortress*⟩. 1973.

Future Glitter. 1973.

The Secret Galactics ⟨*Earth Factor X*⟩. 1974.

The Best of A. E. van Vogt. 1974.

The Man with a Thousand Names. 1974.

Reflections of A. E. van Vogt. 1975.

The Universe Maker and The Proxy Intelligence. 1976.

The Best of A. E. van Vogt. 1976.

The Gryb. 1976.

The Anarchistic Colussus. 1977.

Supermind. 1977.

Pendulum. 1978.

Renaissance. 1979.

Cosmic Encounter. 1980.

Computerworld. 1983.

Null-A Three. 1985.

A Report on the Violent Male. 1992.